Social Movements and Economic Transition

This book examines patterns of political mobilization among groups in Mexico whose livelihoods have been threatened by trade opening, fiscal retrenchment, and market liberalization. Using data from case studies of a worker-based movement and a farmer-based movement, Williams argues that economic transition, in altering modes of state-society bargaining, has altered the form and shape of distributive protest. Williams further argues that social movements make strategic choices in their use of resources to widen their constituencies and extend the length of their insurgencies.

Heather L. Williams is Assistant Professor of Politics at Pomona College.

T0371194

Social Movements and Economic Transition

MARKETS AND DISTRIBUTIVE CONFLICT IN MEXICO

HEATHER L. WILLIAMS
Pomona College

CAMBRIDGE
UNIVERSITY PRESS

CAMBRIDGE UNIVERSITY PRESS
Cambridge, New York, Melbourne, Madrid, Cape Town, Singapore, São Paulo

Cambridge University Press
The Edinburgh Building, Cambridge CB2 2RU, UK

Published in the United States of America by Cambridge University Press, New York

www.cambridge.org
Information on this title: www.cambridge.org/9780521772563

© Heather L. Williams 2001

First published 2001
This digitally printed first paperback version 2006

A catalogue record for this publication is available from the British Library

Library of Congress Cataloguing in Publication data
Williams, Heather L.
    Social movements and economic transition: markets and distributive conflict in
Mexico / Heather L. Williams.
        p. cm.
    Includes bibliographical references and index.
    ISBN 0-521-77256-7
    1. Social movements – Mexico – Case studies. 2. Mexico – Economic policy –
1994– 3. Mexico – Economic conditions – 1994– I. Title.
HN113.5 .W55 2000
303.48′4′0972 – dc21   00-036303

ISBN-13 978-0-521-77256-3 hardback
ISBN-10 0-521-77256-7 hardback

ISBN-13 978-0-521-03282-7 paperback
ISBN-10 0-521-03282-2 paperback

For my parents and my brother

Contents

List of Figures and Tables

Preface

As this book goes to press in July 2000, I am reminded of a remark ascribed to the turn-of-the-century dictator Porfirio Díaz, who lamented as he left the country in the first days of the Revolution, "Nothing ever happens until it happens in Mexico." Ninety years later, another change of power that seems at once inevitable and astonishing will follow the July 2, 2000, presidential elections in which the center–right coalition candidate, Vicente Fox, defeated Francisco Labastida of the Institutional Revolutionary Party (PRI). While many had anticipated that Fox might win, few predicted the wide margin of victory. Fox won handily with a plurality of 43 percent of the vote to Labastida's 36 percent. The center–left coalition led by Cuauhtémoc Cárdenas lagged behind with 17 percent of the vote. As an individual who has made many friends in Mexico and spent much time there, I am glad to see the transition from 70 years of single-party dominance proceed peacefully. As an academic who has just finished a book on Mexican politics, however, I would have appreciated a little more lead time. In the days after the election, I sighed as I looked at page proofs with terms here and there that I knew would soon fall away, such as "ruling party" and "opposition parties."

Oh well, *ni modo*, as my friends would say. This book is about change. It examines the choices of political insurgents in an environment of economic and political uncertainty. I have altered little in the text except a few verb endings in the theoretical chapters, preferring to present this study as I assembled it in the late 1990s. During that time, everyone was aware that the system was in flux, but in truth no one knew when or under what circumstances the long-governing PRI would exit power. Thus, I will ask readers' forbearance if a passage or two seem ever-so-last-year. What I will not do is eliminate all references to authoritarianism in the Mexican political system. Despite Enrique Krauze's recent declaration that Mexico is now a "democracy without adjectives," I remain firm in my contention that there remain many illiberal dimensions to governance. Many people now enjoy hard-won rights to free and fair voting, but significant portions of the population still have little access to state officials and lack services they are supposedly guaranteed by law, including health care, sanitation, education, and housing. Also, many face violence and arrest for peaceful political activities. This is particularly true for members of indigenous groups, as well as workers and the rural poor. To be sure, Fox and his successors face many challenges in bringing about a real and meaningful democracy in Mexico.

What particular impact the administration of President-elect Fox will have on protest and other forms of collective action is unknown. However, I predict that significant cycles of contention and distributive conflict will follow in the coming years, and that groups of workers, farmers, urban residents, teachers, and students will continue to petition the state in recognizable ways for material relief and political rights. In fact, heightened expectations of the new government amid fiscal and political limitations may well make protest a serious problem for a new administration enjoying a broad but thin legitimacy among the populace. Notably, social movements played a relatively muted role in the 2000 elections, signaling a real caution on the part of popular groups to endorse candidates on any side. Many are skeptical about the possibility of electoral politics to provide real change on the issues that matter to them. Most prefer to pressure parties and officials from the outside rather from within party and government hierarchies. This book, I hope, will shed light on how groups with little access to official power deal with systemic change and try through protest to alter the system in turn.

Acknowledgments

This book, which contains much discussion of bankruptcy and social protest, represents a grand and perhaps unpayable debt on my part. The creditors are many, but none lent me so much valuable insight as the many gracious individuals in Mexico who took time to teach me about politics, power, and strategies of dissent. The years I took to research this book, spanning 1994 through the summer of 1999, were extraordinarily difficult for many and represented a time when many aspirations for greater prosperity and political openness were dampened. Despite those difficulties, and despite my slowness at learning many things, people were very encouraging and felt that I ought to write a book about Mexico's economic transition and its impact on popular politics and social organization. This is an initial stab at doing so.

In the United States, James Scott and Margaret Keck gave me exceptionally good counsel and teaching through the years as this project proceeded from proposal to dissertation to book manuscript. Jim had the great gift of listening meticulously and then responding in a way that often shook up the way I thought about crucial issues of power and insurgency. Mimi had the wonderful and terrifying ability to ask me *precisely* the questions I could not answer, thus helping me figure what I needed to know in order to make my case.

At Yale, I must thank my colleagues from my academic "home," the Agrarian Studies program. The people who gave me comments on early papers in student seminars are too numerous to mention. The Agrarian Studies program, along with the Yale Center for International and Area Studies and the John Enders summer grant program, underwrote my fieldwork in Mexico. Also, I thank Cathy Cohen at Yale for her wonderful course on social movements. It came along at exactly the right moment. I took the course between stints of fieldwork in Mexico, and it changed the way I thought about what I was seeing.

In Mexico, Professor Francisco Zapata at the Colegio de México provided many hours of advice and teaching. He made many suggestions about research methods and about possible contacts for my research; without them, I would have learned a lot less. Also at the Colegio de México, I wish to thank Ilán Bizberg, Kirsten Appendini, and Gustavo Vega for their counsel and their research suggestions. Through the Colegio, I also met Sarah Babb, who has been a great friend and colleague, and whose observations and advice have touched many parts of this project.

Some of the people in my case studies later became good friends, such as Selva Daville and Estela Rios. In Mexico City, Asa Cristina Laurell provided me with materials and contacts, and in Michoacán, Jorge Martínez Aparicio did the same. Steve Dubb and Enrique de la Garza also gave me very helpful suggestions on how to pursue my project. In Lázaro Cárdenas City, José Luis Castellanos, Francisco Zamudio, Guadalupe Corona, Francisco Sánchez Rivera, Florencio Tapia Rosas, and José Luis Equihua each spent hours and hours explaining their involvement in worker politics, helping me to locate union papers and circulars, and finding other workers who were willing to talk to me. They introduced me to dozens of other people, who also spent many hours teaching me about their political work and their community.

Doing work on the Barzón movement and on the farm debt crisis in general, I also benefitted from the help of many people. A number of individuals were especially generous, meeting with me several times, helping me to find sources of information, or introducing me to local Barzón groups. Among these individuals are Juan Figueroa, Armando Chávez Loyo, Francis Mestries, Sylvia Campos, Imelda Castro, Renato Rodríguez, Carlos Gabriel Lugo Camacho, Marcos Gutiérrez, Efrén Bañuelos, Jesus Vega, Manuel Ortega, Juan Manuel Maciel, Luis Medina, Saul Sánchez, Vicente Argüéllez, Antonio Risendis, and José Luis Silva Perez. On two later trips to Zacatecas, my good friend Fernando Robledo was of invaluable assistance in locating specific information to fill gaps in my knowledge, as were Clara Castro and Raul Delgado Wise.

After my fieldwork, I had the good fortune to spend a year at the Center for U.S.–Mexican Studies at the University of California–San Diego. Alejandro Alvarez Bejar, Bong-Hyun Chun, Jeff Cowie, Armando Fernández, Fred Krissman, Aida Hernández, Stephen Lewis, Shannan

Acknowledgments

Mattiace, David Myhre, Ligia Tavera, and Van Whiting, in particular, read and listened to parts of my project and gave me wonderful feedback. At the university, Anne Craig graciously took time out from an unbelievably busy schedule to read my work and give me very insightful comments and advice. Kevin Middlebrook also was an unflagging source of support and incisive feedback for all of us at the Center. Finally, my spirits were always buoyed by fellow lunchtime runners C. R. Hibbs, Jim Hawkins, and Tamara Riquelme.

As I was writing my dissertation, I had a second round of good fortune, when I was able to join the "Invisible College of Contentious Politics," a four-year project sponsored by the Mellon Foundation and the Center for Advanced Study in the Behavioral Sciences at Stanford University. The founders of the project were enormously generous with their time and support. I cannot begin to say how much I owe the founders of that project. Ron Aminzade, Jack Goldstone, Doug McAdam, Elizabeth Perry, William Sewell, Sidney Tarrow, and Charles Tilly read my work, introduced me to new ideas and literatures, and also gave me exceedingly sound practical advice.

I must also thank my new colleagues at Pomona College, who have sustained me through the stressful last stages of preparing manuscript. The college provided research funds for a final month in the field in 1999, and the program in international relations provided funds for me to employ my marvelous research assistant, Kirk Shelton. I also wish to thank the two anonymous readers at Cambridge, whose comments provided very helpful guideposts in revising the manuscript.

Finally, a word of thanks to my family and friends and to my college mentor, Deborah Gewertz, who many years ago convinced me to continue asking questions about power and social change. This was the most challenging project I have ever undertaken, and the first one I often doubted I would finish. You all kept me honest and sane through these last few years. I always knew that if I succeeded in writing the book I meant to write, I'd always have all of you.

Introduction

As I finish this book in the summer of 1999, I find myself drawn in by an ongoing news story in Mexico. A strike has shut down the national university for five months, paralyzing the activities of the vast National Autonomous University of Mexico. This, the longest strike in university history, was sparked by university officials' attempts to raise fees to the equivalent of about U.S. $150 per year. The strike continued after that particular demand was won, which provoked much criticism. Nonetheless, the language of strikers and sympathetic onlookers revealed much in the way it echoed larger social and political crises confronting the nation. First, protesters invoked the problem of worsening distribution of wealth that has accompanied Mexico's market revolution. They argued that the fee proposal signaled the imminent privatization of the university system, and the exclusion of poor and working-class students from higher education. Second, protesters pointed to the crisis of government accountability, contending that the fee proposal was one more scheme by which the wealthy and the connected skimmed resources from the poor and middle classes. They pointed out that the annual budget for the university – about the equivalent of U.S. $950 million (Sánchez 1999) – was dwarfed by the staggering sums assigned recent bailouts of troubled banks and bankrupt private sector elites – about $80 billion. Finally, considering the dearth of professional positions available to new graduates in recent years, very few in Mexico have argued that fees were sound investments in students' professional futures.

Indeed, as a professor watching students who could be in my own classrooms, it strikes me that individuals coming of age today in Mexico are likely to have an alarmingly dim view of national economic affairs and may have few notions of doing better financially than their parents. Unlike

1

RECURSOS SUFICIENTES ■ Helguera

Sufficient Resources, **by Helguera** Tattered Mexico playing poker against wealthy countries, betting with the last of its chicklets: "Let's keep playing, what the hell!" From *La Jornada*, July 21, 1995. Reprinted by permission.

previous living generations who saw rising prosperity in the years after World War II, anyone under the age of twenty in Mexico has witnessed an ongoing series of national political and economic crises, interrupted only by brief periods of incomplete recovery. Historically speaking, there is little doubt that the young have lived through an epoch that will be understood in future years as a time of rapid change and watershed events. Alongside a factious transition to multiparty politics, the economy has tumbled through several cycles of crisis and painful policy readjustment. Despite some recent growth, the years following a sovereign debt crisis in 1982 have been marred by repeated episodes of negative and near-zero growth rates, depression-level unemployment, massive capital flight, inflation, falling buying power, rising taxation, and periodic shortages in vital goods and services.

Introduction

During this time, analysts have characterized Mexico through the use of many images, but none has stuck so well as the image of the ailing patient, plagued with malignancies, unable to carry on financial business on its own. Mortal sickness, of course, begs a severe cure, and that image too has stuck.[1] What many in financial circles have called "radical surgery" for the economy has indeed delivered unfortunate side effects in the form of acute hardship of vast numbers of people. Macroeconomic stabilization and market liberalization, often alternately called the "modernization of the economy," have entailed much sacrifice from the population.

The imagery of cure replacing sickness, and modernity replacing backwardness, surely has helped preserve a measure of social peace that might otherwise not have been possible in the face of massive dispossession. Both crisis and market transition have savaged household incomes in Mexico, particularly among workers, small merchants, and farmers. By the end of the 1980s, many business elites and members of the urban middle classes had begun to be publicly optimistic about the possibilities of market-oriented policy to solve problems linked to currency instability, capital shortage, and low productivity in industry and farming. Meanwhile, however, the cure raged on among the bottom two-thirds of the population, who scrambled harder to maintain even a modest standard of living. At the inauguration of Mexico's entrance to the North American Free Trade Agreement (NAFTA) in 1994, the average wage-earner could buy only 35 percent of what he or she purchased in 1980. And for workers at the lower end of the pay scale, a minimum wage salary covered only one-third of what it cost to feed and clothe a spouse and two dependent children (Gómez Salgado 1994). Rural communities, meanwhile, were no refuge for the poor. Decline in the small farming sector was so dire that tens of thousands migrated north and to the cities, as the sum of money in expired loans owed by producers in agriculture grew by 2,000 percent,[2] and the area of land financed through the government had fallen by two-thirds in the late 1980s.[3] In addition, by 1994, 60 percent of all so-called microenterprises (family or individually run businesses) were estimated to be in or near bankruptcy.[4] Though official figures on unemployment

---

[1] A Nexis/Lexis search of all major English-language news articles on the Mexican economy published between January 1988 and August 1995 that also mentioned the terms *cure* or *surgery* brought up 533 entries. A Nexis/Lexis search of articles on the Mexican economy that also used the terms *ailing* or *sick* yielded 899 entries.
[2] Rural Bank figures, cited in Pérez (1994a).
[3] Ministry of Agriculture figures, cited in (Rudiño 1994).
[4] Study cited by Chávez (1995).

hovered at 4 to 6 percent, the International Labor Organization placed the level of effective unemployment and underemployment nationally at more than 25 percent by 1993 (Zanella Figueróa 1994).

Painfully enough, these phenomena continued – in some cases worsened – even as Mexico's vital indicators rebounded from ruinous macroeconomic performance in the 1980s. By the early 1990s, international observers declared Mexico under the rule of President Carlos Salinas de Gortari to be a success story among developing nations – a likely candidate for rapid industrialization and emergence from the status of Third World nation in the manner of ascendant East Asian nations such as Taiwan or South Korea. Unemployment, low wages, massive farm debt and declining domestic manufacturing aside, many still felt that Mexico's future was bright. After years of capital flight and negative or near-zero growth rates, Mexico became a worthy credit risk for private financial institutions. Mexican treasury bonds sold briskly on international markets. The sale of state-owned enterprises filled the government's coffers again. New, direct antipoverty grants from the Executive branch to communities under the National Solidarity Program appeared to open the possibility for poorer communities to bypass the graft and extortion so common in ossified corporatist agencies.

Along with lingering social problems among the lower and middle classes, certain other troubling factors were visible by 1994 in Mexico. A $31 billion deficit on current account was putting pressure on an overvalued national currency and putting further economic growth at risk. To finance its consumption of imports, the Mexican government was paying bondholders a hefty annual interest rate of between 25 and 30 percent, it was indexing peso yields to the dollar, and it was fixing bond maturities at intervals between six months and two weeks. As is now well known, Mexico's reliance on "hot money," or highly liquid short-term debt instruments to balance its trade accounts, control inflation, and capitalize its domestic financial system was in no way a sound scheme for long-term economic growth.[5] In December of 1994, shortly after the inauguration

---

[5] Certainly, after the crash of the peso and the Mexican bond market, multilateral banking officials and financial experts acknowledged that mistakes had been made in the management of the Mexican economy. The International Monetary Fund chief at the time, Michael Camdessus, for example, spent much of his time in public in the early months of 1995 explaining what had gone wrong in Mexico, and why international authorities had done nothing to avert the crisis. The Economic Commission on Latin America, which in recent times has advocated market-oriented development policy, declared in hindsight that

of President Ernesto Zedillo, a series of currency devaluations designed to ease pressure on the peso provoked investor panic in Mexico; within the space of weeks, tens of billions of dollars exited Mexico, the peso plummeted to less than half its value against the dollar, and interest rates on consumer and industrial loans shot up to over 100 percent annually. Now once again, Mexico was in deep crisis, and in need of a $50 billion loan to cover its obligations to its creditors.[6] The faithful among financiers and free market economists maintained their position that with some adjustments, the same curative regimen of adjustment and market liberalization was necessary to bring Mexico back once again from the edge of sovereign economic disaster. Fewer inside Mexico, however, had great faith in the power of modern medicine to make them well this time.[7]

These years since the early 1980s will be painted as a time of vast political tumult, as opponents of the government's policies conglomerated in new political groupings and as actors outside the ruling party came closer to playing a substantive role in determining the affairs of the nation. Mexico's crisis, surpassing in severity and duration the Great Depression of the United States in the 1930s, shook the timbers of an entrenched set of distributive arrangements and, in turn, put pressure on a government long controlled by the Institutional Revolutionary Party (PRI) to make democratic reforms, including changes in electoral procedures, legislative representation for opposition parties, and human rights enforcement.

But the greater question at hand – that being what these new political freedoms will produce in terms of a reequilibration of material distribution – is yet unclear. Misery has, indeed, created new company among civil groups demanding distributive policy reforms, but the gains made by various actors are still local and not systemic. The distribution of wealth in Mexico has grown more unbalanced: by 1995, the wealthiest 20 percent of Mexicans came to control 58.2 percent of all income, whereas the poorest 40 percent controlled just 11 percent, a change from respective

currency overvaluation combined with liberalization of imports – a policy pursued by Argentina and Mexico with the implicit blessing of international financial authorities – was "now seen as a dangerous policy" (Economic Commission on Latin America 1995: 7).

[6] For an overview of the "December Error," including a discussion of how certain particularly risky policies were linked to the dynamics of the presidential elections in 1994 in Mexico, see Castañeda (1995: Chapter 10).

[7] For a summary of various sectors' reactions to the 1994–5 economic crisis, see Williams (1996).

figures of 49.5 percent and 14.3 percent in 1984 (Chávez 1994, World Bank 200).

These hard times, or their post facto records, are fertile historical junctures for social scientists. This is so, it must be hoped, less for the spectacle of human misery and makeshift adjustment than for their implications for the future of distributive politics and civil-political prerogative. Crises are, in some sense, the practitioner's looking glass, reflecting long-standing conflicts over interests and ideology and revealing the juxtaposition of various sectors of society. The basic axiom: when times are bad, leadership loses its luster, and the criticisms of its opponents gain new validity in the growing ranks of beleaguered citizens. Hard times are, in fact, history writ large – a moment in which all the possible balances of governance and dissent, control and freedom, rights and privileges come to be understood as concrete alternatives. As Peter Gourevitch writes of hard times, "Patterns unravel, economic models come into conflict, and policy prescriptions diverge. Prosperity blurs a truth that hard times make clearer . . ." (1986: 17).

This work seeks to illuminate how Mexico's crisis and market transition have altered the way groups pressure the state for distributive reforms. Rather than constructing the political economy merely as a landscape of opportunity affecting the choices of individuals or firms, or simply affecting the fortunes of industrial sectors – as most classical economic and rational choice theories posit – this discussion focuses on the way that Mexico's shifting political economy has affected the way groups challenge the state for resources. Primarily, I focus on the impact of economic changes on the character and location of social protest, as well as the constituencies of organized social movements.

New modes of economic organization and government spending have altered forms of association among social groups. They also have changed various forms of state-society negotiation over distributive issues such as taxation, subsidies, employment, prices, and wages. In response, movements have continued to pressure the state in historically recognizable ways but have adapted to changes by organizing along new lines, pacting with unlikely political groups or parties and even changing their identities or issue frames to maneuver more adeptly.

This type of inquiry is not entirely original. Theories abound of what, in fact, determine the outcomes and/or the fault lines of conflict between regimes and opposition movements in these moments of economic crisis and political rupture. Unfortunately, there remain stubborn gaps among various bodies of research in the social sciences on the subject. Divided in the simplest terms, it could be said that some literatures emphasize large processes and historical outcomes, whereas other literatures examine the construction of groups and the logic of individual participation in collective action. The former examine the role of structural variables in fomenting collective action, consciousness, and mass resistance, explaining historical outcomes from post hoc analysis of long-term processes. The latter extend fewer conclusions about historical outcomes but seek instead to explain the construction of action within particular classes, sectors, and distributive coalitions. Because the two poles of research begin with disparate points of departure, comparative works on structure and ideational frameworks rarely address the fundamental dispute engendered by their conclusions.

Representing the former tendency are works that seek to indicate the aggregate conditions, which lead to collective action and, ultimately, various political economic outcomes – fascism, communism, or capitalist democracy. Outcomes of political conflicts, in these works, are generally determined by the configuration of state institutions vis-à-vis social classes, the nature of national wealth, social and demographic factors, or elite cleavages.

Much of mid-twentieth-century comparative political science, for example, was centered on questions of how industrialization and emerging world markets would affect political arrangements in developing nations. And while certainly many of the works grouped in this genre actually drew quite different conclusions, most tended to assume that demands generated by new international pressures or domestic economic arrangements would produce, in short order, determined political responses. Ted Robert Gurr (1970), for example, provoked much discussion with his theory that rising expectations in changing economies produced a sense of "relative deprivation" among social groups that in turn provoked unrest. Gabriel Almond and Seymour Martin Lipset also stressed that perceptions and values were key to explaining political outcomes in changing societies. In contrast to Gurr, these authors tended to focus on the groups whose actions would stabilize participatory regimes – principally elites and the middle classes. Additionally, Samuel Huntington predicted that industrialization and global market pressures might produce unrest in developing countries. However, instead of emphasizing political attitudes, Huntington (1968) argued that the functional capacity of governing institutions to aggregate and channel new demands was key to governability. Monarchies and colonial orders with undifferentiated systems of material distribution, he argued, were insufficient to represent the demands of new groups for representation in political processes.

Alongside academic debates about modernization were analyses that shunned the more economic determinist or functionalist formulations for historical-comparative analysis. These authors tended to argue that historical processes that resulted in given configurations of class and group power in national contexts constituted the historical antecedents of modern political arrangements. Barrington Moore (1967), for example, changed the direction of much thinking about political history arguing that social outcomes were determined not so much by industrialization itself but by the array of social groups that guided and controlled industrialization. Amending Moore's thesis with the incorporation of the state as an autonomous actor, Theda Skocpol (1979), too, shifted the course of social scientific research, arguing that revolutionary moments emerged when external pressures of the war and the market weakened the power of centralized states, alienating elites from ruling structures and provoking the formation of revolutionary alliances.

In quite a separate vein of macrostructural research, theorists of trade and international sociology tend toward even greater reliance on structure as explanation. Peter Gourevitch (1986), for example, argued that the economic distributive regimes that emerged from the crises and political conflicts of the 1870s, the 1930s, and the 1970s in Europe were a result of the various needs of dominant industrial coalitions inside nations. Similarly, Ronald Rogowsky (1989) argued that ideological conflicts over trade and distributive policy are superfluous, with state policy instead being determined by national endowments of labor, land, and capital. In both works, the authors argued that social mobilization was most likely to occur among groups or industries whose welfare was threatened by crises, or by prevailing economic orders.

The works that seek to explain historical outcomes through the ongoing interaction of political and economic variables remain fundamental in social scientific investigation. Despite some substantial movement in recent years in comparative politics toward quantitative analysis of voting patterns and public opinion and toward the use of formal theory in explaining political choice, the classic comparative-historical works remain central because they make it possible for scholars of the local to speak to one another's work, to participate in common conversations about historical process and outcome in vastly different situations. However, inherent in many of these works is a problematic assumption – specifically, that the mass organization and mobilization necessary to consolidate new ruling coalitions during a time of upheaval are produced on time and on demand. Works that treat societies in their entirety tend not to elaborate on the processes by which particular civil or state actors come to see one another as allies or enemies or come to believe that their group will be included in any old or new political economic regime. Also, insofar as peasantries and populist blocs exist in such works as monolithic "detonators" of insurrection and revolution, there is little means to understand the process by which people of limited resources with no significant political clout may come to challenge powerful state or private actors. After all, even if it can be argued convincingly that a necessary condition for the success of popular insurrection is sponsorship in some manner by elite factions, it must be remembered that this sympathy in no way can be said to produce mass insurgency. The fact remains that vast numbers of workers, small farmers, and petty merchants have failed to mobilize in certain "revolutionary situations" – or those moments in which repression presumably might have been mitigated by elite sponsorship. And, by the same token, workers, farmers, or the poor have also launched uprisings when – disastrously – there existed few cleavages among governing elites, and insurrection was quickly put down through repression.[8]

Clearly, the class structures or sectoral configurations that social scientists have measured with such meticulous detail have limited power to explain protest and insurgency as whole phenomena – in their timing, in their social makeup, in their degree of militancy. As Scott (1985) observed, political economic changes may provoke resistance or rebellion in peasant communities insofar as they affect *local* systems of hierarchical obligation and mutuality, but they may or may not be linked in their timing to larger regime transitions. His work suggests that there is some methodological

---

[8] Examples of the former might be Paraguay during the period of transitions to democracy in South America and Albania during the early 1990s. In both cases, the peasantries and small urban proletariat were fairly quiescent during a period when international events might have been expected to open up elite schisms and corresponding opportunities for insurgency. Examples of lower class insurgency crushed by a unified power structure, on the other hand, are perhaps more common. Slave revolts in the New World had few if any elite sympathizers. The Tomochik rebellion in Chihuahua in 1891 also reads as a quixotic episode of almost purely underclass action squelched by the powerful Porfirian government. In addition, few elites attempted to attach their own political fortunes to the actors involved in the food riots of the 1980s in South America and the inner-city riots in the United States in the 1960s.

problem in comparative work that begins with large historical outcomes and seeks evidence that explains precisely those macrotrends. Various types of disorder and collective action, which among vulnerable subordinate actors may assume heterogeneous forms of sabotage and subversion, may not lend themselves to quantification or to easy cross-regional or cross-national comparison. Acts of insubordination or waves of petty crimes that Scott argues are most likely to be utilized in the most repressive settings are precisely those acts that are most likely to carry on without being identified by officials as collective action, being instead dismissed by authorities as the result of the general depravity and ignorance of the poor.

Timing and duration of local unrest is also best understood in reference to local arrangements and historical expectations of actors. Rebellion – even that which is nominally connected to national political groupings – may be mobilized through a demand structure in which communities essentially seek the reestablishment of certain subsistence arrangements and social guarantees. Victor Magagna (1991) similarly argued that peasant revolt was most likely to occur when outside forces of some sort encroached on the autonomy of individual community institutions. Also, Walton and Seddon (1994), in their comparison of late twentieth century antiausterity riots and eighteenth-century food riots, point out that similar material conditions may prompt very different types of protest with distinct targets and varying narratives of popular justice.

Questions of why a group organizes and mobilizes protest at any given moment are most convincingly answered through analysis of the local and the particular. Scholars of resource mobilization theory in the 1970s and 1980s argued that the collective action depended on institutions, forms of organization, personal networks, and social movement strategies. Oberschall (1978) and Snyder and Tilly (1972), among others, helped establish a striking counterintuitive axiom of social mobilization: there is, they argued, little direct relationship between economic strain and aggregate social conflict. Accordingly, the focus of social movements research turned increasingly to factors of agency, or the process by which movements themselves were constructed. How movements got access to resources, or how they forged alliances with elites, for example, became key elements in the study of protest and contentious politics.

Mancur Olson (1965), likewise, argued against earlier theorists who imagined that the "push forces" generated by mass material demand propelled collective action. Instead, he argued, collective action could not be expected to emerge without the "pull force" of an ongoing supply of group resources. Pointing out that maintaining collective action requires significant expenditures of time and money, he maintained that people would participate in collective action only if the benefits exceeded the costs. In highlighting the so-called free-rider dilemma, whereby no single actor could be expected to expend resources in the pursuit of a public good that both participants and nonparticipants in collective action would enjoy, he argued that people organized resistance not simply out of frustration but also out of anticipation that their efforts would yield positive results. Though certainly many argued that his initial thesis did not allow for the social and cultural factors that may effectively mitigate the free-rider dilemma and enable groups to work for larger goals,[9] it is important to note that his argument implies that the local and the particular may be essential to understanding why movements emerge. Instead of thinking of collective protest as having been detonated by external forces, Olson and other theorists of similar focus saw movements as having been built by rational actors. That is, the means by which movement members broker information, participate in groups, and even provide the selective incentives to convince others to join are very important to understanding why movements emerge and sustain activity over time.

What rational choice and resource mobilization theory did not explain well, however, was the pattern by which social movements emerged, and the crucial relationships among groups that affect the timing and character of protest. That is, if one sought to argue that collective action was a matter of organization and group strategy and was not a direct result of scarcity or mass anger, then there remained some empirical puzzles. There was little explanation, for example, as to why movements protested in the way they did or how people mediated conflicts inside groups. It also explained little about why contention historically appeared in clusters, rather than evenly distributed across time. A rational choice explanation, applied systemically, tended to assume a rather homogenous field of play for collective actors in a national context and seemed to imply that, once movements emerged, they continued to exist until swept away by external forces such as war or revolution (Olson 1982).

Modeling the interplay of states and economies with social movements is a difficult business, fraught with a nearly unsolvable methodological problem of determining the proper level of analysis. Accounts of the

---

[9] See Ferree (1992) for a review of various lines of criticism of rational choice and resource mobilization theory.

emergence and life spans of individual movements may be of considerable use to comparative models, but only when they are accompanied by an accounting of their antecedents and how they relate to regional commercial arrangements and local arrangements of governance and power. Charles Tilly's survey of four centuries of contentious politics in France suggests that markets can be incorporated into analysis without obscuring the complexities of local agency (Tilly 1992). If, *as such*, industrialization and commercial expansion cannot be easily characterized as immediate causes of rural or urban unrest, Tilly argues nonetheless that the component parts of those forces still may be expected to transform the structures of power and collective action. "Urbanization and industrialization," Tilly writes, "are by no means irrelevant to collective violence. It is just that their effects do not work as [classical] theories say they should. Instead of a short run generation of strain, followed by protest, we find a long-run transformation of the structures of power and of collective action" (quoted in McAdam 1982: 41). His data suggest that the reaction of various rural groups to capitalism and the consolidation of the modern state varied widely, in part because commercial agriculture affected people with differing degrees of severity and in part because social organization was altered in a heterogeneous fashion.

In Mexico, as in Tilly's France, a rearrangement of capitalism and the transformation of the state's role in the economy likewise are not taking place in a vacuum. Instead, new policies and external market pressures are interacting with preexisting hierarchies and local systems of material negotiation. By analyzing contentious group politics that accompany market transition, we may better understand the long-term implications of crisis and adjustment for systems of control and participation. Studying political economy as it affects but does not determine group choices or government response to protest helps explain why distributive conflict may have such an erratic character among affected classes and sectors. Although groups are in some fashion shaped by external events and pressures, the abilities of social movements to launch critiques of the regime or simply to gain selective settlements from the state will likely not develop uniformly inside a set of political economic conditions. The Mexican national case reinforces this principle: to date, no "dominant coalition" corresponding to a set of logical structural principles has emerged to claim a hegemonic position over distributive economic policy. Grassroots initiatives that are able to mobilize new members, organize collective action, and make credible claims to be the designated representatives of significant numbers of people have emerged in wildly disparate sectors of society and remain divided by parties, personalistic factions, historical feuds, region, class, and ethnicity.

I intend in the following presentation to demonstrate how one might generate plausible hypotheses about the impact of economic transition on social organization and attendant forms of protest and political bargaining. I do so by identifying – in two distinct regional and sectoral settings – how a changing political economy affected the everyday worlds of people within them. I examine new obstacles that confronted people who sought to dispute distributive policies as well as what new weapons of nonviolent dispute emerged as a result of political changes. In one case, a rapid expansion of industry and then a series of fiscal cutbacks and privatizations in the western state of Michoacán established and then dissolved the terms of state-society negotiation for tens of thousands of workers and squatters who worked and lived at and around a vast steel mill complex. In another case, situated in the north-central state of Zacatecas, trade liberalization and the termination of production subsidies changed the way grain farmers could expect to make a living from their properties. In both cases, regional movements emerged from motley cross-class assemblages of people who temporarily shared both real material interests and notions about who was to blame for their losses.

The two case studies were chosen for selected differences and similarities. As I began my fieldwork, I sought cases where one could likely establish clear links between policy changes and income or production. Departing from the highly intrasectoral emphasis in Mexicanist scholarship, I juxtapose workers' and farmers' disputes in order to bring out parallels as well as differences in forms of protest and countervailing systems of political control. Despite the fact that channels of bargaining and patterns of association are linked to institutional forms of representation as well as the spaces people work in, protest also implicates communities, neighborhoods, and families. Most often, protest is organized when workers leave the factory and farmers leave the fields or growers' unions, and this frequently draws others into their disputes in some manner. As I argue throughout the following chapters, launching and sustaining collective struggles has as much or more to do with cultivating local ties across sectors than with mobilizing dissent inside economic units.

I also selected these case studies because of similarities among the sectoral groups directly affected by policy changes. Although neither were elites as such, both grain farmers and union workers in Zacatecas and Michoacán were initially better off than many of their cohorts, and thus contributed to local economies not only as producers but also as significant blocks of consumers. In this manner, the disruptions to livelihoods of workers and farmers affected other local groups around them, such as shopkeepers and suppliers. Before the collapse of farm lending in the mid-1990s, growers in central Zacatecas, for the most part, were cash-based farmers and ejidatarios[10] and had more access to land, guarantee prices, and government finance than the majority of grain-farming peasants in the nation. Base workers in the steel industry in Michoacán, likewise, had better-than-average pay and benefits. Assuming, then, that if people chose to contest policy changes or their direct impacts (farm bankruptcy, for example), I hypothesized that gaining concessions from the government or even maintaining protest would be dependent on groups' abilities to adapt to changing institutional environments (Craig 1990; Fox 1992b). Making protest effective and durable would also likely be contingent on adapting to shifting interests among elites as well as among other local groups (Cook 1997; McAdam 1982). Finally, following the leads of numerous other scholars (Foweraker 1993; Fox 1992a; Bennett 1992; Keck and Sikkink 1997, 1998; Rubin 1997), I ventured that sustaining dissent depended on making resonant claims, forming strong coalitions, and devising means to deal with internal strife and the decision-making process.

This study owes much to a rich body of literature on social movements in Latin America and elsewhere. However, I also seek to expand the analysis of contentious politics by unpacking market transition as a bundled set of phenomena affecting both the structures and ideas that undergird collective action. By presenting privatization, fiscal retrenchment, and trade opening as shifts in modes of resource distribution, I argue that one is able to consider what rapid changes may do, at once, to real group interests and to narratives of justice and state legitimacy. In explaining how economic and political reforms of the last two decades have affected con-

---

[10] *Ejidatarios*, or members of *ejidos*, historically held usufruct rights to portions of collective lands granted by the government under constitutional land reform provisions. Officially, ejidatarios make decisions collectively through ejidal commissions, and through secondary-level organizations called ejidal unions. The degree to which any of these organizations is controlled by growers varies enormously (Fox 1992a, 1992b; Baitenmann 1998). As discussed in Chapter 1, ejidatarios now may go through a set of procedures to gain title to these lands, and may liquidate, leverage, or rent their holdings if they wish. This is a result of a set of reforms made to Article 27 of the 1917 Constitution.

tentious politics, I argue that it is crucial to examine not only levels of protest but also the manner in which policy changes may relocate contention and reconfigure the structure of social demands. By looking at how established modes of patronage affect and are affected by the relocation of contention, we are better able to understand why certain types of new political coalitions emerge with the capacity for mass action but also why such coalitions are so mercurial in nature.

In summary, the studies of contention in Lázaro Cárdenas and Zacatecas suggest two strong arguments about the intersection of markets and distributive protest. First, the retreat of the federal government in fiscal programs, industrial production, and the regulation of prices is likely to channel social demands into new domains. The character of protest and the makeup of dissenting groups then may change where groups demand the creation of new distributive channels or where bargaining shifts toward pools of social development resources brokered year to year by municipal and state governments. This process, which *fuels and is fueled by* the expansion of opposition parties and more autonomous civil associations, has ruptured many iron-clad fiefdoms among ruling party elites. However, because resources of states and municipalities remain tied to highly volatile and politically manipulated outlays from the federal government (Quiñones 1995; Willis, Garman, and Haggard 1999), protesting groups often face serious strategic dilemmas between pursuing longer term access to institutions and short-term settlements for immediate problems.

Second, the rearrangement of government jurisdictions effected by market-oriented changes has rendered the state environment highly unstable. Because the municipal and state-level agents who deal with protesters have unclear jurisdictions and variable budget lines, struggles over microlevel issues tend to last for very long periods of time and require repeated and costly mobilization on the part of protesters. As a result, insurgent groups must find ways of externalizing the cost of protest itself. They do this by making alliances with other groups, by making deals with political parties, by courting the sympathies of the media and portions of the public, and even by altering the internal practices of the group.

The following work is organized in two parts, beginning with an analytic framework and background and concluding with case studies. Part I introduces the problematic of social movements in a transition context. In Chapter 1, I discuss the factors that may shift the location of contention, the constituency of protest movements, and political narratives under-

15

girding them. In contrast to the macro-level formulations of modernization theory or early social movements theory, which predicted cycles of
unrest as a result of market development with a broad brush, the following study departs from the position that one may argue that such a causal
chain of events exists only if the concrete triggers of social movement
activity can be identified. Moving to a level of analysis closer to the ground,
I examine how regional bottlenecks and relatively localized changes in
resource administration may in fact be the precipitating factors in the
formation of insurgencies that go on to challenge established patterns of
state-society relations. Conceptualizing the political economy, then, as a
changing game board of obstacles and pathways to action that present
themselves to would-be social movement organizers, Chapters 1 and 2
discuss why movements coalesce when they do. Chapter 2 examines what
movement participants do after some collective demands and measure of
organization have emerged. Given the fact that participants in social movements are most vulnerable to selective repression when they are the least
visible, I argue that many movements' strategies of action and confrontation have as much to do with avoiding repression as with actually winning
their demands. I present a second set of hypotheses about movements'
strategies of survival. Allies, friends, inclusive rhetoric, and careful selec-
tion of protest repertoires may provide movements greater protection,
more collective resources, and ultimately more power vis-à-vis the state
than they would otherwise have.

After several years spent researching and writing this book, I remain
convinced that contention provides a singular window on the larger
problem of compromised citizenship in countries officially counted as
civilian democracies. If, as Tarrow argues, contentious politics are used by
people who lack regular access to institutions (1994: 2), then scholarship
on contentious politics in semiauthoritarian contexts reminds us that petition, protest, and collective pressure will likely assume a central axis of
political life where vast and increasing numbers of people are shut out of
formal institutions of arbitration, regulation, or distribution. Pointing out
the potential for heightened contention in an environment of scarcity,
Vilas notes, for example, that "an important and usually very aggressive
part of the 'new poor' in Latin America is recruited from . . . urban and
middle-class sectors, including those who are relatively well educated and
informed. These are the students without diplomas, professionals without
patrons, technicians without techniques, families without homes, and businessmen without businesses" (1997: 25).

Introduction

Contention, as a hard form of bargaining, of course, has long been a component of clientelist politics in Mexico. In a system in which layers of authorities, political bosses, and elite classes typically have controlled resources through the use of partially informal means, protest is a recognizable and sometimes successful means of negotiating for reforms or one-time settlements. At the same time, collective demands are not simple input-output machines. Protest, as it mobilized, repeated, and extended, also transforms politics. Collective demands, as they are fueled by basic narratives of rights or responsibilities, challenge established doctrines, practices, and configurations of power. As observers of Mexico have pointed out, contention is a site where collective identities and narratives of justice are both established and contested. It is also a juncture at which groups form lateral and vertical ties with one another in ways that may change the stakes or meaning of protest.

At the turn of the millennium, many acknowledge the existence of a permanent zero-sum arrangement in poor and middle-income countries wherein macroeconomic stability depends on policies that also leave many unemployed or underemployed, and outside the umbrella of public services. As a result, economic actors straddle formal and informal modes of exchange. In a similar manner, politics also involves official and unofficial forms of bargaining and control. Thus, I argue in this book that market transition, in bringing about many visible changes in the stewardship of policy and institutions, may change the character, location, and stakes of informal politics, including petition, protest, and disruption.

I

1

Markets, Machine Politics, and Protest in Mexico

It is an ironic aspect of much work in the social sciences that the conceptual terms used to describe the logic of protest or policy often obscure the texture of what is being talked about. In this case, terms such as *political opportunity*, *choice*, or *market liberalization* hide as much they reveal. *Opportunity*, for example, is a word social movement theorists have used when referring to political or institutional circumstances external to a group that prompt the emergence or expansion of collective action.[1] However, in reality the term is quite distant from what people in movements experience emotionally or physically as they engage in public assemblies or occupations. Protest, for most people, is at best inconvenient and at worst terrifying. And protest often is priced regressively; that is, to be seen by officials, the poorest often must carry out much more aggressive or prolonged actions than wealthier citizens. As I discuss the ways in which privatization, fiscal retrenchment, and trade opening affect the terrain of contention, one must keep in mind that the concept of "opportunity" is

---

[1] As of late, scholars have begun to debate the conceptual utility of notions of "political opportunity." Goodwin and Jasper (1999) argue, for example, that the variable of opportunity as it is employed by theorists such as Tarrow (1994) is excessively broad and tends to lend a false structural cast to nonstructural factors. He notes, for example, that opposite sorts of phenomena may both be labeled social movement "opportunities." An example of this might be the opportunities Tarrow describes in the suppression of state violence on the one hand (lowering the costs of acting collectively) or the increased use of it on the other (radicalizing groups and creating more effective forms of organization). In the same issue, Tarrow (1999) and Tilly (1999) respond to Goodwin's arguments, acknowledging the shortcomings of the concept and the dangers of reifying this metaphor of opportunity, but contend that Goodwin misrepresents the concept in his critique and presents no alternative explanation. Such an argument, writes Tilly, "implicitly claims that the deep causes of social processes reside within individuals, in some interplay of emotion and consciousness (1999: 58)" – a notion Tilly heartily rejects.

APRENDE JUGANDO ■ El Fisgón

Learn While Playing, by **El Fisgón** The two drawings depict "old bossism" on the left, and what state officials call "new federalism" on the right. Instructions for the game on the margin read: "Hey little friend! See if you can find the six differences between these two drawings. And if you *find* the six differences, please let the leadership of the PRI know." From *La Jornada*, January 9, 1995. Reprinted by permission.

quite imprecise – it is a concept that is useful to a point but that should not be fetishized. For example, I interviewed one group of urban slum residents in Lázaro Cárdenas City who might be said to have mobilized protest for clean drinking water in an auspicious opportunity environment because they had allies in a powerful steel workers' union and because a few local elites were disposed to negotiate with them. What the residents of the slum remember is not opportunity, but instead a time of disease and horror in which forty-two children died from contaminated water, followed by a time of protest provoked, they say, by "sheer necessity." Residents view their mobilization over time, which resulted in the installation of running water, sewers, a primary school, and electricity, as a campaign of raw will, deployed because of gross negligence on the part of the government, and not – as the researcher might model the situation – as a series of strategic choices.

"Market transition" as experienced by local communities and individuals is also quite different from its technical representation in charts and graphs, which indicates various adjustments in the economy as a whole. The ways in which trade opening, fiscal cuts, and the liberalization of markets are experienced on the shopfloor, in neighborhoods, or in rural indigenous communities often provoke not only drastic material changes in people's lives but also unexpectedly aggressive actions if crisis and new policies radically conflict with people's understandings of their basic rights and responsibilities and of themselves in relation to others and the state. First, austerity programs, state retrenchment, and market transition do not interact with people and local communities as their metaphorical incarnations would suggest. To a maize farmer who can no longer sell at any profit, open markets are not like the free marketeer's neatly ordered games, creating "winners" and "losers." Many who stand to be dispossessed don't remember choosing to play in the first place. The open market to such an individual might appear more like a tornado that rips through a valley, pulverizing some streets and houses and inexplicably leaving other structures untouched. In reality, crisis and rapid market transition affect populations unevenly and, for many, quite unfairly if historical relationships are taken into account. Insofar as they also are superimposed on preexisting hierarchies and exacerbate inequalities, unencumbered markets are apt to be seen over time as purely evil forces – reinforcing the domination of the *gringo*, the *cacique* (rural boss), the landlord, and the moneylender. At local levels, most who have lost jobs or sources of income are well acquainted with neighbors who make rapid income gains. Rich residents who become richer are rarely admired as smart investors who took advantage of universally accessible opportunities; many see them merely as thieves who have bought off the police.

For subordinate actors in an authoritarian environment such as Mexico, politics are not experienced as landscapes of opportunity, and markets are not experienced as menus for individual choice. I make this statement for more than rhetorical purposes. In the following discussion, I argue that policy changes and industrial trends associated with market transition have shifted the sites of protest and the structure of collective demands.

However, I also argue that despite the success of elites in remaking clientelist relationships, contention has volatile properties, precisely because there are affective dimensions to markets and politics that factor greatly into people's choices to engage in protest or not, to leave their communities or not, or to participate in new market systems or not.

Although difficult to quantify or specify, a change in opportunity is not just a reconfiguration of material risk and benefit; it also entails a transformation of individuals understandings of power and possibility. In localities in which oppositional political action has exploded in the wake of market-oriented policies, the observer would do well to remember James Scott's discussion of "hidden transcripts," or moral discourse that takes place beyond the observation of elites. When subordinates air grievances in an environment in which dissent is normally suppressed, protest is likely to carry with it the energy of long pent-up fury. "The first public declaration of the hidden transcript," Scott observes, "has a prehistory that explains its capacity to produce political breakthroughs" (1990: 227). There is no contradiction, for example, in Zapatista claims to have risen up against the North American Free Trade Agreement (NAFTA) *and* 500 years of colonial and neocolonial oppression. Like a long-unfaithful spouse who finally runs off with a new lover, the exit of the Institutional Revolutionary Party (PRI)-dominated state from maize production, the coffee industry, or paper manufacturing may provoke the airing of long-unattended complaints from the population. Not only is the spouse remembered as having abandoned his or her family – he or she forever will be recalled as an all-around lout, guilty of a lifetime of sins and slights. Likewise, in movements that identify both the new free trade system and the 70-year-old PRI as bulwarks of an unjust, undemocratic, or even abjectly evil system, "opportunity" is made of emotional as well as material and political components. Free trade, in a given community, may provoke new and tenacious episodes of protest because it devastates the incomes of numerous groups at once. Market transition, if it is seen being ushered into a community by regime elites long seen as corrupt and collusive, may provoke an explosion of long-held social demands, long whispered, but never articulated publicly.

In this work, therefore, I argue that opportunity for protest occurs when a particular narrative of good and evil becomes available to a group of people *at a moment when* the state cannot produce an effective counternarrative and is constrained in the use of force against dissenters. In discussing collective action in terms of opportunities, I concur in great measure with theorists such as Cook (1996), Tarrow (1994), McAdam (1982), or Piven and Cloward (1979), who emphasize the importance of variations in the political environment in affecting the fortunes of political insurgencies. Attentive to the fact that protest is a dangerous and costly business, and that it is mobilized inside very small and tenuous spaces of official tolerance, such theorists have pointed out the importance of access to key decision-making venues, shifting alignments or divisions among elites, influential allies, and the structure of official violence. These theorists, as well as others such as Foweraker (1993) writing on the Mexican teachers' movement of the early 1980s, also point out that opportunities may present devastating dilemmas for political insurgents as well. Groups making demands often have to make fatal decisions between settling for relatively safe short-term solutions or risking repression in a long-term struggle for power and assured access to institutions.

Spaces for open dissent in Mexico are narrow, but they tend to occur in different places at different times with considerable frequency. As Cook reminds us, "The concept of political space helps us to think not only of the existence of opportunities for effective political action, but to think of these as both *temporally* and *spatially* located. Political space usually opens up for limited periods of time and can be located in different sectors or at different levels" (Cook 1996: 39).

In a sense, all spaces for political protest in Mexico are constituted by a fundamental contradiction in the logic of patron-client governance: whereas rule is legitimized through an inclusive rhetoric and legal framework, power is in fact maintained through exclusive practices and extralegal transactions in which goods are exchanged for political loyalty. When political insurgents successfully expose practices of the latter nature using the legitimizing language of the state, they may stave off suppression of protest and petition for a crucial period of time. During this time, they will inevitably utilize various political tools to press their demands. Of crucial importance in understanding opportunity in an authoritarian environment is the treacherous proximity between violence and conciliation. As an individual group maintains or escalates protest actions over time, attracting attention and thus belying the state's claims to uphold its obligations to meet the material needs of subordinate classes, it becomes more likely that the group will obtain a positive settlement from the state. On the other hand, the longer a group maintains or escalates protest actions – thereby threatening real, vested interests – the more likely members of the group will be to face repression and cooptive pressures. Thus, the contradictory situation wherein groups seeking to extend protest in order to overcome a negotiations impasse must also retard a growing threat of repression from the state.

What this study suggests is that shifts in economic policy over time will affect the fortunes of distributive movements by making certain types of social demands and certain types of collective protest identities far more prominent than in the past and others more scarce. As the case studies demonstrate, sea changes in economic policy affect elite tolerance insofar as they alter state officials' relationship to local and/or sectoral constituencies and to one another. These shifts also render some problems more visible or more easily grieved, whereas others become less so. Finally, long-run shifts in economic policy affect political actors' ability to mobilize broad protest over various distributive issues because of changing livelihoods, patterns of consumption, strategies of saving, and household divisions of labor.

In this chapter, I begin with the observation that market transition has not ended clientelism, as some predicted. Instead, market-oriented policies have shifted the locus of state-society bargaining and contentious politics and, thus, have altered the narratives people use to challenge distributive arrangements, as well as the coalitions they build to make demands of the government. Regarding the persistence of clientelism, I concur with Judith Hellman (1994b: 128), who contends that despite the broad expansion of representative groups outside corporatist structures of representation, the dominant mode of state-society bargaining remains clientelist in nature. "Although the emergence of a new movement may challenge the old PRI-linked networks based on local caciques," she writes, "it undermines the control of the caciques only by replacing the old networks with alternative channels that, generally speaking, are also clientelistic in their mode of operation." Launching from this point, however, I argue that it is important to examine how powerful actors attempt to remake clientelist structures of control and how insurgents try to undermine that process.

In the ensuing discussion, I briefly outline a logic of clientelism and social bargaining and then discuss how market-oriented policies have shifted the structure of collective demand and the location of contention. I suggest first that protest has been remarkably well compartmentalized during a harrowing two decades of market shocks and radical government restructuring. Subsequently, I argue that reconstituted systems of clientelism are also inherently volatile under free market conditions. Market policies have also drawn upon a discourse of citizenship that degrades local structures of control more readily than in the past. Technologies of civilian control, which implicitly prescribe the use of group petition and peaceful protest to bargain with the state for resources, also leave open risks that local demands may aggregate following market shocks, or following elite defections from the ruling party. Protest may also introduce new risks to markets when it targets private sector actors, when it threatens policy continuity, or when it appears to reflect a crisis of governability in the regime.

On Machine Politics

Academic and literary analyses of the nature of the single party regime that lumbered on in power until the end of the century have occupied tens of thousands of pages of text and countless years of debate. Certainly, all would agree that one factor that distinguished the Mexican regime from other regimes was its extraordinary longevity. The antecedent to the present PRI formed in the late 1920s during the years under Plutarco Elías Calles's control. President Lázaro Cárdenas took steps to consolidate the ruling party in 1938, and organized the corporatist framework of the Party of the Mexican Revolution (eight years later renamed under President Miguel Alemán as the Institutional Revolutionary Party). Notably, the Institutional Revolutionary Party maintained an astoundingly long-lived domestic peace in a nation prone to long periods of civil war, sectoral conflict, and peasant uprisings. Stretching from 1810 into the 1920s, countless episodes of conflict erupted between liberal and conservative forces, monarchists and republicans, constitutionalists and agraristas, federalists and antifederalists, centralists and regional caciques, and landed classes and peasants. Mexicans in the cities and the countryside suffered chronic food shortages, onerous taxation from both Church and state for war debts, and mandatory service in the armed forces. Save for the 33 years of dictatorship under Porfirio Díaz that preceded the Revolution of 1910–17, little infrastructure was built, and transport and industrial facilities were routinely destroyed by war. Schools and hospitals were nearly unknown to much of the population; death rates for much of the first century of Mexico's existence were so high that the population only increased from a plateau of about ten million people during the years through 1877 to about fifteen million at the turn of the century (Katz 1991: 74).

Then, the Revolution depleted the population by one-tenth. Such a harrowing history of violence and human want left many Mexicans with the sense that political and economic unity – indeed civil order itself – were always, in some sense, at risk in this fractured nation. As Octavio Paz wrote, "The function of the new organism [the party] was above all negative: not so much to set up a program as to reduce the clashes among factions and to put down troublemakers. Although it was not a seed of democracy, it was the beginning of a new national political structure, tightly bound to the new state" (1985: 240). The perceived formula for social peace, for many Mexicans, lay in the institutionalization of a single party, a strong and expansive Executive branch, and the election of a new president every six years with no reelection. Even as many became disillusioned over the decades with the PRI's handling of economic affairs and distributive issues, there was widespread fear into the 1990s that the PRI still monopolized the capacity to maintain civilian peace in Mexico. In the 1994 federal elections, for example, one of the ruling party's most effective campaign slogans was *"Vote por la paz,"* – or "Vote for peace." The implication, of course, was that any other party would be unable to control the simmering social divisions that lay just under the surface of Mexican society. The propensity of regime officials to mix conciliatory measures with repression when dealing with collective social demands was very much a part of this history of extended and horrific social violence. On the one hand, the regime retained the use of force in some conflicts to maintain one of the world's most unequal distributions of wealth. On the other hand, the regime made visible interventions into other conflicts to establish and reestablish itself as the unique arbiter of class conflict in a hopelessly divided society.

Collective action not sanctioned by the official party has been very risky in the presence of the pyramidal structure of the ruling party state. Although rights to assembly, free speech, and political organization exist on paper, they have not been enforced systematically over time by tribunals, legislatures, or federal executive agencies. Until 1997, when the PRI lost its majority in the lower house of the legislature, it was nearly unthinkable that the Congress would use its official veto powers on issues of substance. "The strength of the . . . executive branch generally," writes Roderic Camp, "is at the cost of an ineffectual legislative and judicial branch, or any other autonomous authority" (1993:13). Despite the dangers, though, standoffs and skirmishes have historically occurred with a tenacious frequency in Mexico, even among those so isolated or poor that they have little defense against harsh, punitive actions.

Protest and collective action do not occur randomly. In an authoritarian environment in which civil liberties are often violated in disputes, especially those involving lower class actors, timing and location of protest affect groups' chances of facing rapid repression. Subordinate groups also are more apt to stay intact through protest where elite conflicts in local or federal agencies pit state actors against one another. In the 1980s and 1990s, during which vast reorganization of the economy shifted power inside elite circles and altered the source of rents for the state and for powerful private sector actors, opportunity for protest and collective action generally increased. Openings for protest were not evenly distributed, however. The free trade regime brought with it more rigorous social and political control in some areas, particularly in those sectors where market dynamism might have been threatened by popular unrest. This, in turn, forced the political demobilization of certain formerly militant groups as well as a redrawing of political group boundaries that allowed for greater maneuverability in collective actions.

Despite heterogeneity in local systems, certain principles of social control have governed material allocation by a centralized state. Mexico's patron-client system, which began consolidating substantial regional control in the 1930s, has patterned state-society bargaining through officially designated peak organizations. Corporatist entities representing workers, the peasantry, and urban sectors officially bargain with central executive powers for wages, housing, production subsidies, and public services. Unofficially, the same entities regulate how members participate in politics and the terms upon which individuals advance politically and economically inside the ruling party.

Where patron-client systems of government remain in full force, local politics in Mexico are likely to be marked by at least three major characteristics. First, rewards are distributed in exchange for explicit political support. In the days and weeks before elections, one may see "goodies" such as free lunch, housing materials, or bonus pay given to attendees at political rallies. In the most egregious instances, payments are distributed to (presumably loyal) voters at polls on election day. Second, brokers of employment and subsidies condition the distribution of those goods on support for the ruling party. Leaders of union locals, heads of neighborhood associations, or chiefs of farmers' cooperatives are most often responsible for "turning out" workers, housewives, and peasants to voting polls, parades, and rallies. For a leader who is particularly effective in mobilizing support, the party may consider offering him or her a position higher up in the party hierarchy. On the other hand, failure to organize such support on the part of a leader (particularly one whose position is due to ruling party favor) may result in the termination of his or her charge. Failure of the rank-and-file to accept leaders' "invitations" to participate in events or to be bussed to the polls may result in receiving docked pay, being labeled a "troublemaker," or experiencing general difficulty in obtaining individual items in the future (such as a farm machinery subsidy or an official's recommendation for college admission). A third characteristic of Mexican machine politics is an allocations system in which greater amounts of federal goods and services are granted to neighborhoods or villages loyal to the ruling party. Areas that pledge support for the ruling party in the future or that have demonstrated ability to organize on behalf of the ruling party may expect greater largesse from regional governmental authorities. Residents of areas favored by party officials may expect to see roads paved, wells dug, and schools and health clinics built.

The PRI-led regime's great hallmark was its ability to outlive severe crises of economic insolvency and political impasse without ever relinquishing power or reforming class inequalities or the degree of elite corruption. The PRIista order outlived the horror of the military assassination of several hundred students in the center of Mexico City in 1968. In the early 1970s, multiple terrorist and guerrilla movements peopled by the rural and urban poor, and allied with students from the 1968 movement, were put down in Guerrero and Nuevo León. In the middle 1970s, widespread worker insurgency permeated workplaces and threatened to dismantle a several-decades-old PRI monopoly over organized labor. In addition, land invasion movements by landless farmers and urban poor rocked local business and ranching elites around the country and provoked considerable violence into the late 1970s. On a macroeconomic level, Mexico's troubles long have been quite serious as well. Even before the 1982 debt crisis, which would mark the beginning of Mexico's trajectory toward market-oriented reforms, Mexico had suffered serious problems in its external accounts. A devaluation in 1976 took a bite out of household incomes and permanently marred the reputation of outgoing president Luis Echeverría. Economic activity subsequent to that, bolstered by exploitation of newfound petroleum reserves in Tabasco, probably contributed to an over-leveraging of future oil profits during President Lopez Portillo's administration in the years 1976 to 1982.

Attesting to the power of machine politics to contain political opposition at local levels, the most obvious effect of the subsequent crises of subsistence has not been mass disruption and regime collapse but instead an explosion in informal economic activity. A depressed consumer economy that is saturated with producers has put ever-downward pressure on the price of rural and urban labor, prompting many families to draw greater portions of household income from *tianguis* (sidewalk stalls), informal services, and migrant labor. Wives and children often contribute to family incomes by selling food or crafts or other small items on the streets or out of their homes.[2] Indeed, informal activity is so prevalent that shopkeepers in cities complain that their businesses are threatened from rising numbers of sidewalk vendors hawking their wares outside the shops at impossibly narrow profit margins. One study in Mexico City commissioned in 1994 counted nine illegal merchants for every ten formal businesses. Researchers estimate that by 2000, the informal sector will employ 44 percent of all urban workers (Gómez Flores 1999).

Managed Scarcity, Functional Dependence

A system in which political control is exercised through the selective allocation of material resources has proven to be, in comparative terms, quite a stable system type in the developing world. It is not seamless, though; protest and dissent often lodge themselves in the contradictions of governance embodied by an authoritarian-corporatist regime. There is, for example, an inherent dilemma between the state's need for short-term electoral support and its need for long-term legitimacy. Especially among the poor (notably, still the PRI's most solid constituency), a patron-client system is likely to provide channels of resources all the way to what is often called *la base* (a reference to the "base" of the political pyramid), but only to a point where short-term needs are barely met. In that way, the provision of services, such as drinking water, roads, or deeds to land – once promised to loyal constituents – can garner energetic support over many years. Promised services usually arrive in target areas at some point – illustrating some good faith on the part of the organizer, but they may be delayed over several election cycles, during which the dependent constituency can be counted on to faithfully deliver votes and attend official rallies.

---

[2] For an accounting of economic survival strategies of the poor during the 1980s, including a discussion of immigration, household compensation, and self-help, see Mercedes Gonzalez de la Rocha and Agustín Escobar Latapí (1991).

An account of makeshift settlement told by squatters best illustrates the principle. In a given year, tell the *colonos* (members of the neighborhood), a certain number of people had come to live on a narrow piece of land by a river, informally renting the land from a group of ejidatarios who had official use-rights to the land. A nearby company (owned by the government at the time) did not want the settlers on that place but lacked the legal authority to demand that they exit. The government did have water diversion channels and would open the gates at night, flooding the settlers' houses. Finally, the colonos left in desperation. Lacking a place to go, the group petitioned the local government for another piece of land in the vicinity. The government agreed, and the *damnificados* (homeless people) were then ceded the use of a hillside plot, with the additional promise that the government would promptly give them official titles to their plots. Although officially this land was also owned by ejidatarios, regional urban authorities effectively regulated use of the land, as the adjacent area was being developed for industry and planned residences. Grateful to the government, they said, the settlers set about making the eroded land into a neighborhood. Two years went by before the settlers got outside spigots with potable water. Two additional years passed before titles to the land were issued. And still two more years went by before electric wires were installed. And still in the realm of promises were a primary school in the area for the growing number of children among the young families of the neighborhood and pavement for the streets in their hillside colony that turned to mud six months a year in the rainy season (Interview C-11, 1994).

The shortages and delays in resource distribution that so infuriate people – but that often serve to organize vast electoral support for the ruling party – periodically have spurred the emergence of oppositional movements in localities. Interestingly, the didactic power of the "institutionalized revolutionary" state began to work against itself in these cases. Thousands of local level insurgencies in the six decades of one-party rule testify to the fact that, given the opportunity, groups opted to bite the hand that was feeding them badly. The organization that the state requires of neighborhoods and collective farms, workplaces, and business sectors so that they can petition for resources in the first place, worked against the ruling party's goals of social quiescence when those organized groups decided to use that organization to demonstrate against inadequate state administration.

In most communities at most times, clientelism is peaceful. Rising aggregate demand for redistribution may fuel group anger and propensity to mobilize, but risk of retribution through fiscal deprivation remains ever present. Put simply, people have less to lose than before by mobilizing protest, but they still have something to lose. Although Mexico is said to have been a "model" of market-oriented reform, the degree to which liberalized markets determine distribution of credit, goods, housing, employment, and production has actually varied considerably. And, of course, health care, schools, and the provision of basic infrastructure remain explicitly in the visible hand of the state. In this manner, one can well expect distributive movements to ebb and surge over many of the same basic needs as in past decades; crisis and economic transition alter the timing and physical location of contention, the makeup of coalitions, as well as the relative likelihood of elite defections that provide crucial cover and resources for the maintenance of protest.

Shifting Locations of Protest

The links between market-related shocks are not so intuitive as one might think. It is especially important not to assume, for example, that declines in salaried income will necessarily produce wage-based protests, or that liberalization of land tenure or trade will produce land-based protests or calls for protectionism. Instead, with respect to dropping wages, acute crises of consumption combined with blocked access to substantive salary negotiation have prompted many income earners and their household counterparts to turn to neighborhood-based forms of collective protest and petition as a means of making up for lost buying power. With respect to the impact of changing land tenure and trade policies in contention, one finds embattled farmers mobilizing largely around immediate problems of debt and low commodity prices. In both case studies in Part II, radical policy changes altered not only what it was possible or worthwhile to demand but also of whom it was possible to demand resources or assistance. Income declines and debt were products of fiscal retrenchment, privatization, and trade opening, but those processes shifted protest out of older federal and corporatist channels and into a much more volatile and experimental political terrain.

In Lázaro Cárdenas City, as I demonstrate, the government's privatization of the steel mill provoked a Pyrrhic battle to preserve employment and hard-won union contract victories from years past, but within eighteen months of the transferral of the plant to the private sector, the mobilizational capacity of labor had been nearly exhausted in the city.

Contention then shifted from factory to neighborhood. Often led by steel workers and ex-steel workers, protest movements emerged over housing, urban infrastructure, and the environment. A number of protests also emerged in which people demanded direct monetary compensation for a variety of claims, including industrial contamination of fisheries and decades-old expropriation of land for railroad easements. Notably, with the dissolution of federal institutions of management in the region, protesters frequently occupied the municipal government buildings in their insistence on gaining a hearing with authorities.

In Zacatecas, by contrast, privatization of agricultural credit and liberalization of input prices drove producers into bankruptcy. In this region, growers who had previously negotiated independently and even at odds with one another through federal or corporatist agencies united in the mid-1990s over the issue of farm debt. The change in demand is striking. In this impoverished region, rural demands – although contentious and even violent at moments – typically were channeled through a well-oiled partnership of federal agricultural and buying agencies and the ruling party's corporatist associations for ejidatarios and private landholders. As the federal government receded in the regulation of production and finance, sudden bankruptcy unified the demands of groups which previously had operated separately. Protest spilled into new public arenas, as farmers challenged the governor, marched on Mexico City, and even confronted powerful private banks with direct actions and physical takeovers of buildings and properties.

In an authoritarian patron-client system, the discussion so far suggests that people will demand the possible. However, it is important not to reason backward and fall into the trap of imagining that contention could have taken no other form or trajectory during economic transition and the attendant devaluation crises. Also, insofar as the discussion in this book implicitly posits that these two cases suggest important things about how similar cases ought to be examined, it is worth situating these cases, at least briefly, in national trends and parallel events that have broadly affected both patron-client control structures and the building blocks of collective action.

Wage-Based Contention and Urban Protest

Explaining changing patterns of protest from wage-based to consumption-based demands in far-flung localities requires examining whether market-

oriented policies and industrial trends have made struggles via labor channels less relevant to very immediate struggles of people inside and outside
the formal economy. Certainly, there is the question of whether organized
labor was ever really that relevant to social demands in Mexico. Fewer than
20 percent of workers are unionized, and ruling party-controlled unions
in turn have most often cooperated with management to police the workforce and suppress demands rather than work with union members to
represent demands (La Botz 1988, 1992). Furthermore, the centralized
nature of wage bargaining, in which labor leaders negotiate salary caps that
function as ceilings on the demands of union locals, has limited what
unions could demand.[3] Linked to that, leaders at the helm of the most
powerful union nationals – Confederation of Mexican Workers (CTM),
the Regional Confederation of Workers and Peasants (CROC), and
Mexican Regional Labor Confederation (CROM) – did little to mobilize
protest among workers during the worst episodes of inflation and real
salary decline in the 1980s and 1990s. Instead, despite some sabre-rattling,
regime labor leaders ultimately allowed real salaries to decline, usually in
exchange for price-control guarantees on basic goods (Middlebrook 1989).

Nonetheless, one must ask why insurgent movements that did arise
among electricians, steel workers, railroad workers, airport workers, auto
workers, miners, and textile workers were not more significant conduits
for protest over distributive issues. Not only had such movements fought
for better wages and benefits, but many had also pioneered a discourse of
union democracy among constituencies that previously had little exposure
to politics outside routine authoritarian arrangements. Many outsiders
place the coalescence of a national movement toward multiparty democracy and government accountability at the electoral juncture of 1988;
however, more than a decade before that rank-and-file workers in insurgent movements were demanding union autonomy and linking that
process to a national project of democracy. Also, insofar as such intra- and
interunion movements had linked local demands to national aspirations,
the labor movement became an important emblem of actors outside union
circles. University students, professors, lawyers, writers, and journalists
drew language and modes of protest from such movements as well as
contributing amply to them.

---

[3] Prior to the mid-1980s, the government's minimum wage increase was supposed to serve
as a reference point for union contract negotiations. However, under President de la
Madrid, that percent wage increase became a *tope*, or wage ceiling (Middlebrook 1989: 198).

At least three important factors bear mention. First, plant closings and labor roll readjustments that accompanied privatization were by no means random. The purge of unionists who had fought for greater union autonomy and democracy in the 1970s were inevitably among the first to go (Laurell 1989a). This impeded the ability of workers to draw on regional and national networks of people who had learned over time to negotiate the very complex legal and political terrain of strikes and strong labor actions.

This trend was, of course, strengthened by dramatic sectoral and regional shifts in employment from domestically oriented manufacturing in the center of the country to export-oriented and maquiladora production in northern and border regions. In a ten-year period spanning the greatest portion of industrial restructuring, employment in the maquiladora sector – largely located in the northern border of the country – expanded at an average of 12.1 percent per year. By contrast, employment in forms of manufacturing other than export assembly contracted by an average of 2.1 percent per year (*Business Frontier* 1996). In most newer export-oriented manufacturing plants, factory owners have consciously sought to employ very young men and women – usually first-time employees – to forestall labor demands.[4] Unions, where they exist on the books, are in some cases created and controlled directly by the companies (a practice known in Mexico as "white unionism," or *sindicalismo blanco*). In many other cases, the titles to the unions are held by CTM, CROC, or CROM affiliates but are all but nonexistent as representatives of workers.

Second, the temporal axis for labor mobilization, the annual contract negotiation, was eliminated in many thousands of work sites as companies under strain refused to renew contracts, claiming that doing so would bankrupt the enterprise (Méndez 1987). In such cases, workers presumably were left as day laborers, or in better cases with simple take-home pay, state health coverage, and federally mandated severance provisions. In newer factories in the north, this has been paired in thousands of cases with the use of protection agreements in which corrupt union officials bargain secretly with private companies for union registrations. Then, in cases where workers have attempted to form their own unions, they have

---

[4] This is true not only in very low-paying jobs in the maquiladoras but also in better jobs in the automotive industry. Harley Shaiken (1994) found in his study of four northern manufacturing plants that managers consciously sought workers with less experience, preferring to spend resources training them, but presumably also avoiding worker agitation.

Table 1.1. *Government Spending over Time, by Sector (in millions of 1994 pesos)*

Year	Agriculture	Regional Development*	Urban Development	Industry
1985	4,817	2,123	6,121	3,644
1986	3,307	2,250	5,281	2,360
1987	2,428	4,468	1,178	2,340
1988	2,299	5,607	1,205	3,010
1989	2,987	6,366	818	1,896
1990	3,463	3,574	6,052	1,592
1991	3,652	4,896	6,640	1,219
1992	3,385	5,958	8,514	412
1993	2,855	6,779	8,481	171
1994	3,123	7,020	12,879	76
1995	1,628	4,643	3,080	64
1996	1,870	4,092**	4,092**	N/A

* Includes Solidarity.
** Budgets merged with agency changes.
Source: INEGI 1997, *Anuario Estadístico.*

faced long and violent battles with CROC, CROM, or CTM officials (Bacon 1997; Brooks and Cason 1998; Williams 1999b).

Third, severe reductions in federal spending, as well as a reallocation of spending within the federal budget, have sharply reduced the provision of housing and urban infrastructure, particularly through industrial sector spending. As Table 1.1 shows, federal spending on social development and production was quite volatile throughout the 1980s and 1990s, declining precipitously in the mid-1980s and again in the mid-1990s, mostly owing to currency devaluations. However, one also sees the impact of a conscious budget restructuring in which policymakers replaced spending in government sectors such as urban industry and agriculture with spending in urban and regional development. Notably, social welfare and development funds are generally channeled through state and municipal agencies rather than through labor or farm-sector channels. This further reinforces a shift in contention from institutionally bound protests in federal corporatist arenas toward local and state authorities.

Growth in the number of people seeking work, coupled with decline in the creation of better-salaried jobs with guaranteed benefits made it virtually impossible for vast numbers of people to obtain housing and small-scale credits. Thus, greater percentages of workers were left to self-help strategies for housing, which in turn implied mobilizing around a very different set of demands and through very different channels. If they turned to political means at all to address household crises, such wage-earners were more likely to put energies into seizing land and then mobilizing for some years to obtain basic urban amenities such as water, electricity, and sewage systems.

Certainly, the connection between the expansion of urban protest over services or for short-term goods and the exhaustion of insurgent energies in key portions of the labor movement is by no means absolute. There is no question that even if organized labor had remained a significant channel for collective demands and material bargaining, urban protests organized around consumption-based demands would likely have continued afoot. As scholarship on urban development and social organizing in Latin America reminds us, a significant portion of the economically active urban population in Latin America has never been incorporated into the formal workforce but instead has drawn its principal income from informal-sector sales or day labor (Mainwaring 1987; Castells 1977, 1983). Thus, even if formal-sector workers' demands had not been folded into urban protests in many cases, urban protests in turn likely would have continued to expand in an environment of scarce housing, tenuous incomes, and inadequate urban amenities. What is more significant is that labor insurgencies in Mexico ultimately played a small role in organizing urban protests or in building movements out of urban protests.

In this sense, economic transition can be characterized as a revelatory as well as socially disruptive process. Insofar as crisis and policy change press people to organize around different demands and to solicit government intervention through new channels, contention may lend salience to long-standing problems that have affected people in very different ways for some time. Latent conflicts involving subtle class distinctions, ethnic difference, and gender may emerge, transforming the terms in which people talk about crisis and personal needs. In urban environments, the increasingly prominent role of working-class women in contentious politics, for example, speaks to a long-standing set of problems women have dealt with as managers of scarcity (Bennett 1995; Hellman 1994a; Núñez 1990). Accompanying the new prominence (if not widespread leadership) of women in urban politics, the combativeness of informal-sector merchants reveals much about long-standing structures of inequality.

At the turn of the millennium, the "urban question," or the emergent political activity of working classes around housing, infrastructure, and services, has become the most significant locus of state-society politics in Latin America. It is important, however, as Portes (1990) suggests, to trace the links between state policies that facilitate or inhibit certain types of collective action and people's attempts to mobilize distributive protest. What the account of changing patterns of contention in Lázaro Cárdenas City should illustrate is the link between the suppression of labor demands and the intransigence of many other forms of distributive protest. In that city, market-oriented policies shifted contention in such a way that activists could no longer draw credibly or effectively on narratives of labor justice. Distributive politics shifted over time from institutionally bound, longer term union struggles around contract gains to more ad hoc struggles ending in one-time cash settlements, land titles, or urban infrastructure. The continuities in contentious politics, however, are also notable. In many cases, individuals who had participated actively in local unions spearheaded urban protests. In addition, the city remained combative: the percentage of the electorate loyal to left-of-center parties is twice the national average, and the sheer number of protests in the locality is extraordinarily high in comparison with other municipalities. The persistence, then, of certain threads of combativeness helps explain why groups may venture new demands in a dramatically altered policy and institutional environment.

Markets and Contention in the Countryside

As in urban wage-earning sectors, market transition has dealt a punishing blow to incomes in the countryside. It has also shifted the structure of contention in the countryside over time, with protest flaring over at least three general sets of issues, including (1) access to land, (2) autonomy and control over production, and (3) commodity prices and debt. Although each of these issues has a long history in farm politics, market-oriented policies have made such struggles more visible and more resonant nationally.

First, in southern regions, particularly in the state of Chiapas, a complex set of circumstances has fueled battles over unsettled land claims. These battles are linked to a larger set of demands, including calls for greater autonomy and decision-making power in indigenous localities, for fairer treatment in courts and government bureaucracies, and for better government policies in health, education, agriculture and social services.[5] Second, in some of the same regions and elsewhere, growers have mobilized against the political manipulation of productive resources, demanding fairer buying arrangements, access to credit, and production guarantees. Finally, high interest rates, low prices, and subsequent debt have prompted growers to use direct action against banks and government agencies. Notably, these latter mobilizations have drawn from wealthier farmers, many of whom formerly had rejected collective action as a means of gaining resources or concessions from the government.

Making sense of the impact of market-oriented policies on collective action in the countryside is a difficult task. Here, official accounts of liberalization and fiscal policy trends are deceptive because there has long existed a startling disparity between official and de facto policy events in Mexican agriculture. Land tenure is an excellent illustration of the ambiguities of real and official policy change. Many have spoken of the 1992 agrarian reforms, for example, as a dividing line between state-led and market-led agriculture. Journalists reporting the 1994 uprising in Chiapas sometimes even attributed the rebellion to the government's amendments to Article 27 of the 1917 Constitution, which established a commitment of the state in perpetuity to distribute land to the peasantry. This, however, was only one blow among many for the rural poor in Chiapas. The government's real disposition to distribute viable agricultural land to petitioners all but ceased by the mid-to-late 1970s. This had partly to do with the scarcity of land that could be requisitioned and redistributed without risking bloodshed or internecine battles inside the ruling party,[6] and it had partly to do with the declining profitability of small-scale farming. By the late 1970s, as well, real wages were increasing rapidly, and many small farmers chose to migrate to the cities or to the oil fields for work (Collier 1994).

With respect to land tenure arrangements and the supposedly "inalienable" status of existing land grants to ejidatarios, there has seldom been strict compliance with official laws. As classic studies of the Mexican coun-

---

[5] Such claims now occupy a much more prominent place in national politics, but none are new. In fact, the demands that much of the Mexican and international population became aware of after 1994 had begun materializing at least two decades before, largely in communities where Maoist organizing, radical catechist work, and national indigenous congresses took place (Harvey 1998).

[6] See, for example, Steven Sanderson's work on violent battles over land in Sonora (1981), in which regional elites fought against federal authorities who sought to intervene on the side of land-seeking peasants.

tryside by Warman (1980), Hewitt de Alcántara (1976), Grindle (1977), or Barkin and Suárez (1982) attest, growers have long traded, rented, and mortgaged acreage off the books; real control of land and votes is often maintained by rent-seeking middlemen who perform a sort of political and economic arbitrage between federal agencies and isolated rural communities. Notably, the inalienability of land, which was supposed to prevent speculators from consolidating large properties, also had the perverse effect of preventing ejidatarios from obtaining steady credit, as none had any tradeable land to post as collateral. This left them unable to improve their properties and soil and kept them hostage to undependable and politically manipulated sources of government credit and inputs such as fertilizer and seed. Making do from year to year in agriculture, then, inevitably involved the use of many layers of legal and illegal transactions, rendering property, production, and credit regimes highly heterogeneous.

Local regimes under such circumstances are often powder kegs, and the introduction of new policies or new scarcities stands to affect different communities in very different ways. Land-based contention, which has surged once again since the Zapatista uprising in Chiapas, is tied to coercive wage labor relations, police repression, lack of public services and education, and the absence of rule of law in the countryside. Legal changes per se are less significant than the latitude such changes may give to elites to violate laws more easily or to legalize title to what was gained through coercion. Zapatista leaders simplified their claims for the international press when they claimed that the privatization of land and the North American Free Trade Agreement provoked their uprising; they later clarified their demands in longer communiques and interviews and, ultimately, in the 1996 San Andrés Accords negotiated with Congressional intermediaries (Hernández and Vera Herrera 1998).

Provisions that allow farmers to privatize and sell land introduced another confusing and politicized layer of government intervention, conspiracy, bribes, and forums of contention. As López Sierra and Moguel (1998) show in the isthmus of Tehuantepec in Oaxaca, for example, popular reactions to Article 27 reforms had more to do with the peasants' assessment of the capacity for graft the titling process would give to corrupt authorities than with their assessment of how property titles would work in theory. In general, a change in federal policy may disrupt or end existing claims for government arbitration of property disputes, or may give powerful actors in the countryside new means to consolidate large landholdings.

Land struggles today are often linked historically and ideologically with the struggles of what are referred to as independent campesino organizations. Many of these organizations emerged in conjunction with reformist federal policies in the 1970s[7] and sought to displace the power of rural bosses in the ruling party's corporatist peasant peak organization, the National Peasant Confederation (CNC). Victimized by exclusionary rural administration as well as violence (Hellman 1983: Chapter 5), such groups varied over time in their relative proximity to ruling party circles. Over time, however, the increasing plurality of representation in the countryside produced a political discourse that eventually changed the way vast numbers of peasants and small private farmers inside and outside the ruling party framed local demands. Independent campesino groups and reformers brought into the government in the 1970s and 1980s denounced *coyotaje*, or rent-seeking schemes, which left farmers no option but to sell grain at below-market prices or to borrow money, store grain, or buy inferior inputs at prices above what federal agricultural agencies intended. Attacking such schemes involved pooling harvests and production in sufficiently large economies of scale that groups of peasants could negotiate directly with private sector buyers, sellers, or lenders rather than relying solely on government channels.

The implicit premise of independent organizing was that growers of basic grains, primarily ejidatarios on small plots, need not be considered irremediable victims of poverty and treated by bureaucrats as an unproductive welfare sector. Instead, leaders asserted that small-scale growers were eminently capable of sustaining themselves, given the same access to credit, high-quality production inputs, storage facilities, and grain markets as larger, private sector growers. Notably, this discourse was antistatist in important ways and, as such, dovetailed with the language that market-oriented technocrats were employing to legitimize the project of market liberalization.

Since the 1970s, when a set of policy openings had given independent peasant groups greater freedom to organize, groups had learned to winnow small gains from the government through a process of courting reformist elements inside the state. As Fox has argued, this practice of working with certain officials while at the same time engaging in aggressive struggles against others to gain power over local resource allocation was at the very

---

[7] The Federal Reform Law of 1971, which was part of an attempt to eliminate corrupt intermediaries, encouraged ejidatarios to join together in ejidal unions, offering them preferential credit arrangements and input subsidies (Harvey 1998: 76).

crux of democratization in the countryside. This power over decision making, or "associational autonomy," Fox argues, is constructed through iterative cycles of mobilization and conflict between three key actors: autonomous social movements, authoritarian elites reluctant to cede power, and reformist state managers (1994a: 156).

The contradictory character of struggle among independent campesino organizations – fighting in some sense for both independence *and* inclusion – helps explain what on the surface seems a paradox in the nature and levels of contention during market restructuring. In 1982–3, and 1985–7, protest broke out in the countryside over falling real prices with protest most often in the form of occupations of the government's National Company for Popular Subsistence (CONASUPO) stores. However, in the early 1990s, when permanent and far-reaching constitutional changes were being proposed in agrarian and agricultural policy, response in the countryside was relatively muted.

By the early 1990s, campesino activists were divided over proposed legal changes in government land policy, as well as proposed changes in the structure of ejidal representation in federal arenas. On the one hand, ongoing crises of low productivity and lack of credit and infrastructure necessitated universal changes in agricultural policy. On the other hand, conceding changes in Article 27 risked undermining a set of agrarian guarantees that had lent legitimacy to rural struggles for decades. This dilemma was sharpened by the politics of market restructuring during the Salinas administration. Shortly after he took office, President Salinas began a process of engagement, or *concertación*, in which he invited independent campesino organizations to form a plural, consultative body, known as the Permanent Agricultural Congress (CAP). He also appointed several campesino leaders long known as radicals to bureaucratic posts. Organizations debated among themselves over both the organization and the appointments – some argued that this would provide new means of democratization, whereas others contended that such changes facilitated the abandonment of small-scale agriculture and masked ongoing PRI-linked assassinations of rural leaders affiliated with the new opposition party, the Party of the Democratic Revolution (PRD) (Hernández 1990).

Despite some ongoing opposition, President Salinas successfully seized on the discourse of independent groups in an effort to harmonize domestic markets with commitments inherent in the General Agreement on Tariffs and Trade and with the ongoing negotiations around the North American Free Trade Agreement. What President Salinas appeared to be offering in the early 1990s was a reasonable quid pro quo: in exchange for greater managerial autonomy, expanded access to credit and marketing guarantees, and democratic representation in the bureaucracy, such groups would support a modest liberalization of land tenure and the formal termination of the government's commitment to land distribution. This process, which was accompanied by an intricate set of negotiations and rural forums, appeared to be an viable opening for many groups who hoped to concentrate their mobilizational energies into commercial organizing rather than protest. In the case of the Article 27 reforms, the leadership of almost every independent campesino group in the CAP, save for the Independent Central of Agricultural Workers and Peasants (CIOAC), endorsed the changes alongside the PRI-linked CNC.

A disparity remained, however, between the rhetoric of state-society consensus building and the reality of government policy in the countryside. Even though independent campesino organizations had gained some official consultative powers early in the policy process over Article 27 reforms, they had very limited impact on the final stages of the government initiative (Fox 1994c). Meanwhile, in real terms, agricultural investment in the countryside had dropped by over 80 percent between 1980 and 1990 (Asociación Mexicana de Uniones de Crédito del Sector Social 1994, unpublished paper), and the total acreage covered by government guarantees and programs had dropped by 60 percent (Rudiño 1994). Finally, a Draconian reorganization of finance and rural administration excluded vast numbers of growers from production assistance altogether. Reforms pushed hundreds of thousands of poorer grain farmers into programs that essentially cast them as a large welfare sector. Direct cash payments through the National Solidarity Program's (PRONASOL's) "instant credit" program (*crédito a la palabra*) or food coupons known as tortibonos tended to exclude farmers from markets and production schemes rather than give them new options to pool resources. Chronic cutbacks along with shifts in the way that resources were channeled to poorer farmers tended to atomize rather than aggregate production-related demands among poorer grain farmers.

Meanwhile, structural changes in other portions of rural finance drastically changed the stakes of economic policy for farmers who had historically counted on yearly production loans. Large swaths of the countryside dubbed as minimally productive were excised from the bureaucratic domain of the government's rural bank, which historically had been the only source of credit for the minority of farmers[8] who had been lucky enough to access formal credit at all. As Myhre reports, from 1989 to 1992, the client base of the government's rural bank fell from 800,000 to 224,000 (1998: 42). Meanwhile, agricultural lending through other channels doubled, and wealthier farmers borrowed heavily in hopes of expanding profits. The Agricultural Trust Fund (FIRA) funneled the greatest portion of finance capital and guarantees through the new private banks. This initially benefitted large private farmers, as well as more profitable small and mid-sized farm enterprises in the private and ejidal sectors.

Within two years of the Article 27 reforms, however, falling commodity prices, rising production costs, and high interest rates bankrupted large and small-scale growers in private and ejidal agriculture. These bankruptcies approached a staggering 6.6 billion pesos by the summer of 1995 and affected at one point between 40 and 60 percent of growers who had loans (Pérez 1994, 1995). The magnitude of debt, and the marginal status of agriculture in a free trade regime with volatile interest rates, posed a serious threat of massive land and property loss in the countryside. Protests by farmers needing restructuring terms, emergency credit, as well as price guarantees targeted not only the CONASUPO and the government's agricultural agencies but also the finance ministry, the central bank, state governments, and the newly privatized commercial banks.

As the case study of the Barzón movement will demonstrate, the reasons for this mass bankruptcy are complex and had much to do with contradictions between Salinas' stated intentions in the agricultural sector and higher priority projects of controlling urban prices, raising money on international securities markets, and liberalizing domestic markets in service of ongoing foreign trade negotiations. The peso was overvalued, for example, which gave urban consumers and businesses greater buying power, but at the same time imposed unfair competition on Mexican farmers, who could not compete with artificially cheap grain imports from the United States.[9] Meanwhile, the Direct Rural Support Program (PROCAMPO), a cash-per-acre program designed to provide some additional measure of finance to the countryside, was widely used as a vote-buyer in the countryside, arriving to farms in time for the election, not in

---

[8] One estimate by the Confederación Nacional de Productores Rurales (Rudiño, 1995b) is that about 29 percent of all producers have had access to formal credit.

[9] For a more detailed discussion of the impact of international prices and trade agreements on agricultural markets, see López Ortiz (1995).

time for planting. This imposed a second level of usury into rural production, as loan sharks and unscrupulous financiers fronted PROCAMPO money to producers at planting time and took high percentages out of the funds when they did arrive from the government. By 1993, debt radicalized new constituencies in the countryside, notably among more privileged groups of growers. Direct defense actions against repossessions and banks introduced a powerful new discourse about property, markets, and production. This discourse in turn would resonate among urban constituencies shortly thereafter when the devaluation crisis of December 1994 plunged millions of urban merchants and consumers into massive debt.

Ruptures in Control: Scenarios of Insurgency in an Altered Environment

Transforming the economy into a viable investment climate for global capital while time maintaining control through tested forms of clientelism is a contradictory process, politically and ideologically. Managing protest, on the one hand, implicates the use of an older language of patronage and government stewardship of resources. Limiting claims, on the other hand, involves using a legitimizing language of market citizenship and political autonomy. As I have argued, protest is not necessarily anathema to free market policies. In fact, a system of managed and local petition and protest remains a crucial means of controlling aggregate demand. It compensates for the political and economic difficulties inherent in building solid and inclusive institutions of arbitration while also attracting fickle private capital to national markets.

Compartmentalizing protest in volatile market conditions, though, can be difficult, particularly when protest provokes defections from incumbent powerholders, when it challenges the private sector, or when it aggregates protest in ways that threaten the appearance of governability. The following discussion considers in turn these types of events that may undermine the ability of authorities to compartmentalize protest. As I argue, sharp cycles of market volatility, new scarcities in state budgets, and the particular nature of risk in global capital markets may alter landscapes of bargaining and control at local levels. At given moments, the unequal power relationships that are maintained fairly well most of the time can give way when sudden shifts in production or in the allocation of power enable new coalitions to form and facilitate the diffusion of potent narratives to new audiences.

Shocks

I have pointed out the revelatory capacity of market transition in exposing long-standing divisions inside communities, neighborhoods, and families. Market-borne shocks, however, may also reveal common ties among groups that formerly had associated very little with one another. Rapid privatization and trade liberalization, combined with punishing inflation-control policies, are likely to cause quasi-disaster situations in certain local contexts. A community disaster such as a market downturn in grain prices, a rise in input prices, or a sudden industrial shutdown may bring together groups that routinely have had little to do with one another. Certainly this was at play in the Barzón movement. In the states of Jalisco and Zacatecas, for example, the growers who banded together in protests over debt in the summer and fall of 1993 included groups that had fought bitterly with one another over land and resources in previous years.[10] In the state of Sinalóa, a similar phenomenon occurred with the umbrella group called Productive Sectors in Action in the spring and summer of 1995. Thousands of farmers, including some with highly capitalized farms and export possibilities, occupied the government square in Culiacán alongside ejidatarios with very limited assets and little or no access to international markets. Their demands included higher prices on basic grains, especially wheat, greater government investment in the farm sector, and restructuring programs for compounding debts.

Even though policymakers may distinguish such events from natural disasters (which would merit relief), people in hard-hit sectors or localities often do not see such a difference. In many rural Indian communities in cash-poor Chiapas, for example, such a distinction made by a technocrat in the capital city would be absurd and irrelevant to people. Metaphors used by people to describe and make sense of the processes of disruption and dispossession, for example, often invoke images of the natural world and of ongoing battles dating back for centuries. To such people, government programs are never neutral exercises in prudent policy making. They are instead understood as successive rounds of *engaños* or "tricks." Consider for example Zapatista Army of National Liberation (EZLN) Comandante Ana María's way of describing the impact of the global economy on the Mayan peoples of the eastern highlands and the Lacandón jungle:

---

[10] I am indebted to Gabriel Torres for this insight with respect to Jalisco.

Social Movements and Economic Transition

Every day and . . . night, the powerful want us to dance the *X-tol* and repeat their brutal conquest. The *Kaz-Dzul*, the false man, rules our lands and has giant war machines that, like the *Boob* – which is half puma and half horse – spread pain and death among us. The trickster government sends us the *Aluxob*, the liars who fool our people and make them forgetful (Comandante Ana María 1996).

Even if one were to argue that the case of Indian villagers constituted an extreme case of differential conceptualization of events by citizens versus policy makers, a general principle still applies. In instances where people's descriptions of disruption come closer to the language used by national officials, many continue to believe that, in situations of community disruption, the government should rebuild housing and services if areas are devastated and also should create employment or emergency markets (say, for damaged crops) where livelihoods have been disrupted.[11] Organizing that capitalizes on widely familiar knowledge of constitutional mandates requiring the state to intervene in the economy to provide employment, land, housing, and health care may be particularly fruitful at moments of acute need.[12]

Schisms Among Elites

Market transition threatens the power of incumbent party militants, government officials, and elites in the private sector.[13] Fiscal retrenchment

---

[11] In Zacatecas in the summer of 1994, for example, the Barzón movement capitalized on discontent in northwestern municipalities of the state that stemmed from farmers' anger that the government would not purchase their bean crop. Adverse weather conditions had damaged the beans so that they were stained but not inedible. The government buying agency, CONASUPO, maintained for some time that it would not buy crops at full price and then take a loss for the lowered quality of the beans when it resold the produce to merchants.

[12] The earthquake of 1985 in Mexico City is a good example of this. A wave of urban mobilization arose against the federal government after the earthquake, precisely because people felt that the government had not fulfilled its duties in providing relief to the populace. In the hours and days after the earthquake, government response was disorganized and inadequate. Tens of thousands of people had been killed and needed to be buried, hundreds more were buried alive under rubble, and millions more were left without water, electricity, or basic services. In the midst of this chaos, hundreds of citizens' brigades took over the jobs that the government ought to have performed, and also began mobilizing politically around issues of housing and urban services.

[13] Theorists of social movements have long emphasized the role of elite conflicts in the creation of political opportunity for social movements. Some integrate the variable of elite conflict into their explanations for movements' success or failure, whereas some examine the role of elite conflict in creating or fueling insurgency itself. On elite fractures as a

48

and more effective tax collection, for example, provoked open dissent among many individuals whose loyalty in the past had helped maintain the appearance of political consensus in a one-party-dominant Mexico. The willingness of opposition parties to receive defecting elites and run them as candidates in high-priority elections accelerated this process and contributed to the recent fracture of the ruling party.

Elites who seek to reestablish their power after party defection often seek leverage through popular mobilization, either siding with already formed groups or associations or providing resources to would-be leaders who go on to form pressure groups or distributive movements. One sees this, for example, in the case of the 1998 gubernatorial election in the state of Zacatecas, in which long-time PRI strongman Ricardo Monreal bolted the ranks of the ruling party and eventually won the governorship as a PRD candidate. In that state, as I discuss in Chapter 6, leaders of the debtors' movement were key brokers in that defection. They rapidly negotiated the defection with Monreal, on the one hand, and the opposition party leadership on the other. Promising change and greater government dialogue with social groups, Monreal's election, in turn, provoked many more groups to take their demands to the streets in the year following the election.

Market transition and political reforms profoundly altered cleavages and patterns of hierarchical loyalty inside the PRI. In some cases, market transition decreased the ability of traditional party actors to counterbalance presidential programs and sponsor claimants at the rank-and-file level. In *Democracy within Reason*, Miguel Angel Centeno argues that the administration of Miguel de la Madrid marked the beginning of a presidential dynasty of a class of people who constituted, as he writes, "a cohesive elite with specialized training who claimed the ability to maximize collective welfare through the application of a set of instrumentally rational techniques and success criteria" (1994: 39). These elites, who came to exercise vast power in the system due to the dominant role of monetary and trade institutions in a free market order, nonetheless faced serious problems of defection and dissent inside the PRI. Many viewed the *tecnicos* (technocrats) with great suspicion and gained considerable political capital by casting aspersion on their

determinant of movement success, see, for example, Tarrow (1993); on the role of elite fracture in fueling political insurgency, see McAdam (1982, especially discussion on pp. 40–2); see also Meyer (1993).

foreign PhDs from the University of Chicago or at Ivy League universities. Few technocrats had held elected office before taking high-level positions in the Executive branch.

While many during the Salinas years from 1988 to 1994 predicted the inevitable disappearance of more traditional elements inside the PRI, including professionals whose credentials came from Mexican institutions and whose ideological orientation was more developmentalist and Marxist, and *políticos* (persons who have advanced in the party through electoral means), who may have had very little formal education and derived power from the ranks of labor and peasant organizations, the death of traditional wings of the PRI was greatly exaggerated. Even though President Zedillo's inner circle remained largely foreign-trained and loyal to principles of free market economics, PRI politicians and corporatist bodies outside the highest ranks showed increasing proclivity to disagree publicly with the president and to use implicit threats of defection. What bolstered such threats was the prospect that such defections did not necessarily end the political careers of the defectors or cause social chaos where they occured. So far, in three gubernatorial races in Tlaxcala, Baja California Sur, as well as Zacatecas, where PRI defections have resulted in electoral losses to opposition alliances, PRI-cum-opposition strongmen have taken thousands of rank-and-file supporters along with them.

This tension has altered the PRI's internal governance in ways that expanded openings for dissent from below. In September of 1996, for example, a meeting of some 4,500 rank-and-file members of the PRI staged a minor mutiny of sorts, introducing party legislation that supposedly would require that candidates for federal office hold elected positions prior to their nomination. If such bylaws had been in place in the past, for example, Presidents De La Madrid, Salinas, and Zedillo never could have assumed the presidency. The PRI also adopted an open primary system, replacing the mystified and near-sacred rite of the "dedazo," in which the outgoing president hand selects his successor.

In an interesting parallel to recent U.S. elections, in which many candidates have tried to convince voters of their outsider status and of their contempt for status quo politics, it has of late become a public sport for PRIista candidates to declare their opposition to neoliberalism because of its negative impact on poorer urban and rural constituencies. Coverage of the presidential primary campaigns in the summer of 1999 showed candidates with purportedly outside chances of winning the nomination, including Roberto Madrazo, Manuel Bartlett, and Humberto Roque, condemning the incumbent.[14]

With events carrying increasing significance during the electoral season in 2000, tensions inside the ruling party increased steadily. Exigencies of economic management in the present era will doubtlessly require the ongoing participation in government of the técnico class, without whose presence in diplomatic and business circles there would be little chance of maintaining any significant inflows of private capital from abroad. At the same time, though, the exigencies of domestic control will require the participation of elites drawn from working and peasant classes and educated in Mexican institutions. As long as lower- and middle-class audiences remain unconvinced of the power of unencumbered markets to improve their material lots, schisms in elite circles will continue to provide openings for collective pressure from below.

Protest and Global Finance

I have argued thus far that the breakdown of a patron-client system, which in and of itself is often precipitated by economic strain and fiscal shortfalls, begins to dissolve a field of widespread but often shallow public loyalties. In conditions of low or negative economic growth, the state may find itself unable to respond to increasing numbers of local disasters and mass bankruptcies. Austerity policies and market restructuring exacerbate this phenomenon. In addition, a reconfiguration of distributive channels entails a shakedown in state agencies and political circles. Significant numbers of party insiders find themselves unable to procure rents from government budgets or the private sector as before. This field of uncertainty alters the perceived calculus of cost and benefit for loyalty to the party and/or the federal government hierarchy. Local officials and strongmen who find their fiefdoms in decline may consider it convenient to side

---

[14] The seriousness of such candidates' opposition to privatization, fiscal retrenchment, and trade liberalization is questionable. As Labastida pointed out regarding his rivals, all had shown great loyalty to upper echelons of the party and their policy programs throughout the 1980s and 1990s. The antisystem rhetoric, however, does indicate a dilemma of internal solidity inside the party whereby market-oriented policies put a strain on middle-level supporters in the PRI. As for those Centeno called the "ward bosses" of the system, the politicos' participation is essential in party activities at ground levels. It is they, after all, who assess local conflicts, balance competing demands, identify troublemakers, organize party functions, and speak an identifiable language to ordinary people.

with disgruntled social groups in an effort to gain new political leverage and influence; meanwhile, subordinate actors become aware of new pathways to conciliatory negotiation with state agencies.

With regard to the impact of economic transition on contention, one must finally consider the relative risks of certain types of protest to the market itself. Although the direct vulnerability of any powerful capital interests to protest actions or localized disorder is not great, the Mexican state clearly has become more vulnerable to some sorts of groups since the exit of large-scale external commercial bank lending to the public sector after 1982. With the emergence of publicity sensitive industries such as tourism and export-processing manufacturing as principal motors of economic growth, day-to-day reports of events in the foreign press – particularly foreign business press – carry more serious political implications than in decades past.

Market transition has shifted the location of this sort of political vulnerability. In decades past, social actors most closely affiliated with prominent national enterprises such as railroads, petroleum installations, transportation, and utilities were more likely to gain leverage by threatening physical structures or interrupting production and services. Now, a more diversified economy makes such installations less important politically, automation makes them harder to occupy, and privatization (where it has occurred) makes them more difficult to threaten without the looming prospect of capital exiting altogether from a given locality or sector.[15]

Groups that may gain greater leverage now are those that somehow become emblematic of what is wrong or illegitimate in the Mexican political system generally or that appear to be pied pipers of mass disobedience. In a business climate where finance capital and currency trading determine crucial margins of profit, companies or investment firms may hesitate to place financial resources in "high-risk, high-yield" Third World markets in the face of reports of mass protests, contested elections, regional violence, or human rights abuses. Where groups can implicate the state or elite business actors in such events, they may affect the flow of financial resources into securities markets or into fixed investment schemes.

Particularly because Mexico's program of market-oriented economic recovery in the late 1980s and early 1990s emphasized portfolio invest-

---

[15] This last scenario would be entirely possible in the case of installations that have gone to seed, and where there are alternative services or installations that can replace them. Minor ports or railway lines are examples.

ment over foreign direct investment, the Mexican state has become not only politically vulnerable but also financially vulnerable to mass collective actions. In a world of volatile capital, the very hint of regime weakness or civil unrest given off by newsworthy protests has serious consequences for the performance of national securities in international markets. Thus, although physical facilities may be controlled tightly, now the state faces the issue of policing its national image for investor consumption because portfolio investment in the form of stocks and bonds may exit national markets in short order.

As in the United States – when the news of a presidential illness or a terrorist action will spur a bearish cycle in financial markets – so too in Mexico do incidents such as killings, municipal crises, and insurgencies affect securities performance. When the Zapatista army launched its offensive in the southern state of Chiapas on New Years Day 1994, the Mexican government was quite vulnerable to the flurry of news stories going out on international wires to audiences around the world. At the end of 1993, about 80 percent of all investment in Mexico was in portfolio investments and government bonds. As demonstrated in Figure 1.1, this represented a new trend: only two years before, foreign investment was at one-third the level it would reach in 1993, and money market investment was only somewhat higher than foreign private sector direct investment – a slower moving type of financial enterprise in which, as the Inter-American Development Bank defines it, "the investor (foreign or domestic) has a permanent and effective share in the management or control of firms outside the country in which he or she resides." After the calamitous events of 1994 and 1995, which included both financial and political tumult, investment plummeted once again to 1991 levels, only with foreign direct and money market investment reversed in quantities.

Mexico's market transition, which stressed the use of portfolio investment to attract capital and thereby finance domestic economic activity, opened up new but probably not permanent vulnerabilities for the state. In response to the Zapatista uprising, Mexican securities values immediately plunged when the markets opened on January 3, 1994, shocking the Mexican stock market into a 3.4 percent drop (Carroll 1994). While the market subsequently recovered ground later that week, investors were edgy, waiting for word on how "serious" the guerrilla was. When, by January 12, the government was sending signs that it would negotiate a cease-fire with the rebels, markets again took an upward direction (Torres 1994). It was as if, in a sense, the EZLN were occupy-

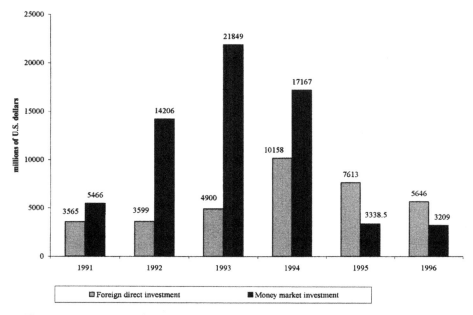

Figure 1.1 Foreign direct investment and foreign money market investment in Mexico, 1991–96. Source: SECOFI statistics.

ing part of the Mexican Stock Exchange over 1,000 miles away from the gunfire.

As talks reached an impasse, however, and it became clear in subsequent weeks that the rebellion had genuine grassroots support in the Chiapan countryside as well as widespread national support among leftists and the poor, Mexico's investor attraction declined. Then, after the assassination of presidential candidate Luis Donaldo Colosio in late March 1994, a significant number of investment houses sensed the potential for further instability and signaled their intent to decrease the share of Mexican securities in their Latin emerging markets portfolios (Myerson 1994).

Certainly, the extent to which popular movements can hold the state hostage at will should not be exaggerated. The risks are exceedingly high, and the likelihood of conciliation declined as coverage of Chiapas fell, and mainstream observers abroad lost interest. A learning curve on the part of the state also must be assumed; the police and military likely will suppress conflicts earlier and more thoroughly when unrest emerges in other localities. Preemptive militarization of the state of Guerrero after 1995 is an example. In the case of EZLN, communities have paid a high price in pain, humiliation, and human lives for their insurgency in January 1994. Though government officials have claimed that the conflict in Chiapas has been bloodless – merely involving a war of words on the internet – reports of continuing abuses in the conflict zone from human rights authorities support a different conclusion. What Chiapas does illustrate, however, is that a changing political economy does indeed alter the access of government "soft spots" to groups in the general population.

The Impact of Economic Crisis and Market Transition on Contention

Mexico's market transition, in idealized terms, is a set of policies and processes that decreased government intervention in the economy by freeing most domestic prices, lowering tariffs on imported goods, cutting programmable public spending as a percentage of total economic activity, privatizing industry and credit markets, and eliminating most subsidies. In the various ways that they affect local systems of patronage, market transition and fiscal retrenchment create a variety of political outcomes. They place pressure on many provincial party fiefdoms, and they also change the incentives and the ability of different groups to demand concessions from the state and resist repression. In some cases, the decline of fiscal channels of distribution has provoked an increase in the use of violence and police repression against civil movements because politicians have no other means to coopt or assuage demands. In other cases, the decrease in public spending has provoked acts of open disloyalty by leaders in the lower echelons of the PRI on behalf of distributive movements. In still other cases, local shortages associated with market transition have reinforced authoritarian enclaves by increasing the relative power of quasi-military strongmen in drug corridors.

Most importantly, market transition must be understood as undermining systems of material distribution and systems of clientelistic political control. Where groups may rise up in protest of shortages, they may also seek to undermine older party hierarchies. At the same time, however, local party elites may seek to protest shortages as well but may fear the power of protest to provoke mutiny that upends party power altogether in the locality. Groups may therefore be expected at times to act in sync with local functionaries whose political survival is threatened and at other times to take advantage of those functionaries' vulnerability in order to impose a thoroughly oppositional order – opposed to both a patron-client past and a market-driven present.

This chapter has outlined an argument about how the emergence of social movements in transition-era Mexico can be understood. With respect to local level organizing, the market's force destroys much in its wake, but at the same time it knocks open spaces in structures of control. The next chapter opens the insurgent's toolbox, examining the means by which organizers may widen the spaces that may appear at given moments and begin to build amidst the wreckage left after the storms of crisis and market opening have destroyed both elements of top-down control and modes of popular subsistence.

2

The Insurgent's Toolbox

Market-oriented policies, fiscal retrenchment, and compounding disorder in the ranks of the ruling party have altered distributive protest in Mexico, shifting contention into new terrain and changing movement constituencies. In sectors or communities where officials successfully compartmentalize protest and reestablish clientelist relationships, groups making demands of the state may continue to use forms of direct action and protest but will likely remain divided as they compete with one another for dwindling pools of discretionary state resources. By contrast, where distributive demands or collective identity attract widespread attention or provoke turf wars among state elites already threatened by state retrenchment and declining material resources, groups may find temporary means to unify demands and leverage greater power vis-à-vis authorities.

In the midst of market-oriented restructuring, many groups have recognized and seized upon what new opportunities exist, exploiting cleavages among party bosses and gaining greater leverage inside gaps in declining patronage systems. Urban and rural demonstrations over purely local matters – such as land titles, contracts for grain or small machinery purchases, school buildings, running water, municipal election outcomes – have ballooned in numbers in most localities. Though the connection between the opportunity for mobilization and levels of protest cannot be proven unequivocally without more systematic information on contentious events nationally, popular recollection of protest change over time, and even business association records suggest a wave in confrontational actions by local groups in recent years probably unprecedented in sheer size. In the site of the decade-and-a-half-long workers' movement in Lázaro Cárdenas City chronicled in Chapters 3 and 4, for example, citizen occupations of local government offices shot up from none or perhaps one a year

EN CIRCULOS OFICIALES ■ El Fisgón

In Official Circles, by **El Fisgón** Mexican official on the left: "For me, it's a lot harder to negotiate with the Zapatistas than with the gringos." Mexican official on the right: "Of course. At least the gringos speak our language." Official on the left (in English), "Oh yeah!" From *La Jornada,* May 12, 1995. Reprinted by permission.

in the early 1980s to an average of over twenty per year by 1994. Or, in the Zócalo (central plaza) in Mexico City, protests have become so great in number that downtown merchants cite demonstrations as a major factor in the decline of their businesses. In 1993, the number of protests in the Cuauhtémoc delegation was said to be at 1,240; by 1996 (Rodríguez 1994), government sources said that the number of protests in that same area stood at well over 3,000 (Sheridan 1996).

The previous chapter outlined a process in which a volatile and still-evolving field of partisan competition, combined with fiscal retrenchment, privatization, and trade liberalization, shifted the structure of demands as well as the political liabilities that provoke combative collective action. These factors, however, do not explain differences in durability of collective action among similar types of movement campaigns. This chapter presents the argument that groups in Mexico sustain protest only when they devise methods to resist threats and repression by the state, and when they harness resources to sustain participants physically and morally during extended standoffs. In the simplest terms, opportunity for public dispute may occur by chance, but longevity of dispute is forged through conscious strategies to hold off police and state pressure to disperse. To maintain protest in the face of dwindling personal resources and a growing threat of repression, groups in the midst of a struggle must work quickly and somewhat haphazardly against two inevitable phenomena: a state counter strike and movement members' moral and physical exhaustion.

Groups that seek to make distributive demands often must employ a variety of organizational and mobilizational methods to compensate for minimal political-institutional access and perennial shortages in material resources. In the same manner that a trekker depends on a fishing pole to provide food on a long journey, social movement participants bring to protests a range of political and mobilizational tools during an ongoing confrontation with the state. Holding out in a battle with the state – a dubious enterprise in the best of circumstances – most often entails forging a variety of functional alliances with parties, communication agents, or groups with similar demands. Additionally, groups may take steps to reinforce decision-making procedures that preempt both real cooptation on the part of leaders, as well as fears among new recruits and potential movement recruits that leaders will be coopted.

Without reducing groups' motives to purely instrumental dimensions in their choices of alliances, protest venues, and rule-making procedures, it may be useful to imagine that strategic concerns are never fully absent in the construction of dangerous and costly campaigns of political action. Externalizing costs of protest is essential, particularly for workers, farmers, street vendors, or urban dwellers, for whom the costs of nearly any activity out of the ordinary are prohibitive. Friendly individuals and groups are also barricades against police, hunger, and moral isolation. Sympathetic newspaper coverage is a screen against denunciations that may appear on more controlled media. Propaganda and progroup graffiti on walls and windows remind the public of the existence of dissenting opinions. Committee hearings in state and national legislatures pertinent to group demands generate media and force crucial issues before the state and pressure the Executive branch more directly. Cases brought to court by sympathetic lawyers may end in impasse but may also generate more visibility and bolster the legitimacy of a given cause.

In the following section, the analysis provides a sketch of four tools that may be useful in keeping repression and cooptation at bay. I argue that protesting groups are likely to employ one or all of the following strategies as a means of pressuring powerful public or private actors and evading backlash: (1) solidary assistance from sympathetic individuals or from other groups with similar demands, (2) performances designed to evoke outrage and sympathy from external audiences, (3) pacts with political parties, and (4) nominally to fully democratic decision-making procedures. The discussion touches upon the nature of the strategy, what it can provide, and its relative availability.

Examination of social movement strategies in Mexico brings home to the observer the enormous difficulty inherent in mobilization and protest by subordinate actors. The tools that bring in the resources to extend the viability of any challenger movement confrontation are flimsy and ad hoc compared to the resources wielded by the state and the ruling party. The observer occasionally wonders about the sanity of participants in social movements in an authoritarian environment. That individuals who may have little or no real inside access to formal institutions will risk confronting the state with demands and disobedience underscores the importance of explaining why and how movements ever appear in the first place.

It should be remembered, of course, that each strategy that may yield strength to a movement campaign may also entail some long-term costs. Strategies often clash with one another and backfire on the movement. An example is the potential contradiction between cultivating external audiences and practicing internal democracy in a group. What rank-and-file members in a given case may be inclined to demand of the state may not match the sympathies of outside public observers. This is of particular concern to the most marginalized of political actors, who have been more likely than others to seek transnational assistance (Brysk 1996). For instance, a Mam or Zapotec community seeking land distribution and production resources may find that external support is more forthcoming when demands are framed in terms that resonate well cross-nationally and are closer to the agendas of external funders. These may include forest conservation or cultural rights or women's education, perhaps. On the other hand, if the movement were to curtail participation in order to override majority concerns and gain the sympathies of outsiders, leaders might well find themselves the target of rank-and-file accusations of being no different from the enemy (perceived as the Institutional Revolutionary Party and/or the state in most cases) in ignoring popular demands or of being the puppet of elite outsiders. In this manner, different weapons of struggle may simultaneously serve to fend off repression and cooptation in the short run while working at cross-purposes in the long run. This uneasy relationship among strategies lends increasing volatility to already tension-filled periods of confrontation and may cause fracturing of movements or internal power struggles. Thus, any tool – even when used skillfully – may also contribute to movement setbacks or even total movement collapse.

Instruments for Mobilizing Protest and Gaining Conciliation

Solidary Support from Individuals and Groups

In Mexico, the externalization of various components of mobilization is particularly important in light of the blistering poverty plaguing many individuals who participate in collective political action. Beginning with Tarrow's observation that "mobilizing structures can exist prior to, and autonomous of, movement leadership and, in some cases, operate through other organizations or within institutions" (Tarrow 1994: 136), it may be useful to first consider those resources that a movement lacks – and that it needs in order to confront authorities in a dispute.

A frustration of the author, upon embarking on research on social conflict in Mexico in the early 1990s, was that formal histories and official statistics never explained how families in everyday circumstances subsisted through chronic unemployment, insolvency, and prohibitive credit arrangements. Even less clear was how groups with limited or nonexistent emergency funds stayed for weeks in protest camps and occupations far from home. Still less clear was how so many people found out about other movements and took steps to assist them, despite the fact that most did not have telephones and many did not have access to independent mass media. Interviews with movement members and onlookers were peppered with questions asking, "But *who* paid? . . . *who* brought food and water? . . . *who* made the banners? . . . *who* had access to a bus? . . . *who* brought the tarpaulins during the rains? . . . *who* knew a doctor when that person collapsed during the march? . . . *who* knew a lawyer when twelve of your cohorts were jailed? . . . *who* leaked crucial documents to the movement?" Questions were answered in terms both vague and specific; by and large, however, it became apparent that movements are simply never autarkic and must be considered as part of a complex and decentralized web of organized and unorganized political resistance. Accounts of protest would seem to indicate that more diverse or better-off protest groups – such as some of the urban cells of Barzonistas, or groups of middle-class students – might internalize some of these functions. Among poorer groups or groups limited to a single social sector, such as workers in a politically isolated plant on the U.S.-Mexican border, or urban slum dwellers, extended confrontation entails a greater dependence on resources furnished by allies and sympathetic strangers.

Material alliances may be crucial for protesting groups that often must travel on foot, hitchhike, or take buses to municipal seats, state capitals, or even Mexico City to pressure state elites to hear their demands. Often, groups need food, blankets, and material for signs and banners. During blockades, protests, or strikes, additional numbers of people in actions help deter police and attract media and the attention of bystanders. Alliances also expand the range of skills available to a protest. Lawyers, students, shopkeepers, and housewives, respectively, may help by auditing government documents, writing press releases, circulating petitions, and cooking for large actions. Finally, a diversity of supporters necessarily renders any set of demands less parochial in nature, making it more difficult for a movement's adversaries to accuse a movement of inconveniencing the public for purely self-serving demands.

Material alliances, as described here, are those links forged by a protesting group with other groups or individuals that provide direct assistance during confrontational periods. Such alliances may be formed through loose confederations of sectoral- or class-based groups or may be formed spontaneously through chance contacts or events held by the protesting group for the express purpose of gaining alliances.

Although historical accounts of movements tend not to chronicle small, singular acts of solidarity in a confrontation, oral accounts of past standoffs and protests and observations of recent ones indicate that anonymous acts of support may be quite important to the viability of extended protest actions. Sustaining protest usually involves soliciting *cooperaciones* ("cooperations" or material donations) as well as *apoyo* (support in more general terms, which may involve moral or physical presence as well as material assistance) from the public. As touched upon in later chapters, members of steel workers' Local 271 mentioned soliciting donations on the street when they traveled to Mexico City during a strike in 1989. Interestingly, when I interviewed a professor and resident of Mexico City on a wholly different matter, she recalled by coincidence that she had heard about the very same Lázaro Cárdenas Steelworks (SICARTSA) steel workers' demonstration and had gathered together blankets and some food to take to their downtown occupation site. She said that she did not know them, but that she did what she could because she liked their politics. She noted that many other strangers spontaneously did the same, explaining that during such protests, "*hay gente que coopera* [there are people who cooperate]."

Loyalties invoked during a struggle are multiple and cross-cutting. Extended kin are called upon to provide support for extra costs incurred in protest actions. Class identity also figures in. Strikers or protesters on a street corner may board a city bus or *pesero* (a small privately owned bus or van) with the intention of collecting donations. The driver may then quietly cooperate by not preventing the protesters from boarding, perhaps quickly negotiating a small cut of the donations or perhaps not. Passengers, mostly working class, are likely to make small donations, despite their own very limited resources. (If asked why, an individual usually summons a properly pious explanation for the observer – "Because those *muchachos –pobrecitos*, they are even worse off than I.") Catholic pity aside, it may also be that material and other forms of support flow from a vast underground reservoir of public anger and discontent with the government;[1] many view protests as speaking for their own demands in an environment in which institutionalized channels of voice are often compromised and suffused with corruption.

In addition to spontaneous donations of physical presence or material resources that a movement may gain through approaching strangers or family connections, a group may also draw on personal or group ties. During confrontation, those ties are severely tested; many speak of confrontation events as moments that cemented or dissolved friendships at once. Oftentimes, if a group foresees a confrontation (as a labor movement may before contract negotiations or a campesino group may before planting season), its members may take steps to seek out potential allies or

[1] In a fairly reliable recent opinion poll, four-fifths of respondents indicated, for example, that they believed the government did what was right only sometimes or hardly ever; on the same poll, two thirds of respondents indicated that they believed Mexico was either making no strides toward greater democracy or was becoming less democratic. (Source: *Los Angeles Times/Reforma* poll, taken August 3–6, 1996. Fifteen hundred adults were surveyed in face-to-face interviews August 1–7 in twenty-five states.)

to call in favors from groups whose actions members of the former group had supported. Militant steel workers of Local 271 in Lázaro Cárdenas, recall traveling extensively in the months before a strike campaign, arriving at universities or in Mexico City or in other mill and mining towns with the name of a potential contact.

Groups may cultivate allies by essentially offering reciprocal help to cooperating individuals or may make a commitment where possible to include allied groups in any settlement won with the state. Particularly in enclave economies or less diversified local economies, where a settlement won on behalf of a central sector may automatically benefit the community in terms of cash flow or employment or services, resources and support may flow in a seemingly spontaneous fashion, fueled by a web of informal social ties and ascriptive networks virtually invisible to the outside observer.

Alliances sealed by the understanding that groups will help one another during struggles may be formalized somewhat through confederations (examples include various uniones,[2] coordinadoras, asambleas, federaciones), although interviews with movement participants would indicate that such confederations are so informally incorporated that membership alone in such umbrella organizations in no way guarantees automatic mobilization of the network encompassed by the confederations. Many such confederations are founded through national or regional assemblies or may stem from a particularly successful mass protest, as was the case in the formation of the May Day Inter-Union Committee in 1995. What is most notable about mutualist networks is that they may be quite effective in amassing mobilization resources at certain junctures – for example, in convening large protests or in putting together aid – but considerably less effective in homogenizing ideological outlooks among affiliated groups. It would appear that ties implied by such confederations are merely as strong as individual protesting groups make them through individual visits with other group leaders, and personal assurances of future reciprocity.

Group-to-group support is instrumental in expanding local movements into municipal, regional, and national insurgencies. In certain cases, groups that begin a struggle may merge into a single movement, eventually sharing a name, as was the case in two separate movements in Jalisco and Zacatecas that became the Barzón debtors' movement. Despite

---

[2] The Spanish word *union* is sometimes confused with the English word *union*. The Spanish word is used in Mexico to mean an umbrella association of groups. *Sindicato* is the translation for labor union.

sharing a name, however, ties between local groups in such movements most often retain the same local leaders and are better described as alliance structures than singular organizations. This leads to a situation in which a movement under a single name is seen by the public as one organization, but in administrative and organizational terms, it is effectively two or more entities. Oscar Nuñez, for example, argues the following about the Urban Popular Movement – often seen by outsiders or the press as a singular organization:

The Urban Popular Movement is in reality a federation and/or a front of associated organizations with different levels of politicization, and with different propensities to make demands and protest. Since its beginnings, it has been independent associated organizations which seek to break with the government's mass politics – even to break with its most backward members (Núñez 1990).

Alliances may also draw on networks connected through common historical-ideological roots. Especially in the case of groups whose origins date to the flurry of radical popular organizing in the 1970s, there may be some access and long-time connections to loose affiliations of free-lance organizers or professionals who do pro bono work and grassroots cells of urban dwellers, campesinos, and workers. People associated with such networks may or may not belong to minority parties; at any rate, such networks are not heavily involved in electoral politics. An example of such a network includes Proletarian Line, an entity formed in the early 1970s by student activists drawing loosely on Maoist doctrine (Carr 1992: 237; Harvey 1998: 81). Groups around the nation affiliated with Proletarian Line, including such diverse actors as indigenous groups in the Chiapan highlands and steel workers and slum dwellers in the northern state of Coahuila.[3] A branch of the Proletarian Line took on the name Mass Line and maintained a significant presence in Lázaro Cárdenas City in Michoacán and among telephone workers. In the case of Mass Line, various steel workers in Michoacán recalled in interviews that Mass Line affiliates in their union called on other urban labor groups affiliated with Mass Line or another branch of the same political group in Coahuila, which retained the name Proletarian Line.

In cases where popular organizations call upon the services of certain types of urban professionals, such as lawyers, physicians, and academics, old loyalties to such ideological lines maintain networks and contacts. For

---

[3] On involvement of Proletarian Line in Chiapas and its relation to later insurgencies including the Zapatista uprising, see Hernández Navarro (1994) and Harvey (1994, 1998).

example, two networks of left-leaning attorneys, the National Association of Democratic Lawyers (ANAD) and the Democratic Lawyers' Front (FAD), serve different networks of clients. The former organization is said to be more moderate and less confrontational in orientation and has clients among loyal opposition in Institutional Revolutionary Party (PRI)-linked groups as well as among affiliates of the center-left Authentic Labor Front (FAT) and fledgling labor groups in the northern border area. The latter attorneys' organization is said to represent a more radical, confrontational left contingent. The FAD has prominent ties, for example, among former transport workers, whose union was dissolved by force in 1995, as well as among the transport workers' urban popular wing, the Independent Proletarian Movement (MPI).

Between networks forged from strangers' and family members' cooperaciones and networks constituted from a motley assemblage of political affiliations, groups may significantly expand their ability to maintain protest and generalize disorder in a given space. What people cannot amass among themselves, they depend on others to furnish. Ironically, a small certainty that uprooted protesters carry with them even when protest takes them far away from their localities, they will likely be able to tap a generalized reservoir of disillusionment with the government and the incumbent party.

Cultivating Sympathy Among External Audiences

Positive public opinion is an extraordinarily valuable resource to social movements. Many times, the existence of external audiences, or what Michael Lipsky (1968) called "reference publics," are so crucial in given national historical contexts, in fact, that they may tip the balance – at least for a short time – between tolerance and outright repression for participants in opposition organizations or protest actions. Many credit attention generated by timely press releases with saving the lives of both activists and bystanders in conflictual areas. Also, insofar as such media has also heightened public participation in reform groups or intermediary solidarity groups – in Amnesty International or Witness for Peace, for example – media coverage has acted as an enormously important pressure mechanism for conciliation of protesting groups.

But the cultivation of external audiences (usually but not always through mass media) goes beyond short-term human rights work. It is also crucial in changing the minds of strangers about what is acceptable behavior, what it is possible to demand, and what rights citizens ought to enjoy. A dignified protest thwarted by a thuggish police in full view of the public may turn the world upside down for a time, opening up possibilities for unprecedented concessions and reforms. In his study of student antiwar mobilization in the United States, Todd Gitlin argued that media coverage of protest events may put cracks in the sheen of hegemony:

The routines produce news that no longer harmonizes with the hegemonic ideology, or with important elite interests as the elites construe them; or the elites are themselves so divided as to quarrel over the content of the news.... [At these moments,] Opposition groups pressing for social and political change can exploit self-contradictions in hegemonic ideology ... (1980: 12).

Although media freedoms and institutional roles in Mexico are quite different from the U.S. environment upon which Gitlin drew, the argument is still quite useful, particularly if we construe "news" more broadly to include popular discourse and communication that in many cases constitute information sources for many who have limited access to formal mass media. Despite a dearth of traditional mass media coverage, groups in Mexico have long engaged in public protest and have placed enormous weight on the opinion of onlookers. Long prior to internationally visible protests such as the Zapatista uprising in 1994, the practice of protest has been a means of calling into question the government's legitimacy on the grounds of a discrepancy between constitutional mandates and actual patterns of governance. Oddly enough in a country whose nineteenth-century history was peppered with violent peasant insurrection, the balance of many struggles in past decades has rested minimally on actions that involve physical resistance (such as barricades and rock throwing) or the threat of riots by dissenting groups. Notably, this civility on the part of protesting groups has continued, despite alarming rises in the use of official violence against peaceful protest (Amnesty International 1999). Often, action and counteraction played out by a protesting group and the state becomes a morality play in which each party attempts to demonstrate who, on balance, is the more law-abiding. Where challenger movements successfully coopt the concepts and rhetoric of revolutionary nationalism and gain wide visibility, agencies of the state will often back down from frontal attacks, refraining, for example, from arresting a group's leadership or evicting a group forcefully from an occupied area.[4]

In Mexico, the state's formal, initial reaction to any protest is crucial. Due to the highly personalistic nature of governance in Mexico, there is a prevailing sense – reflected in protest – that institutions, laws, precedents, and codes themselves do not dictate outcomes; rather, identifiable individuals do. In a system without an autonomous judiciary system or legislature, without systematic due process of law, and – perhaps most importantly – where a substantial portion of decision making at executive levels leaves no paper trail, a prolonged confrontation may assume a symbolic drama comparable to that of a public courtroom. Some protests, like minor cases in a lower U.S. court, receive scant attention. Other protests, however, may rivet a region or the entire nation and, also like major court cases, are often used as measures of the tides of mass politics. Protest size, militance, group makeup, diversity, and durability are apt to be discussed among observers. In addition, the coherence of the performance itself at an action is often commented upon widely, as is the presence or conspicuous absence of certain key opposition leaders or reformist elites affiliated with the PRI.

May Day 1995 is an example of protest as public hearing. Hundreds of thousands of people marched in actions around the nation in defiance of official government Labor Day ceremonies discreetly held indoors. The size and apparent spontaneity of the protests was gauged by observers at the time as a sign of deep discontent with the state's low wage-caps in the wake of the currency devaluation of the previous December. More importantly, it was also seen as a show of popular contempt for official labor centrals, whose leaders had obeyed the president's order to stay indoors for the first time in seventy-four years. Labor leaders' abandonment of

---

[4] It is difficult in most cases to measure the effect of public protest on short-term decisions of elites or police. Transcripts of meetings or documents detailing executive orders, if kept, are not available to the public. However, one can point to instances in which hard-line law-and-order stances became conciliatory after a period of mass protest. In March of 1995, for example, President Zedillo issued arrest orders for the leadership of the Zapatista army, probably underestimating the reservoir of public sympathy for the Zapatistas, even after fifteen months of political impasse. After several suspects were apprehended, three protests of forty thousand to fifty thousand people materialized in Mexico City on extremely short notice, despite the fact there was little or no advance media coverage of the actions. After three major protests, President Zedillo backed off his hard-line stance on arresting the leaders of the Zapatista Army of National Liberation, although military harassment of the Chiapan population in the conflict zone continued indefinitely.

traditional Labor Day marches at a time when real wages had plunged to a sixty-year low and collective contracts were going unrenewed by the thousands was seen as an emblem of an absolute impotence and marginalization from the policy process. Commented the newspaper *Reforma*:

Mounted on *burros*, leading dogs dressed up as bankers and burning effigies of ex-President Carlos Salinas de Gortari, President Ernesto Zedillo, and labor leader Fidel Velasquez, thousands of workers marched yesterday in 14 states around the country to commemorate Labor Day and to protest the government's economic policy (1995: 1).

Analysis of the protest's meaning and implications was also broken down by region. In Mexico City, for example, the protest of 100,000 people, largely made up of supporters and former workers in the SUTAUR, a public transport union that had been dissolved only a few weeks before, was seen as a sign that this was a movement in ascendance that likely could maintain resistance for some time. There was also a considerable amount of negative gossip and public commentary about the protest, even from people hostile to the government's economic policies. Popular and elite analysis identified failings and bad omens in the protest. The fact that leftist leader Cuauhtémoc Cárdenas of the Party of the Democratic Revolution was at the protest but did not speak was noted by many and provoked questions about whether this was a sign of a fractured left, a hostility between opposition labor leaders and the PRD, or perhaps a sense among ascendant popular movements that the PRD was in decline. There was also considerable ambivalence and suspicion about the SUTAUR and the Independent Proletarian Movement to which it was linked – interestingly enough, because it was seen as a group with a mysterious lack of support among leftist groups. Painted by the government as an entity suffused with corruption and run by criminals (the leaders had been jailed upon dissolution of the union), the SUTAUR could not fully shake public suspicion, even among those inclined to mistrust government allegations. According to informants affiliated with a broad range of center-left groups, the union and its urban popular arm had neither contributed to nor drawn upon most leftist groups' mobilizations during the 1980s and 1990s, leading to speculation that the movement was funded through crime or rogue elites inside the PRI who sought to maintain potentially destabilizing social forces for their own benefit.

Certainly, from an abstract point of view, it is curious that distributive disputes should *ever* generate broad sympathy among bystanders. Onlookers in distributive protests, after all, seldom if ever stand to share in gains made by protesters. Yet in Mexico, often a considerable portion of the public displays solidarity with distributive insurgencies. This is due to a long process of protest and performance that have drawn upon and subverted official doctrines pertaining to citizens' rights and guarantees before the state.[5] Even Mexicans of extremely humble means, who may have completed only three or four years of primary school, have been taught that the Constitution of 1917 imbues the government with the power to arbitrate conflict between competing groups. This power of mediation is also explicitly linked to an obligation to defend the rights of workers, farmers, and the poor. There is wide consensus, then, that rights of the population include but are not limited to civil liberties. In fact, popular understandings of state obligations usually give primacy to its redistributive obligations – its mandate to balance class interests. Whether or not the PRI-led regime ever even had the administrative capacity or structural power to fill this role is a complex historical issue and has been addressed by a wealth of literature on the postrevolutionary regime.[6] However, it is probably valid to state that historical group rights *as they are constructed* in the popular public domain include "inalienable" rights to employment, affordable food, housing, health care, and land. Thus, although a significant proportion of the population may not, in fact, enjoy the rights still codified in Articles 11 and 123 of the Constitution of 1917, and stipulated in Article 27 until its amendment in 1991, protests that are able to mobilize consensus[7] by claiming that those rights are being widely violated may enjoy

[5] There is an insightful set of writings among social movements theorists that analyzes the role of these generic motifs of protest that define the cause of vast numbers of unrelated demonstrations. David Snow and Robert Benford, for example, unified a good deal of thinking with the concept of "master frames," or flexible concepts that make "diagnostic and prognostic attributions" among participants and onlookers in protest and that connect the demands of one group to a set of other groups and related principles that are seen as widely legitimate. The concept of civil rights in the United States, for example, has undergirded countless protests since the mobilizations of African Americans in the U.S. South in the 1950s and 1960s. According to Snow and Benford, "The elaborated master frame allows for numerous aggrieved groups to tap it and elaborate their grievances in terms of its basic problem-solving dilemma" (1992: 140).
[6] Hamilton (1982) spurred much debate arguing that President Cardenas' challenges to the prerogative of capital classes in the 1930s were unsustainable in a prevailing capitalist system. Several excellent works on agriculture explore issues of land reform and of state and popular subsistence. See especially Sanderson (1981) and Fox (1992b).
[7] Bert Klandermans (1988) utilizes the term "consensus mobilization" to refer to the process of provoking public sympathy or collective action through the use of widely agreed-upon values. These public values, or "collective definitions of a situation," form through a diffuse

a priori validity in the public eye. That is, if a given group of people claims publicly that they do not have land to settle on or that they have no means of feeding their families, then state officials (hard-liners or not) are unlikely to respond that the landless do not necessarily have a right to land or that the hungry do not have a right to food subsidies or jobs. In the United States, claims to subsistence may be seen as equally or less legitimate than counterclaims that such redistribution violates taxpayers' liberties. In Mexico, revolutionary nationalism is still a hegemonic public ideology and generally precludes any outright denial by officials that protesters' claims are legitimate. In a confrontation, state officials and participants in protest will likely both invoke the same concepts of revolution, patriotism, constitutionality, and social justice and claim to be the defenders of the public good.

The state may defuse compelling protest performances and discourage similar protests through a number of methods, including negative media reports and mobilization of counterperformances by groups calling for law and order. Private elites or hostile officials may also seek to mobilize public prejudices about the social groups or classes to which protesters belong. Campesinos and/or Indians, for example, may be portrayed by a hostile press as dirty, sneaky, and lazy, and thereby unworthy of consideration by public officials.[8] They may also be portrayed more subtly as having been cruelly manipulated by subversive outsiders. Another process that may occur over time is a gradual appropriation of legitimizing claims utilized by protesting groups in official performances and rhetoric. One can identify a state-society mimesis in the formulation of groups in different sectors, in which dissenting groups may form groups independent of progovernment organizations but call their group something similar to or identical to the progovernment group. Or, on the other hand, government

process that he calls "consensus formation." Most importantly, he notes that the process of consensus formation occurs quietly and does not, in and of itself, produce collective action. Social movement actors, he argues, consciously draw upon these collective values through symbols and performances, thereby utilizing public sympathies to pressure for given demands.

[8] Anne Schneider and Helen Ingram (1993) identify a similar process in their work on the United States. They argue that inequitable distributive policies are reproduced not only because selected groups have greater access to government officials but also because public images of groups perpetuate notions about who is worthy of government largesse. Groups that are well-regarded, such as homeowners and retirees, rarely face harsh public criticism of their tax breaks and infrastructure subsidies. Prisoners or welfare recipients, on the other hand, who receive benefits through more visible cash payments, coupons, and aid programs, are often seen as undeserving, unproductive draws on tax moneys.

officials may seek to divide a particularly combative movement by funding the formation of a new group with a similar name and purpose to the combative movement or even to set up an actual decoy organization with the same name and insignia as the movement. Recalls Judith Adler Hellman of her observations in the field in the 1970s:

> The Echeverría period was marked by profound ideological confusion as the oppressed peasant (or bewildered researcher) who arrived in Mexico City to seek help from Central Campesino Independiente (Independent Peasant Central – CCI) of Danzos Palomino or the Union General de Obreros y Campesinos de México (General Union of Workers and Peasants of Mexico – UGOCM) of Jacinto López was now confronted with *two* CCIs and *two* UGOCMs, one genuinely autonomous and *muy luchador* and the other co-opted by the regime (1994b: 128).

The presentation of new fiscal programs or policies by the state or the public petition for specific demands by a dissenting group may also lend itself to this type of rhetorical and visual state-social movement imitation. An example is the battle for public opinion in 1991 and 1992 over a proposed set of amendments to Article 27 of the Constitution of 1917, in which both advocates and opponents used nearly indistinguishable rhetoric, dress, and ceremony to support radically divergent viewpoints. A month after President Salinas announced his intention to present the Chamber of Representatives with a draft of the constitutional reforms, he staged a final, high-profile bid for support for the reforms. At Los Pinos, the Presidential residence, Salinas gathered representatives of 268 agricultural organizations to ratify a document entitled the "Campesino Manifesto."[9] Photographs in the national press featured Salinas and the Minister of Land Reform, Victor Cervera Pacheco, looking on as Mateo Zapata signed the Manifesto under a luminous painting of his father, Emiliano Zapata, dressed in full battle gear (*Uno Mas Uno* 1991). The same day, groups opposing the reforms, including the CIOAC (Independent Central of Agricultural Workers and Peasants) and various regional and national peasant groups organized a protest in Emiliano Zapata's birthplace that culminated in the signing of an opposition manifesto, the *Plan de Anenecuilco* (Mexico Service 1992).

The construction of public protest in Mexico, drawing on culturally and historically based rights, process, and causality, bears much similarity to

---

[9] Jose Luis Calva contends that many of these representatives at Los Pinos were deceived into attending the ceremony. According to Calva, some who attended the ceremony were brought in trucks by government officials to the ceremony and had no intention of endorsing Salinas' reform proposal (1992: 129–30).

processes described by observers of protest in other national settings. However, the extreme distributive inequality of Mexican society, paradoxically coupled with the broad legitimacy of revolution-based material guarantees of employment, housing, schooling, and land, produces a striking set of outcomes. Interestingly, though demands may change, the bases or "frames" for claims are extraordinarily durable, lasting for decades rather than rising and falling as described, for example, by Snow and Benford (1992). Rationales for protest are also perversely portable. The degree to which protesting groups, embattled elite targets, and state-backed patronage organizations all masquerade as one another in public demonstrations, speaking of the same injustices in the same terms and yet ultimately striving for such different distributive ends, is notable. On certain national holidays, when discontents and regime-loyal foot soldiers alike march in parallel protests of patriotic indignation, each claiming the mantel of the past and the key to a just future, one remembers Paco Ignacio Taibo's famous line that in Mexico, Kafka would have been a gossip columnist. Promises of distributive justice may remain unfulfilled, genuine protests may be subverted with state-backed decoy protests, and political commentators may objectify protest and examine it as they would the evening news, but public demonstration over historically based claims continues to evolve and repeat itself in an obstinate fashion in Mexico.

Pacts with Political Parties

A strong literature is emerging on the role of opposition parties in the process of democratization and economic liberalization in Mexico. A number of scholars have focussed on electoral strategies and the dynamics of party affiliation (Bruhn 1997; Mizrahi 1995) or on public opinion and voter choices in elections (Domínguez and McCann 1996; Lawson 1997). It may be useful, however, to examine for a moment how political parties may be viewed by protesting groups with specific sets of material demands. I argue here that the relationship of distributive movements and opposition parties in a democratizing environment is likely to be a volatile one. It is likely to be conditioned by many factors, including the laws that govern political parties' structures and practices and the obstacles that opposition parties encounter in solidifying their presence in national politics (Fox 1994b; Keck 1992). As opposition parties evolve from broad protest fronts into consolidated organizations with real stakes in the electoral system, distributive movements may find that inclusion in opposition parties becomes something of a quid pro quo in which a party's support comes at a price.[10] Tying a distributive movement to a party also entails considerable risks if a party fares badly at the polls or performs poorly in a mediating role in institutional arenas.

In the space of less than a decade in Mexico, state and national elections have run the gamut from virtually uncontested PRI landslides to highly fractured contests in which the results were so highly disputed that officials were removed from office and interim outcomes were eventually negotiated by elites.[11] In national elections, a tense two-party contest took place between former PRI-member Cuauhtémoc Cárdenas's breakaway National Democratic Front and the PRI in 1988. A three-party contest ensued in the mid-term elections in 1991 with the PRI becoming dominant once again over the Party of the Democratic Revolution (PRD) and the National Action Party (PAN). By 1994, the PRD still led by Cárdenas had slipped far behind the more right-wing PAN, and still farther behind the ruling party.[12] In 1994 the PRI got 48.7 percent, the PAN 25.94 percent, and the PRD 16.6 percent [Federal Electoral Institute statistics cited in Harvey Serrano (1994: 13)]. In July of 1997, the PRD came back to life with a set of stunning victories in mid-term federal elections, and with a victory in the first mayoral elections ever in Mexico City since the Revolution. Perhaps as significant as volatile aggregate numbers is the constantly shifting nature of party constituencies. Studies of voting behavior in municipalities indicate that even where a given party may retain the same number of total votes, it is quite likely that the party may not be capturing the same voters as before (Guillén 1991, 1995).

[10] Kathleen Bruhn (1997) illustrates this principle in her study of the PRD. She argues that the PRD encountered many difficulties in the process of party consolidation, evolving from a broad opposition front (such as the Frente Democrático Nacional, FDN) into a stable party organization. She points out that the FDN included civil groups unconditionally, but once it embarked on the task of becoming a party, it had to confront the differences among those groups. It also did not continue to support popular organizations unconditionally. Organizations that affiliated with the PRD generally gave up some autonomy in decision making.
[11] As noted by Harvey and Serrano (1994: 11), by December of 1993, seventeen out of thirty-two governorships in Mexico were in the hands of interim governments.
[12] Voting patterns were as follows: in 1988 the PRI claimed 50.74 percent, the PRD 31.06 percent, and the PAN 16.81 percent, although most analysts put the PRD's actual vote count much higher – perhaps in excess of the PRI's actual votes. In 1991, the PRI got 61.4 percent of votes, the PAN got 17.7 percent, and the PRD fell to 8.26 percent. In 1994, the PRI got 48.7 percent, the PAN got 25.94 percent, and the PRD got 16.6 percent [Federal Electoral Institute statistics cited in Harvey and Serrano (1994: 13)].

In this shifting landscape, local groups challenging the state more often than not maintain some considerable distance between themselves and parties; at specific junctures, however, they may form coalitions with parties in order to mobilize the vote or contest electoral outcomes. In this manner, the dynamic between parties and social movements not only echoes a general instability of party electoral bases but also plays an active role in reproducing it. With notable exceptions, such as the Exodus for Dignity led by Manuel Andrés López Obrador (elected head of the PRD from 1996 to 1999), and now the Barzón movement headed by Alfonso Ramírez Cuellar, groups protesting economic policy often remain at arm's distance from both the PRI and the two primary opposition parties – a situation that at best yields short-term support from movement to party and party to movement.

The erratic relationship of organized groups to parties can be attributed not only to divergent goals and tactics conceived inside organizations and parties, but also to a democratization process that has remained stalled in various realms. While parties have diluted the PRI's power in the legislature to a plurality and now may realistically aspire to capture some governing seats in municipal posts, and even state governorships, budget purse-strings remain effectively in the hands of a strong central Executive. Therefore, opposition parties' power to sponsor the claims of protesting groups remains weak. Even if elected and permitted to assume office by the ruling party, an opposition party official may find no means to fund a promised solution to a dissenting group that may have supported his or her candidacy. And, as discussed in Chapter 1, local and state officials with the PRI have greater power than minority-party officials to sponsor claims of protesting groups in certain cases, although decline in programmable public spending has diminished even the PRI's power to conciliate protest. Thus, vast numbers of dissenting groups of farmers, small merchants, workers, and urban dwellers, among others, express little confidence in elections or parties as a means of gaining permanent or institutionalized access to state actors and budget allocations processes.

The relationship of movements to parties – oscillating between antagonism and cooperation – underscores how forms of resource mobilization among grassroots groups in pluralist-democratic versus corporatist-authoritarian environments differ in important ways. American sociologists have described the process of resource mobilization of social movement organizations as a process of working toward greater institu-

75

tionalization and entree into policy-making arenas.[13] In Mexico, however, political mobilization often requires that leaders work an organization *out of* standard partisan and bureaucratic channels and toward *de*institutionalization.[14] Without, then, discounting their contributions toward understanding the logic of social movement strategy and organizational evolution, we must recognize that the models suggested by the U.S. studies assume a constitutional system anchored by a neutral court system and a routinized system of legal reform and legislative procurement.

Synergism between distributive protest and electoral mobilization reached a peak in 1988, when Cárdenas's National Democratic Front aggregated a massive vote against the ruling party. Since that time, cooperation between national parties and grassroots groups in mobilization and confrontational protests has been far more uneven. In part, this has to do with the unlikely nature of the PRD itself as a long-term presence in Mexican politics. Emerging from a pragmatic alliance of left-leaning defectors from the PRI and members of what many call the "old left," including ex-members of the Mexican Socialist Party,[15] party members remain deeply divided over questions of ideology and internal practices. Personal loyalties also pervade internal party disputes. A long-running conflict between the two most prominent candidates – Porfirio Muñoz Ledo and Cuauhtémoc Cárdenas – exploded in the spring of 1999 as Muñoz Ledo accused Cárdenas of having secretly negotiated with members of the ruling party in July of 1998, resulting in a retreat of popular protest over the elections. Internal PRD elections in the spring of 1999 were annulled because of vote-buying and fraud.

[13] Piven and Cloward (1979), however, argued that it is precisely this very process of institutionalization that dissipates the force of social movements in a capitalist democracy. In this perspective, distributive social movements of marginalized sectors would actually be more similar than opposite in Mexico and the United States.

[14] Jonathan Fox (1994c) discussed this dilemma, arguing that as social organizations begin to play the role of local political parties, they risk subordinating long-term social and economic goals to short-term political exigencies. Their challenge, then, is to participate in civic and political movements without losing their identities.

[15] The Mexican Socialist Party, and its predecessor, the United Socialist Party of Mexico, had in turn united a number of smaller left parties during the 1980s. Founded in 1981, the PSUM merged five political parties, including the Mexican Communist Party, the Mexican Workers' Party (PMT), the Movement of Socialist Action and Unity (MAUS), the Movement of Popular Action (MAP), and the Party of the Mexican People (PPM). For two excellent analyses of groups on the Mexican left, see Carr (1992) and Moguel (1987).

Despite the relative newness of multiparty electoral competition in many localities, links between parties and social movements have existed for many decades. Ironically, links between minority parties and social movements may have been the strongest in past decades when the parties were, in electoral terms, the weakest. Opposition parties have long played a part in organizing and mobilizing local cells in certain economic sectors (Carr 1992; Hellman 1983; Moguel 1987). Communist and socialist parties have longtime roots in radical factions of railroad workers, telephone workers, teachers, electricians, steel workers, and landless agricultural workers, among others. However, many factors that condition the relationship between parties and local groups have changed. As the possibility of electoral success has increased for opposition parties, party activists' organizing goals have diverged somewhat from direct organizing around popular demands.

This shift in emphasis has provoked much debate among leftists. Many committed socialists and communists remain contemptuous of the PRD, and some of the more minor leftist parties have put their energies into mobilizing votes and reforming electoral institutions rather than into supporting direct action at local levels. Unlike in other democratizing nations – Brazil, for example – there were no sizable independent labor blocs that publicly rejected the PRD as a project of the left, with the idea that the founding of a communist or socialist party should come about later, when an electoral challenge from a labor-based Left would be more viable. Significantly, however, the Zapatista Army of National Liberation (EZLN) has declined to declare its support for the PRD and has not mobilized its militants to turn out voters for the PRD in local contests in Chiapas.

Mobilizing voter turnout, coordinating electoral observation teams, and manning extended postelectoral protests now occupy greater portions of party energies than in the past, leaving less time for direct organizing around popular disputes. Several opposition party activists for the PRD, whom I interviewed, for example, indicated that they had previously worked in the Mexican Communist Party (PCM), and later the Mexican Socialist Party (PSM), or in smaller regional groups such as the Zacatecan Front of Popular Struggle (FPLZ). Their activism had been of a different nature in those parties, however (Interviews with Jose Luis Castellanos 1994, 1995; with Luis Medina 1995; and with Renato Rodríguez 1995). Leftist party activists' shift toward the more centrist ground in the PRD alliance after 1988 reduced parties' explicit involvement in radical direct action, such as land invasions or production stoppages. Even though these organizers testify that their goals remain much the same as before (advocating land for urban and rural settlers, basic services for the poor, higher crop prices for farmers, or better wages for workers), they describe an array of party-connected activities in which efforts are directed less toward direct action than toward pressing for broader changes in national and state policies. Parties' means of pressure have changed as well: even in areas where a given party may have no hope of winning local or state posts (for example, the PRD in parts of Baja California, where the PAN garners most protest or opposition votes), activists may press demands through print media by denouncing official corruption.

With the decline of organizations affiliated with labor and an "old left," not only have parties distanced themselves from social movements in certain realms, but social movements have taken steps to distance themselves more from parties. What comes through in many accounts of grassroots organizations is that even in previous decades when opposition parties were more involved in organizing direct action and were less involved in national electoral campaigns, friction between parties and social groupings was often a fixture in those alliances. Barry Carr, in his work on the Mexican Left, suggests that social mobilization around distributive issues has undergone a long-term transformation, with the logic of organization shifting from focus on production-based demands to consumption-based demands. Carr argues that this process pre-dates the emergence of the PRD and the PAN as mass parties. He sees a clash between organic forms of cross-sectoral grassroots organization that often materialized across sectors and along ascriptive and kin lines and pressed for local goals, and parties' continuing insistence on strict definitions of class and proletarian unity.[16] In his account of the emergence of cross-sectoral mobilization under broad umbrella coalitions known as *coordinadoras* in the early 1980s, he describes the following process:

The coordinadoras' major concerns are not so much focused on production in factories, mines, and workshops as on struggles over access to land, housing, roads,

[16] Carr (1991: 126) writes of this phenomenon inside the labor movement: "Echoes of a vigorous anarchist and anarchosyndicalist heritage can still be felt in the Mexican labor movement, even though hardly anything remains of the once substantial network of anarchist and libertarian organizations. And despite the universal hostility that the Marxist left has shown toward this anarchosyndicalist tradition, syndicalist and anarchist movements (as Mexico's most original Marxist thinker, Jose Revueltas, once argued) have been consistently the staunchest defenders of the need for independent working-class economic and political activity."

water and other urban services. The coordinadoras have also directly challenged the political left by treating traditional leftist parties with suspicion and occasionally by treating traditional leftist parties with open hostility toward leftist involvement in their activities (1991: 126).

The split between political parties and grassroots organizations should not be exaggerated, however. Despite friction between political parties and many social movements in Mexico, there is also substantial convergence between party activists and social movements in high-profile protests and electoral campaigns. Political parties ultimately play an important part in bolstering social movement campaigns in many localities. Independent social organizations in San Luis Potosí mobilized around statewide elections in 1991, for example. In that instance, the independent Potosino Civic Front organized significant support for an opposition front made up of the PAN, the PRD, and the Mexican Democratic Party (a smaller party with a regional presence), and also participated in postelectoral protests and a march on Mexico City after substantial electoral fraud occurred (Gómez Tagle 1994). Another example is the broad mobilization of protest in Michoacán in state elections in 1989 which included Cardenista groups linked to Cuauhtémoc Cárdenas (as a PRIista and then an opposition candidate), older "hard left" groups, plus more independent or centrist groups (Gledhill 1993).

Most importantly, political parties now offer opposition groups new means to denounce an incumbent local government publicly and to do so in a manner that an ostensibly "democratizing" regime cannot prevent. An opposition candidacy offers a juncture in which activists may gain a foothold in a city councils as *regidores*, or as representatives in state legislatures, or even the national legislature. Even where such individuals remain in the minority, they may access party and state resources to agitate over their groups' issues, convening meetings about their concerns at party headquarters, and seeing their issues debated in public venues.

In cases in which a party's ideological position as stated at upper levels may be an odd fit with a particular citizens' organization, opposition parties still may court a movement leader as a candidate in order to gain a foothold in a region or gain another seat in the national or state legislature. As such, a mobilizational convergence between a party and a social movement or a group of movements may involve a recognized movement leader taking on a party candidacy, even if he or she has not been a member of the party before a given election. In elections in the city of Culiacán in 1993, for example, Mercedes Murillo de Esquer, an attorney and longtime advocate of the urban poor and an activist in civic affairs, became the PAN candidate for mayor. Following the elections in which the PRI claimed victory but opponents claimed electoral fraud, supporters of Murillo engaged in direct-action strategies to force an audit of the vote count. The tenuousness of party-movement alliance, however, became clear within weeks of the election. Despite a sixty-three-day protest, occupation by groups that would later form the nonpartisan coalition, the Sinaloan Civic Front, PAN elites rescinded their complaints and negotiated a solution with the government and PRI officials. As is typical of such conjunctural and pragmatic episodes of party-movement cooperation, Murillo immediately left the party along with the movements who had mobilized around her candidacy (interview with Murillo 1995).

Candidacies allotted to leaders of vocal social movements carry with them some considerable risks for the unity of a movement, and this, in turn, contributes to many movements' reservations about cultivating ties to political parties. In cases where the leader has little history of association with the party, and the candidacy wears a somewhat mercenary sheen, he or she may have little means of mobilizing support under duress from the national organization, as was the case in Culiacán. Rank-and-file members of a movement in turn may bristle at having been linked quite suddenly to a political party during a campaign. In Lázaro Cárdenas City, for example, informants in various political groups expressed frustration at the practices of a local opposition government that had ruled somewhat incompetently from 1991 to 1994. "The PRDistas are all PRIistas," said one resident in conversation with me. Sensing my confusion about what he meant, he continued. "It's true," he said, "they all came out of the PRI, and they do things the same way. The only things that are important to them [local party leaders] are money and capturing votes." Particularly as the prospect of winning local and state elections has become more real, opposition parties have welcomed votes from poor neighborhoods run by old-style caciques in the same manner that the PRI has done traditionally. As one PRD candidate in Zacatecas lamented, such deals cost his party's reputation as a reformist entity among onlookers. He explained that in top-down groupings, most common among the poorest of urban and rural residents, "They can go to bed PRIistas one night, and they wake up told they're PRDistas the next day."

Democratization is popularly conceived by the press or even by most social scientists as an incremental process in which participation in the public sphere broadens to include greater numbers of actors and opinions.

In official international circles, assessment of the democratization process often privileges the measurement of direct fraud, voter turnout rates, and levels of reported preelectoral violence. As reflected in the erratic relationship between parties and civil groupings, political parties' performance in electoral episodes may provide deceptive indications of entrenched citizen preferences and even less of ideological alignment. When observed at the level of local settings, there is every indication that parties' constituencies are conjunctural and quite often mobilized by anti-incumbent sentiment, and alliances between party and other mobilizing agents are often tenuous and pragmatic.[17]

Nominally to Fully Democratic Decision-Making Procedures

Popular and academic accounts of civil mobilization in Mexico often incorporate some description of decision-making procedures inside social movement organizations. Interestingly, though, until recent years, such descriptions were often set apart from analysis of the efficacy of strategies and movement campaigns. More recently, scholars including Cook (1997), Fox (1992a), and Keck (1992) have argued that organizational democracy may be instrumental to the duration of protest under authoritarian circumstances.

This part of the discussion suggests that even though decision-making processes often reflect normative values of the people who participate in a given movement, they also reflect practical responses of the movement to the immediate political environment. A rough comparison helps illustrate the point. In the United States, for example, formal parliamentary procedure is often used in organizations. This is partly because many people believe in it and feel most comfortable with formal procedure as a means of making decisions and resolving internal disputes. Nonetheless, it also shields the organization from challenges that may come from the outside. Because challenges may well be carried out in the court system or may involve harassment under the guise of some formal investigatory pro-

---

[17] A substantial number of studies have emerged since the late 1980s, analyzing the emergence of limited multiparty competition in local and national elections and governance patterns in cities and states where opposition party members have assumed power. However, many researchers lament that analysis remains somewhat hobbled by the debility of the standard measurement instruments of party politics, principally opinion data and exit polls. Public mistrust of surveys and survey-takers, plus general volatility in the electoral arena itself, has led to somewhat tentative and diffuse conclusions about the evolution and future of multiparty competition in Mexico.

cedure, detailed accounting and tax forms, minutes, voting, and membership all help establish the group to be what it tells the state it is – a non-profit group, a private school, a citizens' lobby, or a party-affiliated entity. In Mexico, formal parliamentary procedure is used less consistently in organizations. Fewer people insist on its use, and challenges in the form of legalistic internal or external investigations over dues-collection and tax status do not arise in the same manner as in the United States. In Mexico, movement members are more likely to be arrested on charges of theft or treason or of inciting riot than they are to be investigated for tax evasion, illegal campaign contributions, or failure to install proper fire exits in a building.

Leadership structures and decision-making procedures in groups outside the official corporatist network vary widely, ranging from PRI-like caciquismo to painstakingly nonhierarchical systems in which members work out differences until nearly everyone in the group is in agreeement. Variance even exists inside movements: local cells within the national Barzon movement whose beginnings are profiled in Chapters 5 and 6, for example, vary substantially in their everyday organizational practices. Insofar as decision-making procedures differ at all in any group from the autocratic practices normally present in political organization sponsored by the ruling party, it is useful to examine what capacity of disruption or of resistance this may or may not lend to a group.

The kinds of threats a group faces may impact how a group chooses to organize itself. Because repression in Mexico often takes the form of selective repression or cooptation of leaders, centralized leadership and/or charismatic leadership present practical risks to organizations. Although many popular organizations nonetheless maintain a centralized structure or remain associated with a single well-known leader over time, others have been absorbed into official organizations as a result or, in other cases, have disappeared where leadership was threatened, discredited, jailed, or even assassinated. Where groups, by contrast, spread out administrative and leadership functions through committee structures and so forth, and changes in leadership are made routine, the cost of repression for the state may rise.

Increasing the number of participants in movement affairs in some cases may have a practical use insofar as it may counteract an enduring cynicism among lower and middle classes about political action in general. Complicating the business of social movement recruitment is the fact that a ruling party itself survived nearly unchallenged for seven decades in part through the logic of the *política de masas* – by organizing and mobilizing the Mexican citizenry in cells of workers and peasants and guilds and neighborhood organizations. In this way, the PRI was like so many social movements, only exercising far less power vis-à-vis the central state than President Lázaro Cárdenas, the architect of inclusionary corporatism, likely imagined they would. Many of the activities of social movements are all too familiar for those sectors of the population who have been brutally dispossessed by economic policies of the 1980s and 1990s. Workers in the most controlled cells of official labor centrals were used to marching on cue, holding up signs and banners, protesting when labor leader Fidel Velásquez decided to flex his muscles. Peasants remain accustomed to regional leaders asking them to organize "spontaneous" demonstrations of gratitude for visiting federal officials coming to inaugurate public works or road-building projects. The very acts that are associated in many cases with the modern social movement – demonstrations, marches, placards, meetings, and revolutionary slogans – are, in Mexico's case, the bread-and-butter politics of the regime itself. In some cases, the only thing that distinguishes an official group from an opposition group may be the opportunity for the rank-and-file to participate in decisions about group demands and strategy.

Researchers visiting a region or locality in Mexico in which there is an abundance of independent mobilization and of political conflict will undoubtedly be pulled aside by many separate individuals claiming to know the inside scoop on all the groups and leaders. Each story told by each individual "in the know" is unique in its tawdry details, and many times, information brokers are aware that one has spoken with other information brokers telling different stories. Commonly, one such individual will point out that another story-telling individual is a "spy" for the government or the ruling party or for some unscrupulous large landowner and should not be trusted. In this context of both effervescence and widespread unease, accusations fly. Presumably, the power of such gossip has an effect on popular sensibilities, and not just outside observers. The idea that no source of information is objective, and that any leader ultimately acts *"por interés personal"* (in his own interest) is a powerful demobilizer in any case and is only heightened when decision-making procedures are centralized and the activities of high-ranking committees are mystified. In *Mexican Lives*, Judith Adler Hellman illustrates this in her chapter contrasting the lives of two women residents of urban slums – one who chooses to participate in a citizens' movement and one who rejects political action. "A neighbor of mine told me about the Asamblea de Barrios," says the latter woman. "But the way it works is that you have to go every day to demonstrations and meetings and sit-ins and after you do this for a year or so, they put your name on a list and you get a house" (1994a: 72). In that case, a desperately poor woman who obviously had some incentive to join popular actions did not, viewing the activity as something of a scheme rather than a form of valid political participation.

Beyond the practical considerations of avoiding selective repression and of convincing onlookers that a movement is actually better than the official groupings that it may resemble, participatory decision-making processes may in certain cases diversify a group's resistance strategies in a useful manner. As will be discussed with respect to both case-study movements in the next section, a more diffuse leadership structure that encourages rank-and-file participation runs the risk of incubating internal division but at the same time generates greater organizational innovation. A movement with several committees gearing up for a campaign or a demonstration does run the risk that separate factions will not cooperate in the end, but at the same time, factions or different-minded subgroups that unite against a common enemy after a period of semiautonomous organizing may have greater resources to bring to a campaign or strike or long-term occupation. In the SICARTSA workers' movement, for example, one faction cultivated ties to other independent trade unions nationally and internationally, while another faction organized in the city slums. Another faction favored some entente with municipal officials, and garnered support among local elites inside the ruling party. All bickered with one another – sometimes bitterly – but union rules dictated that no faction could prevent the others from participating in committees and elections. And, in strike episodes, differences between the factions usually receded in the face of what was perceived as the larger enemy – the SICARTSA management and hostile official labor leadership in Mexico City. In the case of the Barzón movement, where strategy and demands are largely worked out by local organizations, a diffuse leadership has lent the national leaders an oddly fortuitous bargaining chip: they have no power to stop Barzonistas' disorderly conduct in states and municipalities by decree. They can only recommend cooperation with the state if members' debt problems are demonstrably solved.

Internal democracy, for many who participate in social movements in Mexico, is important in and of itself. It affirms the intrinsic dignity of the individual, and empowers people to resist exploitative and patriarchal

84

arrangements. Quite separately though, it also may act as a means to prolonged collective action. This helps explain another paradox of social
movements and democracy in Mexico: many people who participate quite
actively in distributive social movements may be quite indifferent or
cynical about campaigns for national democratization. Diffusion of leadership and transparency in group activities and finances may be, as much
as anything, an important assurance game in which members and potential members of a movement organization are better able to ascertain for
themselves whether the organization is likely to represent and defend their
demands in long and dangerous confrontations with the state.

Conclusion

Clearly, power is woven between material structures and ideational frameworks. For example, the ability of the small, militarily weak Zapatista army
to make demands at all of the Mexican state had to do with the ability of
that movement to utilize symbolic capital to harness public sympathy and
solidarity. The EZLN, unlike, say, a union or a mass rebel army, has no
power to blackmail capital or the state with strike or embargo. Nor, like
a movement in the United States, can it harness power through constitutional precedent and an autonomous court system that counterbalances the
power of the executive branch. As they launched their January 1, 1994,
offensive in Chiapas devoid of material, structural, and institutional leverage, the Zapatistas owed their power to make transformative demands on
the economic-distributive regime without immediate, total reprisal to their
ability to create localized ungovernability and damage the legitimacy of
the PRI-ruled government. By the same token, however, the EZLN's lack
of structural weapons conditioned the types of collective action they had
at their disposal at any given time. If their ability to demand substantial
redistributive reforms hinged on using external resources of national and
international media, nongovernmental organizations, networks of expatri-
ates, students, and the like, they clearly had to tailor their strategies of
action as a movement to maintain and expand those resources. These
exigencies, in turn, undoubtedly had an effect on what the movement
demanded, how it represented itself, what it settled for (or didn't settle
for), and even who it identified as its members.

Like the Zapatista Army of National Liberation, very few social movements have the power – by virtue of structural, numerical, or institutional
leverage – to make distributive demands on the state and/or bourgeoisie,

which hold discretionary power over resources. Therefore, social movements that maintain the ability to deploy mass actions over collective demands must overcome this deficit of structural power through use of symbolic resources and selective disorder. The auxiliary resources that a movement may use to compensate for this deficit, I argue, are conditioned in a dual fashion by the national "moment" or distributive ideology of the state and the specific terrain of the industry, market, and place where the movement occurs.

The basic proposition presented here is that political economic structure conditions but does not determine the outcome of social movements. A political economic system affects the size of the "structural deficit" that a movement will encounter by affecting the distribution of wealth and control over the means of production. Also, the political economy affects the powers of government institutions which create public goods such as housing, roads, and drinking water to meet the demands of a social movement. In addition, legal changes that accompany transition from one mode of economic management to another may affect the range of actions that social movements may employ. That is, under certain distributive regimes as opposed to others, people may have greater claims to demand concessions on wages, land distribution, finance, or collective bargaining over production processes. Therefore, it is clear that the distributive system of the state affects *what* a social movement may demand and *of whom* it may make demands. But ultimately, in a system in which capital and resources are perennially scarce, and in which current development policy mandates further restriction of fiscal resources, subsidies, and protective tariffs, there is virtually no group of workers or farmers or debtors or small merchants or slum-dwellers whose protests and actions are guaranteed to gain them access to official arbitration and to conciliatory measures. Their petitions represent, in effect, demands for exceptional state measures. That is, if the government were to meet a given group's demands, it would require appeasing the group with a selective compensatory payment that would almost certainly not be paid immediately to all workers or peasants nationwide. Groups that cultivate public opinion through national or international media, which forge a supply network of material and moral support, which skillfully negotiate pacts with political parties at opportune electoral interludes, and which avoid making themselves vulnerable through an excessive concentration of leadership, are more likely to make successful bids for distributive ends.

II

3

Privatization and Protest in a Steel Town

Three and a half hours north along the coast from Acapulco by bus is the
city of Lázaro Cárdenas. Though a populous area, few outsiders from
Mexico or elsewhere know much about the city or the surrounding industrial area. Travel books on Mexico mention the city of Lázaro Cárdenas
only in passing, listing for the sojourner only a number of bus transfers to
elsewhere, and a few phone numbers for travelers who may be stranded
there for a night. Noting merely that it is a port city gone to seed, travel
guides commonly stress that it holds nothing of interest to outsiders and
urge those who do go there to avoid staying long. It is a concrete city
without museums or theaters or a university, without historical plaques
or signs explaining the purpose or the origins of the area. It also has
relatively few links to the rest of the country. The deep-water port, which
might in other circumstances have brought and retained commerce and
trading activity for the city, is underused in part because the mountainous
land route to and from central cities is treacherous. The railroad that con-
nects Lázaro Cárdenas to the state capital of Morelia and then eventually
to Mexico City is in an abysmal state of repair: just the trip from Lázaro
to Uruapan – four hours away by car – takes some ten hours by train. Similarly, air travel to and from Lázaro Cárdenas is quite limited; only small
aircraft can land on the rustic airstrip outside of town. The final alternative, travel by road, will remain unattractive until the new highway under
construction is finished, as the two-lane highway to Uruapan and Morelia
is now frequently set upon by armed bandits.

Scholars of the region note the same thing in more sophisticated terms.
"The region's industrial development," notes Jorge Martínez Aparicio, "is
characterized by minimal integration" (1993: 7). Factories in this isolated
place have no linkage to one another. Absurdly, the factory that makes steel

DESPEDIDOS ■ Helguera

The Jobless, **by Helguera** Fired workers are standing at the personnel exit. "So this is the light at the end of the tunnel..." From *La Jornada,* July 19, 1995. Reprinted by permission.

does not supply another smaller factory in the same city that makes finished goods out of steel. The farmers who grow fruit and vegetable crops nearby do not sell to local merchants; both buyers and sellers have contracts with a few large merchants who control commerce farther inland in Uruapan and Morelia.

The city remains well-populated, but many of the installations are bankrupt and virtually abandoned. Besides the two steel mills and the iron mine, a fertilizer factory and a small metal parts manufacturer are still working. Little else functions anymore. Empty industrial buildings lie shuttered behind barbed wire fences; here and there, lots once planned for construction lie untended – deforested and empty, with footpaths carving the shortest route through them from one settlement to another. The broad boulevard cutting through the center of the city, grandly divided with landscaped islands and large traffic circles, today hosts children at intersections breathing fire or juggling in clown suits for a few pesos. In blistering lowland heat, tired street merchants sit at stalls along the sidewalk, hawking tape recorders or sandwiches or nail polish. There are few customers. The hotels, once always full with government officials and visitors, now are mostly vacant. Taxi drivers idle at the curbs beside them or cruise through town looking for customers. There are too many taxistas for the small customer base (the result of corrupt officials selling too many medallions), so no one makes a living at that business either. Thirty years of history have not been kind to Lázaro Cárdenas.

There are reasons for Lázaro Cárdenas's forlorn visage. If one were to compile a list of regional economies shattered by the fiscal and trade policies of the Salinas and Zedillo administrations, the city of Lázaro Cárdenas would undoubtedly appear near the top. Built on land that was once mostly remote coastal swamps at the mouth of the Balsas River two decades ago, the Lázaro Cárdenas-Las Truchas Steelworks (SICARTSA) was one of a number of prominent factories built or expanded under state auspices in the thirty-five-year era of import substitution industrialization following World War II. Requiring unprecedented levels of concentrated public investment and vast state and urban planning, the industrial complex embodied nationalist-revolutionary aspirations as few other industrial projects had ever done in Mexico (Zapata 1978; Bizberg 1982). The development of an integrated economy, a "pole of development" as it was called, was meant to demonstrate to the world Mexico's industrial might, its planning know-how, and its commitment to delink its economy from first-world markets. Named for the populist president from Michoacán who originally conceived of the project, the Lázaro Cárdenas-Las Truchas steel complex was to provide employment, replace Mexico's dependence on foreign steel, decentralize capital formation, provide export earnings, and create economic growth and urban services in a remote, poverty-stricken part of the countryside.[1] "Upon the inauguration of SICARTSA," extolled a local newspaper upon the opening of the Stage I plant, "the infrastructure that the country is building will extend on to highways, roads, schools, and the planning of human settlements, beginning the country's true industrial stage" (*La Voz de la Costa* 1976).

---

[1] The project's architects drew heavily on theories of regional de-centralization of development. See discussion in Restrepo (1984), and also Zapata (1985) for a comparative study on four Mexican poles of development.

A project that consumed vast fiscal resources, the urban industrial complex in Lázaro Cárdenas was precisely the sort of item that market-minded technocrats would later identify as a budget boondoggle – as an obstacle rather than a solution to the nation's development problems. As public policy shifted toward open markets and private sector-led industrialization in the middle and late 1980s, fewer and fewer officials in control of economic policy in Mexico believed that SICARTSA had a great deal to offer the nation as long as it remained a state-owned enterprise. At the national level, a devaluation in 1976 and then a rapid diversion of government attention to petroleum-related projects during an oil boom in late 1978 through 1981 made for mixed signals from officials in Mexico City. Also in the 1980s, the government's mounting troubles with external creditors, combined with considerable cost overruns and graft in the project's administration, variable quality in the industrial products manufactured at the plant, and falling steel prices internationally made it appear that the project would remain a net burden to the government for some time before returning profit to the state. By the time it was built, the Lázaro Cárdenas-Las Truchas Steelworks (SICARTSA) was becoming outdated as a model of development policy, even if it was still quite modern as a manufacturing facility. The industrialization and urbanization of Lázaro Cárdenas City, planned in four stages, never advanced past the completion of the second of four planned stages. Projects following the $1.5 billion construction of a steel mill and the development of iron mines at nearby La Mira in 1976 proceeded fitfully. Budget problems and periodic stoppages plagued the construction of a second steel mill that was to manufacture flat steel; several other enterprises that were to manufacture finished and semifinished steel-based products were never integrated as planned into the SICARTSA enterprise.

If one stays for a time in the city – something that very few do these days if they don't live there – other aspects of Lázaro Cárdenas City start to become clearer. Despite the fatiguing heat and flagging economy, there is surprising dynamism and intensity to citizen politics. Since 1988, the city intermittently has been controlled by the leftist Party of the Democratic Revolution (PRD); the area is also the birthplace of a national environmental network of river fishermen whose production has been devastated by pollution from local industries. The city hall frequently is shut down by angry residents of makeshift settlements, or *colonias*, demanding services or property titles. There are marches now and then by federations of the unemployed. Many teachers in the area are dissidents, too – participants in a PRD-linked faction of the national teachers' union. *Barzonistas* – part of the national debtors' group – often break a day's boredom by forcibly recovering properties repossessed by the banks. And when there are scandals or crises in town, as when toxic fumes sickened several dozen children at a local school in the summer of 1995, the demonstrations are fierce and well attended – enough so that the story makes the Mexico City dailies five hundred miles away.

Though many of the organizations active in Lázaro Cárdenas today are fairly new, distributive conflicts pre-date industrial downsizing, urban sprawl, and serious chemical and heavy metal contamination in the area. In fact, the tone of state-society politics in Lázaro Cárdenas was set in large part by workers who were brought to the city thirty years ago to build the port's industries and then to run them. This chapter and the next demonstrate how privatization of the steel industry and the port enterprises altered the field of contentious politics in Lázaro Cárdenas. In this locality, I argue that privatization of the steel industry and trade liberalization set in motion a crucial set of structural and ideational changes in grassroots politics that dissolved the basis for broadly backed union militance centered in the steel workers' Local 271. After privatization, contention shifted from workplace to neighborhood, and from strike campaign to local petition.

Similar to the case study of Zacatecas which follows, the retreat of the federal government in major industries had a deep and largely negative impact on the region. Mass layoffs, debt, and rising prices affected not only workers in the city's factories but also those who lived from industries that marketed wares to workers or who serviced industries. Notably, privatization and fiscal retrenchment did not empty the city of workers or contention, as one finds, for example, in rust belt localities elsewhere. Instead, the city has continued to grow. Meanwhile, as independent labor-based mobilization became less relevant and less viable an option for groups seeking resources or reforms social movement politics splintered into a multitude of small distributive disputes.

Any account of contentious politics that seeks to explain the extraordinarily high rate of protest in Lázaro Cárdenas today, but also the unusually fractious and competitive nature of protest politics, must consider the roots of protest in the city as well as the structures of patronage and resource brokerage that controlled protest and dealt with disputes. Those structures of control are intimately tied up with the sorts of disputes that emerged in this planned city, in which labor insurgents mobilized around the needs of the migrant population for housing, services, and ever more employment. Accordingly, the following account first seeks to explain why the steel workers' Local 271 was able to anchor contentious politics in the region at key junctures, and then why the movement and its cross-sectoral bases of support so rapidly dissolved after fifteen years of combative campaigns.

In brief, I argue in this chapter that the developmentalist language that undergirded the city's creation, the political needs of left-leaning elites backing the project, and the enclave nature of the local economy gave militant Maoist and Communist workers a crucial space and time to build a strong union with unusually autonomous mobilizational structures. Narratives of labor autonomy and democracy, interwoven with the government's own discourse about the social goals of the project, provided militants with a powerful means of linking wage and workplace demands with broader bids for schools, housing, services, and more employment. However, as I also argue, those narratives were fragile in many ways. Throughout the life of the workers' movement, deep schisms divided workers among competing factions with different ideological and strategic outlooks. In addition, increasing proportions of the urban population came to understand the interests of labor insurgents as irrelevant to or frankly incompatible with their own. In this fashion, privatization and massive layoffs disrupted life in the port city and introduced new shortages and discontent. They also brought to the surface underlying divisions that cut across sector, class, and gender.

The Origins of a Worker/Community Movement

Lázaro Cárdenas City, in its early years, resembled by all counts a gold rush city. In the years surrounding the construction of the first steel mill, people seeking employment poured into the region. The population would sometimes as much as double in a year in the early 1970s, rising from some fifteen thousand residents in 1970 to over fifty-six thousand five years later (Bizberg 1982: 127). Rapid in-migration quickly transformed hillsides and river banks. New settlements dotted rural ejidal agricultural lands around the mines, spreading north along the coast going north toward Colima and south toward Guerrero. Houses, dirt roads, churches, and food stands that settlers built did not much resemble the neatly ordered neighborhoods mapped out by a firm of Swedish urban planners in the early years of the project. In part, this was because there were more people than official housing. However, others recall that the housing was not to their tastes, pointing out that the low-income housing was very cramped, that the wiring was often flimsy, and that the walls were thin. Many from the countryside resisted living in such close quarters. Living in urban housing meant that there would be no place for animals or a garden, and that swimming or fishing in the river or the ocean would remain a long walk or bus ride away.

Despite the creation of over ten thousand jobs in the operating first-stage steel plant and in the construction of a second-stage steel plant, which was to produce flat steel, the city's population swelled with people seeking additional jobs, coming principally from surrounding states of Michoacán and Guerrero but also from Mexico City and other parts of the republic (Bizberg 1982: 47). Counter to the recollection of many in Lázaro Cárdenas today who see joblessness purely as a result of government exit from the project, unemployment was a perennial issue of contention in the region, even at the most expansive phase of public investment in the region. SICARTSA itself never employed much more than five thousand union workers. Government officials in the 1970s declared employment creation to be a priority in the Lázaro Cárdenas project; undoubtedly this lent to the expression of public discontent over the fact they could not meet the exploding demand for jobs in the area. From the very beginning of the project, substantial numbers of people worked only sporadically and shifted between day labor and the informal economy (Interviews D-2, D-5, D-6 1994; Nolasco 1984).

Many of the initial outbursts of civic and worker protest in Lázaro Cárdenas stemmed from the fact that the city was not evolving in the manner publicly predicted by its planners. Forward and backward linkages that planners asserted would develop between the core plant and the surrounding rural economy, propelling yet new works in transport, shipping, and retail sales and services, never materialized in the dimensions imagined by the project's architects. As a result of interrupted development and the lack of industrial linkages in the area, the SICARTSA steel plant came to assume a far greater proportion of the city's economy than had originally been projected. In many senses, what wealth existed in the city came directly or indirectly from the plant's operations. Those who did not work for SICARTSA were likely to work for contract companies who worked for SICARTSA, or to work in the services – both formal and informal – that catered to SICARTSA employees and workers. One longtime resident, when asked to explain how she saw the SICARTSA plant in the early days, commented simply, "Everyone ate from steel here."

The Lázaro Cárdenas project was a product of developmentalist policy making that placed emphasis on the generation of employment and on the direct reduction of poverty through the provision of services such as public education, health, running water, and electricity. In the end, however, the provision of such services took a back seat to the exigencies of industrial development. Problems that emerged in the new city, and that in fact persist in aggravated form today, had to do with the very lack of adequate services promised in the formation of the project. Housing did not meet demand, and urban services such as electricity, clean water, sewage systems, and pavement lagged behind the level population growth. The construction of the planned city, administered largely by the Lázaro Cárdenas Public Trust (FIDELAC), lagged far behind the housing needs of the population. Workers and urban dwellers subsequently built dozens, and eventually hundreds, of makeshift *colonias populares*. In settlements around the city in the nearby ejidal and fishing villages of La Mira, Las Guacamayas, Playa Azul, El Bordonal, and Buenos Aires, workers and migrants seeking income built their homes of spare materials of corrugated metal and wood (Bizberg 1982: 116). The situation was also aggravated by the relatively high price of housing built by the FIDELAC and the National Workers Housing Institute (INFONAVIT). FIDELAC statistics from a survey of residents of the aforementioned villages, largely living in "irregular" (unplanned) units, indicated that household budgets accommodated little more than food and clothing, with 48 to 63 percent of income going to food, and 7 to 17 percent paying for clothing (Fideicomiso Lázaro Cárdenas 1980). By the end of the 1980s, the number of informal colonies inside Lázaro Cárdenas would reach 130, and the number in Guacamayas, the next largest municipal entity, was over 74 (Interviews C-1, C-6, 1995).[2]

---

[2] Respondents' comments from Lázaro Cárdenas are almost all cited with numbers, not names. I did this because I judged the political climate to be very tense at the time I spoke with people. Between the two periods of fieldwork I conducted in Michoacán, a number of workers I had spoken with were fired, presumably for insurgent political activities. I do not think that my speaking with them contributed to their dismissal; nevertheless, the incident reinforced my decision to keep names out of direct citations. Therefore, I have chosen not to publish information about who said what. I also will not print the names of people who asked specifically to remain anonymous. I devised a system to give readers a little bit of information about the respondents. Interviews lettered "A-" are workers and ex-workers. Those lettered "B-" are associated with SICARTSA management or labor contract com-

In tandem with the lack of adequate services in the area, nature itself lent a hand in opening spaces for workers at SICARTSA to make demands of the company. The lowland climate and dense swamp lands of the Balsas River delta made for a difficult adjustment among the workers and their families, who were mostly newcomers to the area. People who had migrated from cooler regions – the lovely tierra fría of Michoacán or the springlike highlands of Morelos or Guerrero or the state of Mexico, suffered in the intense heat and humidity of the Pacific coast. Mosquitos and sand flies swarmed; malaria was endemic to the area. "There were still swamps everywhere," says a worker, "and there were scorpions and flies all over. A lot of people left." A housewife from Sinalóa recalled, for example, how in the rainy season her street was full of huge frogs that would come into the house at night.

Early Protest

Original union members and early chroniclers of the area recall that labor disputes broke out in the city's prehistory, during the years the steel mill and local hydraulics projects were still under construction. The first labor disputes in the area were wildcat actions, occurring in the years 1972, 1973, 1974, and 1976, mostly having to do with labor code violations, wage anomalies, and inadequate safety equipment at work sites. A number of trade unions associated with the Confederation of Mexican Workers (CTM) stepped in to mediate these conflicts. Settlements were usually reached within days. Local 271, which would eventually come to represent plant workers at SICARTSA, was formed in 1973 by a few dozen mostly skilled laborers such as topographers, electricians, and welders. By the time labor authorities registered the union, the number of workers had grown to 222.

The most important legacy of early labor organization was a set of union rules that were set up for Local 271. The SICARTSA workers' union central, the National Union of Mexican Miners and Metalworkers, generally controlled workers' locals fairly tightly. Conservative, party-loyal national officials always had the option of expelling troublesome union members. So-called exclusion clauses enabled authorities to fire disobedi-

panies. Those lettered "C-" are political activists in Lázaro Cárdenas at large, and those lettered "D-" are residents of the city who may or may not have been sympathetic to the steel workers' movement.

ent workers easily.[3] However, the statutes written for the new Local 271 were fairly liberal. This was part of a political compromise because workers were initially disappointed at the one-sidedness of the registration process. Rules mandated, for example, that the rank-and-file approve of collective contracts through secret ballot voting; they also required majority quorums for general assemblies. Statutes also provided for a dual committee leadership structure and direct elections of union officials for each of the two committees every four years. Years later, such procedures would enable the union to make contract grievances that went far beyond what authorities were disposed to give to workers. At the time, however, officials did not consider such statutes to be any threat to labor control. The fact that such statutes were conceived at all was undoubtedly due to where the project stood vis-à-vis a particularly tense configuration of national and sectoral politics.

The president at the time, Luis Echeverría, had come to power in 1970 following the massacre of students in 1968. Although (or perhaps because) many people believed him to have been responsible for the military's actions in that episode, acting at the time at the helm of security forces as Minister of the Interior, his presidency took a turn toward the left. He built his own presidential power base by sidelining older segments of the government associated with his predecessor, Díaz Ordáz, and/or with more conservative elements in the central bank and the finance Secretary (Centeno 1994: 76–84; Smith 1991: 366). Working in a personalistic fashion, he conducted a campaign of reformist administration in which he emphasized a national development course of "shared development." Rather than undertaking this national project through institutional reforms, he instead intermittently conciliated the demands of labor and peasant movements who were calling for distributive reforms and organizational independence from corporatist Institutional Revolutionary Party (PRI) structures. The labor union statutes at Lázaro Cárdenas, conceived as an adjunct to a still-restrictive national union covenant, were typical of Echeverría's rather double-edged political opening that gave some encouragement to grassroots organizers while falling short of systemic reform that would render organized labor an autonomous political force.

[3] By law, union shop floors are closed-shop. If a labor leader removes union affiliation from a worker, the enterprise is obligated to fire the worker. Perversely, this makes it possible for coopted labor bosses to do the bidding of management.

Viewed with two decades of hindsight, it is not surprising that the SICARTSA project would become a pariah institution in the late 1980s under President Salinas. The construction of the complex was overseen by Cuauhtémoc Cárdenas, who later became governor of Michoacán. Inside the PRI, Cárdenas was the heir to the left-leaning political legacy of his late father. The first director of the steel mill was also long associated with popular, large-scale public works projects. Adolfo Oribe Alba had been the head of the Secretary of Hydraulic Resources under President Aleman in the 1940s, directing the country's largest expansion of irrigation projects to date. The first head of the union was Rafael Melgoza, who was a long-time friend and associate of Cuauhtémoc Cárdenas. Even more interesting, Adolfo Oribe's son by the same name, was a leader of a number of radical political initiatives informed by a syncretic mix of Maoist populism and anarcho-syndicalist doctrines. According to most accounts, the senior Oribe gave his son considerable latitude to organize among workers, giving rise to what would be the most durable and populous union faction in the factory, Mass Line, or *Linea de Masas*.

Authorities who oversaw the project had little reason to believe that the union at SICARTSA would become problematic for the government or the state-owned enterprise. Most of the workers who came to build the industrial complex and work in the Stage I SICARTSA steel mill had little in common with one another. In a nation where extended family and regional ties constitute economic lifelines as well as social networks, particularly among peasant and working classes, the workers who came to Lázaro Cárdenas formed an atomized noncommunity of strangers. Bizberg notes, for example, that in 1976, the workers who arrived to work in the plant were disproportionately young, and nearly half of them were single (1982: 47). As much as the steel city on the coast was a new frontier for individuals seeking work or higher wages – or perhaps wanting to flee uncomfortable political circumstances in shop floors elsewhere[4] – it was also a place that could be quite alienating for individuals moving away from family and friends. Fewer than 10 percent of the workers contracted in construction and operations were from the area.

---

[4] Some older, skilled workers from urban areas report that they had participated previously with the Mexican Communist Party or other leftist groupings and parties. Although it is probable that people in the Mexican government and/or groups of private sector entrepreneurs were keeping track of communist organizers, it appears that they did not give those lists to labor recruiters for the SICARTSA plant.

As often as not, discomfort prodded workers to leave the area, not to engage in protest. Although no reliable figures on out-migration exist, informants consistently testify that there was a great deal of worker turnover, particularly in the early years. Veterans of the area remember that, when conflicts arose among workers, problems tended to get solved through elite channels. In the early years, Local 271 maintained good relations with national union leadership, allowing the general secretary of the National Mining and Metalworkers' Union (SNTMMSRM), Napoleón Gómez Sada, to intercede with company management on behalf of workers. In a plant such as SICARTSA, where a high degree of automation and complexity in the manufacturing process required a substantial proportion of skilled workers with knowledge of the equipment, turnover represented a production liability. Particularly in skilled positions in departments like the machinists' shop or the area where iron pellets were processed, workers were not fungible. Skilled workers, however, were precisely the individuals who had greater prospects of being hired elsewhere if they chose to leave. As a consequence, older workers recall, it seemed that the company was disposed to accommodate worker demands and petitions in order to retain personnel. As one worker put it:

When SICARTSA started, it gave the workers a contract without a fight. There was no history in the area of labor fights – most workers were at that time getting more money than they would have at home. Also, many people wanted to leave because the heat and conditions were so bad. The heat was terrible, and there were swamps which smelled really awful, and there were all sorts of flies and crocodiles. The company was so anxious to keep us there that they would solve whatever little problem came up. They were pretty relaxed about how you worked. You could bring in a TV set to watch during work and they wouldn't say anything . . . (Interview A-2, 1995).

The disproportionate power of skilled workers presented a dilemma for authorities at SICARTSA. Highly trained laborers, who were the least replaceable on the shop floor, were also more combative and likely to participate in incipient radical organizing in the community.[5] The enterprise was apparently so in need of skilled workers in Lázaro Cárdenas City that

---

[5] Bizberg's factory study conducted in the late 1970s, for example, shows a clear correlation between individuals' level of education and "workerist" political beliefs. Skilled workers, he argues, tended to identify their own interests as being class-based, rooted in a larger proletarian struggle. Such ideologies were more likely to give rise to demands for things such as greater union autonomy and an expanded political role in government. Less educated workers, by contrast, were more likely to be concerned with more immediate economic issues, such as wages and benefits. Also see Bizberg (1990: Chapter 7).

no serious attempt was made to sift out dissident workers before they were employed at the plant. By 1976, such workers began to mobilize their colleagues around a more expansive set of demands than had been lodged before. One self-described radical organizer, a university-educated machinist and maintenance worker, recalled that politics among urban workers with backgrounds in industrial shop floors in other parts of the country were very much affected by national trends in labor organizing. Many of the skilled workers who emerged as important organizers in Local 271 brought with them a radical proletarian consciousness forged in leftist insurgencies occurring around the country at that time. One early radical organizer recalls that his radical colleagues included veterans of the Maoist Land and Liberty movement in Monterrey and the electricians' Democratic Tendency insurgency in Mexico City. In addition, communist organizers in the north, having made inroads into sibling SNTMMSRM locals in Monclova, Cananea, and Monterrey, began to pour energies into solidarity work at SICARTSA, viewing mining and metal workers as a potential vanguard for leftist insurgency.

The physical isolation and lack of established institutional administration over human settlements in the area contributed to various organizers' radical projects for three reasons. First, acute shortages in urban services produced discontent among new residents. Second, the newness of the city made it such that there were no naturalized hierarchies. There were no sacred families, no entrenched elites. Any policing of the population had to be done fairly directly, as evidenced in the extensive military and judicial police presence that was eventually established in the area.[6] Third, most people received services from the common providers, making common public targets fairly easy to identify. Both formal urban or informal networks of distribution were in their infant stages. There was also no established urban private sector – only that which sprung up in tandem with the mass investment of the government. Lázaro Cárdenas was a place where public entities occupied monopolistic control over major functions of material distribution, but in contrast with other mining and enclave economies that were much older, the system of social control had not become naturalized in forms of public discourse or history.

---

[6] Police and military installations in the area include a headquarters for the state judicial police, the federal highway police, the federal port police, and the customs police. There is also an army base within ten miles of the city.

A 1977 strike movement marked a watershed moment of sorts in the city. Its militance and prominent location gave the union local national visibility, and its popular bases of support lent new credence to notions that labor struggles could encompass social demands beyond the factory. A number of aspects of the struggle marked Local 271 as "problem" union, and as a movement sufficiently autonomous from government control to organize political opposition at a local level. Workers began to make demands that extended beyond the spectrum of what central authorities considered legitimate and negotiable within the realm of collective bargaining.[7] Complaints focused not on salaries (acceptable as a worker demand) but instead on issues of job safety and the management of production. Discontent swelled over company pressure to accelerate production beyond what workers considered safe levels, as well as over nonfunctioning antidust/anticontaminant equipment. Workers also demanded public works, land distribution for new settlers, and multiple other measures to address substandard living conditions.

The months-long process of organizing for the strike movement unquestionably moved the union rank and file to the left. It also provoked many hundreds to participate in everyday union affairs. Bizberg (1982) mentions, for example, that as the strike movement built steam, daily general assemblies numbered fifteen hundred or more. Radical members of the union convinced many new workers of the need for organizational and decision-making autonomy from labor elites in Mexico City. This aspect of the workers' platform antagonized labor authorities more than workers' material demands because it threatened political elites' ability to utilize the union as an agent of electoral mobilization. The more radical workers, for example, flouted clauses in the national union charter that required that all affiliates be members of the ruling party and carry out duties associated with electoral mobilization.

Workers' movements had the support of much of the population in the area, effectively because workers' demands that extended beyond pure salary issues effectively constituted demands for public goods. That is, workers in this still-monolithic economy constituted a significant portion of the municipal population as a whole, and their union represented the

---

[7] Labor unions in Mexico, limited to what are considered "economic" demands, run the risk of having strike movements declared "nonexistent" if movement demands are declared "political."

only significant entity for interest aggregation of the lower classes. In purely economic terms, many of the workers' real economic interests were indistinguishable from the those of urban nonworkers around them. More housing, schools, and public works benefitted workers and nonworkers alike. In addition, while unionized workers on the whole received a higher average salary than their non-unionized counterparts, significant differences inside the pay scale of Local 271 workers existed (Zapata 1978: 264–5). Thus, workers in Local 271 did not as a whole constitute a privileged class, as some informants allege. Unskilled workers, laboring as drivers or *peones*, received as little as 20 percent of the pay of the most skilled unionized workers. As a result, Local 271 members were at first interspersed in all but the wealthiest settlements in Lázaro Cárdenas and built ties and mutual interests with residents of colonias populares and planned housing complexes.[8]

The three years following the explosion of militance in 1977 initiated a storm of internal organization and mobilization in Local 271. State response was ambiguous: moves by the government to cease the local's trend toward radicalization and its campaigns for union autonomy alternated with government attempts to appease worker demands. Punitive dismissals of members were interspersed with sporadic federal government attention to health and education, and with conciliatory contract clauses giving workers more benefits and pay.[9] A local entrepreneur with ties to the local ruling party remembers this period in strong terms: "They [the workers] walked all over the bosses. They violated the contracts, they blocked the streets, they took over the Palacio Municipal. They began to create social problems, not just here but also in Morelia and Mexico City" (Interview D-1, 1995). While the strength of Local 271 and the extent of its actions is actually an exaggeration of the facts – there is no record of worker occupations of the local government offices, for example – this

---

[8] Regarding this phenomenon, Robert Aitken (1988, unpublished paper) argues a Chayanovian scheme: his household survey data suggests that workers at Local 271 were differentiated economically by stage in family reproductive stages. That is, families with small children tended to be worse off and less likely to have regular housing than more mature family units.

[9] Bizberg (1982: 62) notes, for example, that while worker actions did not always produce explicit conciliation by the state, extralegal demands often received indirect attention. In 1977, for example, within five months of the strike, officials from state agencies pertaining to health, education, industry, and public works arrived in Lázaro Cárdenas on fact-finding missions.

informant's impression is important because of the power *ascribed* to them in this period.

To a certain degree, workers in prominent state enterprises in the late 1970s operated in a narrow, but palpable space of government receptivity to labor demands. On a national level, the movement for labor autonomy from corporatist control continued after President Echeverría left office, albeit under greater constraints, and provided economic and moral support for local-level militants. In addition, macroeconomic policy channeled ample funds into the sphere of state-owned enterprises: the administration of President López Portillo stressed state-led industrialization with the exploitation of vast new petroleum reserves and raised the level of public investment from the already high 30 percent to some 47 percent during the period 1977 to 1982 (Rueda Peiro, González Marin, and Alvarez Mosso 1990). Labor leaders who attempted to make explicitly political demands of the government, or who initiated campaigns for union independence met with firmly repressive measures. At the same time, the government allowed unions in state-owned industries to inflate their ranks beyond the needs of production. Personnel adjustments for economic reasons were virtually nonexistent (Interview with Rueda Peiro, 1994). At the SICARTSA plant, the five thousand plant workers enjoyed a reasonable amount of job security when they were not openly disobeying the government. During strikes, when workers displayed sufficient unity, their numbers were such that repression of the unit as a whole was unpalatable for the government.

Changing Local Structures and National Economic Policies

The 1977 strike movement shaped the union politically in a number of contradictory ways. The struggle itself established Local 271 as a potentially dangerous political force vis-à-vis the ruling party and corporatist labor elites, the SICARTSA enterprise, and the Secretary of Labor. Inside the union, however, workers argued over how the union ought to be run and what demands merited the mobilization of radical actions. Generally, workers sided with one of several union factions, or *corrientes*: Linea de Masas – a group with Maoist origins – and Democracia Proletaria – a faction with ties to the Mexican Communist Party (PCM) and later the Unified Socialist Party of Mexico (PSUM). Though factional antagonisms were present from the beginning, they were at first surmountable. In 1979, members of both factions participated in Consejo de Lucha, a radical protest movement directed against sympathizers of the national union leadership, who had illegally rigged union elections in 1978. However, they became very distinct in constituency and ideological outlook by 1981.

When the two factions became deeply divided, Local 271 foundered. Two base workers recalling a failed strike movement of 1981, for example, say that members of Democracia Proletaria even acted as strikebreakers in a Linea de Masas-led standoff. Another faction called Coordinadora de Lucha began to grow in numbers. Its membership, generally more sympathetic to the more radical Democracia Proletaria, differed with Democracia Proletaria in its contention that the poorer working classes and the marginal colonias ought to assume greater priority in the union demands. One early leader of Democracia Proletaria, recalling the latter movement, recalls its participants as admirably radical, but less "preparados," a reference that would imply some rift between workers of different socioeconomic backgrounds. This factionalism, discussed in greater depth in the next section, underscored an increasingly complex project of mass movement consciousness. As the apparatus of distribution became more complex and divided among multiple government agencies and state-owned enterprises, so did the possible choice of strategic targets. As the number of distinct economic sectors grew locally, so did the possible choice of allies and enemies.

One is often tempted to attribute coinciding protests in different localities directly to disruptions caused by national policy. An examination of the process of local organization and protest events in Lázaro Cárdenas, however, reminds us that cycles of mobilization have mostly to do with political circumstances inside movements as well as inside local systems of governance and distribution. Whereas one might be tempted to assume that worker organization and strike activity in Lázaro Cárdenas in 1977, in 1979, and again in the 1980s were manifestations of general unrest in Mexico over contracting buying power and austerity policies, closer inspection reveals that such a conclusion is problematic. Workers' disposition to strike in Local 271 was provoked as much by political convictions about labor power and union autonomy as by fluctuations in incomes. Workers' power to mobilize crucial lateral support from the community for strike actions was conditioned as much by the structure of distribution in Lázaro Cárdenas City as it was by the amount of resources available.

As evidence of this, we find that economic conditions did not decline as drastically in Lázaro Cárdenas before 1985 as they did elsewhere in

Mexico. In fact, in June of 1983, workers at SICARTSA actually resisted joining national actions called by Mexico City labor bosses who were responding to currency devaluations and falling real wages. Although workers at SICARTSA were suffering from rising prices, they resented having any action at all imposed upon them by the national leadership (Daville 1986: 109). As the national economy crashed in the debt crisis of 1982, and the new administration of President De La Madrid began to dismantle the preceding models of state-led industrialization, government policy by the mid-1980s also veered toward a slowdown of public operations in Lázaro Cárdenas. Residents of Lázaro Cárdenas living in the city at this time, however, consistently testify that the direct impact of the initial debt crisis was minimal in the city itself. "We lived in an artificial economy," noted one individual. Investment earmarked before the debt crisis for the construction of the port enterprises ensured that ample funds flowed into the area. In addition to the new manufacturing companies, construction resumed in 1980 on the Stage II plant; there were also jobs and contract deals going on with the construction of a thermoelectric plant nearby in Petacalco, Guerrero, providing an additional ten thousand jobs at the height of its construction. This mass capital inflow made the city a rare oasis during the national shortages and monetary instability of the early 1980s.

Ironically, it was state-fueled prosperity and diversification of the economy that first began to limit the relevance of Local 271 as a channel for public demands. With the arrival of more housing, roads, and services over time, for example, the structure of demand and the channels of material distribution in Lázaro Cárdenas became more diffuse and harder to harness in unitary insurgent campaigns. Notably, housing policy by 1980 was beginning to differentiate social classes measurably *within* the bloc of unionized workers, separating better paid, skilled workers from other formal and informal sector workers, both spatially and in terms of standards of living. Houses inside the planned city settlements in Lázaro Cárdenas were mostly in reach for workers and management employees in middle- and high-income brackets (Hiernaux 1982: 118–22). Those informal lower-income housing settlements that were addressed by government policy were done unevenly. A 1977 World Bank loan designed to finance the construction of housing for lower-income residents of the greater metropolitan area resulted three years later in the distribution of deeds to three thousand lots in the more marginal settlements of Las

Guacamayas.[10] However, other lower-income settlements such as Playa Azul and La Mira received no such attention.

In 1980, significant changes occurred in government investment policy and the administration of the urban spaces in Lázaro Cárdenas. The development of a series of port enterprises, including joint state-foreign capital initiatives, gave rise to new sources of employment and a new surge of migration to the area. Construction of several large enterprises began on the adjoining space of Cayacal Island. The new enterprises included a fertilizer plant, an oil refinery, and two steel parts manufacturers (expected eventually to process output from the yet-unfinished Etapa II). Fertimex, Productora Mexicana de Tubería (PMT), Nippon-Kobe Steel (NKS), and Petroleos de México (PEMEX) were expected to generate some eighteen thousand new jobs in construction alone; after they began operation, their projected worker bases would together exceed that of Local 271. This diversification of the economy was accompanied by the entrance of multiple new state actors in the region. For some years after the initiation of construction, the operations of FIDELAC were displaced in importance by the Coordinación de Proyectos de Desarrollo, a creation of the López Portillo administration (Hiernaux 1982: 123).

The diversification of the distributive state apparatus on both the demand side (by 1983, union leadership from PMT, NKS, and other local enterprises also demanded housing and services for their constituencies) and the supply side (in terms of numbers of state actors) modified the initial "natural convergence" of local interests. At this point, the role of internal organization and strategic resource mobilization assumed newly important roles in the maintenance of Local 271 as a social movement with autonomous political capacities. Before 1980, a lesser material differentiation between union members, combined with the virtual monopoly of the union as a representative body of workers, lent Local 271 greater leverage vis-à-vis the government; after that point, they enjoyed a less automatic approval among the greatest part of the citizenry.

Workers at the SICARTSA plant established loose connections with union locals at the new port enterprises. The workers at SICARTSA sup-

[10] This term technically refers to the legalization of urban land tenure. Residents in a "regularized" settlement have been granted deeds to the plots they inhabit. Informants in colonias and the municipal government, however, also used the verb form *regularizar* (to formalize) to refer to a longer process by which colonos apply for and receive basic urban services as well as title to the land they occupy.

ported struggles of union locals at the other plants by supplementing their strike funds and filling out picket lines. However, the ties were loose, and SICARTSA union leaders were critical of what they saw as controlled leadership in the CTM locals. The decision to lend mutual support to other strike movements in this period presented something of a dilemma, with support finally winning out for ideological reasons (support for any union over any enterprise), and for the purpose of compelling local unions to support strike movements of SICARTSA workers in return. "We must use our own resources in order to consolidate this movement," stated one internal union bulletin. "These are the moments in which we must consolidate a permanent partnership [with the NKS union] through a promise of SOLIDARITY and MUTUAL SUPPORT. We must discuss how we can work in a joint manner in order to form a solid, unitary FRONT OF STRUGGLE that guarantees us the ability to fight against our enemies with greater force" (Democracia Proletaria, March 1986).

The factors that appear to have been most crucial in the formation of a radical movement were those existing at the outset of various unions in Lázaro Cárdenas City. Whereas unions established in the 1980s in the city remained fairly subdued, workers at Local 271 continued to make contract and salary gains in the early and mid-1980s, even compelling the enterprise to exceed federal salary caps[11] to settle a strike in 1985. Rare among unions at the time, Local 271 also defied federal labor authorities by continuing to make extralegal "noneconomic" demands for things such as low-income housing and an epidemiological study on worker health in the steel plant. Whereas national labor protests over wage and price policies were waning, Local 271 went on strike for 33 days, demanding among other things a 33 percent raise, a workplace health study and better medical care, new schools, promises of no downsizing of labor rolls through 1987, and a 40-hour workweek (Democracia Proletaria 1985: 61–2).

The years 1986–7 marked a point in which local organizers began to see a connection between themselves and national policies associated with sectors and markets. A study commissioned by President Miguel de la Madrid, conducted by a team of consultants led by Fernando Hiriart, the director-general of the Federal Electricity Concern (CFE), resulted in an

---

[11] To control inflation and/or respond to demands of the business sector during periods of economic downturn, the Mexican federal government often issues percentage caps on salary adjustments. Though businesses are rarely sanctioned for exceeding these caps, managers are usually only too happy to comply. The federal standard allows them to avert direct blame for falling real wages or buying power.

important policy paper known as the Hiriart Report. Made public in 1986, the report called for the rationalization of state assets in the steel industry (*Latin American Newsletters* 1986: 2). Following the report's recommendations, the decision was taken to close Fundidora Moneterrey in May of that year. The Fundidora, with the oldest equipment, the highest debt load, and the lowest productivity of three state-owned steel plants was clearly the most vulnerable to elimination. With debts measuring 230 percent of total assets, compared with respective ratios at Altos Hornos de Mexico in Coahuila and Sicartsa of 52 and 27 percent, Fundidora Monterrey was but an oblique warning signal to workers at SICARTSA (Villareal 1988; Rueda Peiro 1994). In a sense, the sacrifice of twelve thousand jobs in the sector might have appeared either as an indication of things to come or as a measure that protected the jobs of workers in more productive plants, such as SICARTSA. With regard to the impact of this policy on the strategy of Local 271, the extent to which union leaders and the rank-and-file imagined that they would be affected by industrial restructuring is questionable. An internal document of Democracia Proletaria mentions the Hiriart Report in September 1986 (Democracia Proletaria, September 18, 1986), but interviews with rank-and-file workers on the company rolls at the time indicate that many laborers were unaware of the plans to restructure and downsize Steel Holding Company of Mexico (SIDERMEX), the government holding company that included SICARTSA and two integrated steel mills in Coahuila and Nuevo Leon. "Most of us lived in the present," explained one worker. "We didn't have time to research things or predict what the future would bring" (Interview A-10, 1995).

An event that affected Local 271 more directly was the suspension once again of Etapa II in 1987. Though SIDERMEX recommenced construction within a year, the impact on Lázaro Cárdenas was both financial and psychological. The loss of business associated with suspension of construction always had immediate consequences on local services and small contract businesses. In addition, a great deal of local anxiety over the economy put pressure on workers not to strike in 1987 over contract negotiations. A Democracia Proletaria circular in July 1987 warns directly that the decision to strike or not must be made with regard to the "political and economic situation." The circular notes national inflation at 130 percent, a limited strike fund, and recent punitive dismissals of workers at Etapa II (Democracia Proletaria July 29, 1987).

By 1988, international market forces conditioned policy choices at SICARTSA and in SIDERMEX with a new directness. Officials were directed to reduce debt and increase productivity at all costs. All nonpriority companies were to be auctioned to the private sector or shut down (Martínez Aparicio 1992). Though SICARTSA was still regarded as a priority company, the adjustments in the steel and mining sector that followed were unprecedented. In June of 1988, SIDERMEX, with three integrated plants and eighty-seven associated mining and metal manufacturing companies, announced its goal of reducing holdings to two integrated plants and twenty-eight associated plants. An exterior debt of $3.53 billion, coupled with falling national demand and low international prices in steel, compelled state managers to take successively more serious actions to address production, marketing, and finance problems (*La Jornada* 1988). And SICARTSA's commercial competitiveness at national or international levels was fragile at best: SICARTSA's per capita productivity was 40 percent higher than that of the two state-owned steel plants in Monclova but was 50 percent lower than that of the Hojalata y Lamina Company (HYLSA), a privately owned steel plant in Monterrey (Rueda Peiro et al. 1990: 87). Adding to the pressures of fiscal austerity, international steel prices in the late 1980s were falling, as major producers of steel continued to substitute plastics for steel in cars and appliances.

By 1989, leadership of Local 271 began to respond to the pressures of the state to restructure the industry by publicly challenging the competence of company administration. Reproducing the terminology of state managers, on June 9, 1988, Local 271 demanded that the Secretary of the Treasury do an audit of SICARTSA, charging that millions of dollars in profits had been lost due to administrative incompetence. Copies of a letter approved by the worker general assembly denouncing massive fraud in the company were sent to President De La Madrid and the national press (*La Voz de Michoacán* 1988a). The company then responded to the workers' accusations in a public campaign to shift the blame to other parts of the government and back again to workers. The company alleged that its losses of 600 billion pesos were due to changes in the exchange rate and in revenue laws. It also noted that the wage bill was high: its workers, it alleged, had among the highest salaries in the country (*La Voz de Michoacán* 1988b).

Shortly after his succession to office, President Salinas intensified structural adjustment by accelerating the privatization of state industries and instituting a new level of government control over labor. Beginning with the dramatic armed removal and arrest of the petroleum workers' president, Joaquín Hernández Galicia, an event known as El Quinazo (owing to Hernández' nickname, La Quina) President Salinas began to sideline the power of labor leaders inside corporatist circles. General worker access to government arbitration of contract disputes declined as well. By 1992, the number of recognized strikes had declined by 50 percent from a decade earlier, despite a loss of real wages in that time approaching 60 percent (Méndez and Othon Quiróz 1994).

With a state program of privatization and labor restructuring already evident, the biannual contract negotiations due to occur in the summer of 1989 represented a crucial juncture for Local 271. Privatization was a tangible possibility, if not yet a certainty. In the state-owned steel industry, deep spending cuts that included more mass layoffs continued: workers at Plant II in Monclova struck in protest of mass cuts in the labor rolls, winning virtually nothing in a fifty-one-day strike. Locally in Lázaro Cárdenas City, strike movements also foundered: NKS struck in Lázaro Cárdenas in February of that year, only to have the movement declared illegal. In preparation for a company contract proposal that almost certainly would contain personnel cutbacks and the excision of clauses from the collective contract, Local 271 prepared a document in the spring of 1989 proposing various means of augmenting company productivity without cutting worker roles or sacrificing areas of bilateral control. Ignoring the report, SICARTSA released its initial contract proposal on June 11, 1989, offering workers a 10 percent salary raise and 8 percent raise in benefits packages and, in return, calling for the layoffs of 2,138 workers.

The fifty-nine-day strike beginning on August 4 of that year capped the end of yet another political economic era in Lázaro Cárdenas. Unlike previous actions, the 1989 strike was almost completely defensive in its goals: Local 271 this time fought to stave off losses rather than make distributive and/or political gains. Several key clauses that company managers sought to eliminate were precisely those that workers had fought in previous years to establish. Clauses that the company targeted for elimination or revision included those guaranteeing mine workers a forty-hour week and pay for time spent in transport to the mines in La Mira, obligations to build worker housing, pay for piecework, worker training, worker representation on company committees, public lighting obligations, and assistance for repairs on worker houses. In addition, new work regulations proposed by the company would end all company obligations for workers' compensation over and above that required by the Federal Labor Law and would grant the company management unilateral power to interrupt or suspend labor in any area or discipline workers. The company also sought the power to change schedules at any time without union permission (a sensitive issue for workers in a factory with twenty-four-hour operations and eight-hour shifts, six days a week), to deny temporary replacement of vacancies on the shopfloor, and to delay worker vacations for two to six months when deemed necessary (*La Jornada* 1989).

Workers speaking of the strike paint the struggle of autumn 1989 as an action that assumed all-or-nothing proportions. One ex-worker recalls of the fight: "Workers united [behind the effort] because, well, it was felt that if we won [the strike], it was a victory well won. If we lost, at least we fought well to defend ourselves" (Interview A-9 1995). According to accounts of rank-and-file union members, leaders, and witnesses of the strike, worker participation in the strike was very high, perhaps higher than any previous strike. Worker participation, which was at 80 to 90 percent in general assemblies held daily prior to and during the strike, became even higher when the national and local leadership became polarized over the legality of the movement. On September 18, the Federal Bureau of Conciliation and Arbitration declared the strike *inexistente*[12] – that is, illegal – and ordered the workers to return to the factory. The president of the SNTMMSRM central, Napoleón Gómez Sada, declared that as official union representative listed on the contract, he had ultimate authority to end the strike. Workers continued actions and augmented campaigns locally and nationally. Emergency workers running essential operations inside the factory were persuaded to leave. When the company tried to get past picket lines by flying in strikebreakers by helicopter, workers' wives thwarted their efforts by occupying the landing pad. A hunger strike by some one hundred workers commenced in Lázaro Cárdenas and in the state capital of Morelia, and groups of workers occupied protest camps in the Zócalo in Mexico City and Puebla.

Even though workers received donations and support locally, interviews suggest, however, that participation of a number of nonworker sectors in Lázaro Cárdenas, particularly among members of the colonias populares, was more muted than in previous strike movements in 1985, 1981, and before. Because the struggles of Local 271 had grown more defensive in

[12] Under federal labor law in Mexico, workers must petition a bureau in the Secretary of Labor in order to strike. Over 90 percent of strike movements are quelled through this process. When officials in the Federal Bureau of Conciliation and Arbitration determine that a strike movement does not qualify for recognition by the government, it is declared – in Orwellian fashion – to be "nonexistent."

nature, and the authority of single distributive agencies had grown more diffuse, the connection between 271 and the residential population narrowed. One younger member of the corriente Democracia Proletaria commented of the evolving position of Local 271: "The old Democracia Proletaria had . . . the luxury to be more radical. They fought for contract victories. After 1986, the fight was to keep the contract at all. After 1989, the fight was against privatization. . . ." By the time of the strike of 1989, Local 271 members perceived a greater stake in cultivating strategic alliances with other unions locally and nationally than with nonunion sectors in Lázaro Cárdenas. Meanwhile, nonunion sectors in Lázaro Cárdenas had begun by the late 1980s to form organizations of their own.

In terms of contract losses, no juncture in the history of Local 271 was more devastating: workers lifted the strike in October with a settlement that included the dismissal of 1,119 workers, the modification of seventeen work clauses, and a modest raise of 10 percent (Daville 1986: 121). In the year following the strike, the company dismissed an additional one thousand workers and instituted new work rules that augmented the rhythm of production and required the remaining workers to perform a greater number of jobs per shift (Interviews A-10 1995; A-12 1994; A-13 1994; A-14 1994). Workers and ex-workers interviewed four and five years afterwards, however, recall the strike with great pride. Almost without exception, workers and local activists who participated in the strike recall the strike as the union's greatest and last victory, as the ultimate expression of Local 271's autonomy and political radicalism. That the strike was declared illegal and that workers uniformly stayed out is generally one of the first things pointed out to one who asks about the events of 1989. Also, workers point out with great pride the level of open worker defiance to the wishes of the national union and the Secretary of Labor. One ex-worker recalling the strike, for example, emphasized the participation of great numbers of workers in the daily assemblies, and the margins of the initial strike votes. "According to our statutes, strikes are supposed to be approved by 50 percent plus one, but our [strike votes] were something like 70 to 30" (Interview A-9 1995). Another worker leader talked at length about the support Local 271 won from other combative union locals. Several workers pointed out the defiance embodied by the hunger strike, recalling friends, brothers, or cousins who had taken part.

113

Privatization and Dissolution of Central Distributive Channels

Although steel production facilities in Lázaro Cárdenas were not sold to the private sector until 1990,[13] the strike movement of 1989 represented the division between one epoch and another in terms of their ability to make distributive and political demands of the state. Individuals in other sectors in Lázaro Cárdenas, including businessmen, journalists, other unions, day laborers, and residents of colonias populares, also describe time in terms of a "before" and "after," but with direct reference to privatization. Following the privatization of SICARTSA, Fertimex, NKS, and PMT were also sold to the private sector. Labor rolls plummeted: the number of management employees at SICARTSA fell from 3,000 to 600; the number of workers at NKS from 1,200 to 410, at PMT from several hundred to a few dozen, and at Fertimex (Fertinal under private ownership) from 1,500 to 700. Adding to the wave was the completion of construction at the thermoelectric plant in Petacalco, ending work contracts for yet another 4,000 employees.

In the 1990s, new forms for civil politics surged. As federal agencies and institutions left the city or were dissolved, the only permanent channel to state brokerage of disputes was the municipal government. Protest occupations of municipal offices – once an extraordinary act of civil disobedience – became routine, numbering over 20 per year by the early 1990s (Interview D-6 1995). As significant numbers of workers, particularly those who had come from surrounding regions, turned once again to farming and fishing, issues of water and land contamination surged. Colono politics also erupted, with movements populated mostly by women. Movements of unemployed workers called for negotiations with the municipality alongside new organizations of debtors. Organizations that either formed or became militant after the privatization of SICARTSA included groups pressuring for land titles and urban infrastructure (including the Coordinadora Independiente de Colonias Populares de Guacamayas and the Tenencia de Guacamayas), jobs (the Coordinadora de Desempleados), debt relief (three chapters of the Barzón and the Asociación Nacional de Deudores Anónimos), jobs and social services (the Fronte Popular de Lucha Nacional – formed as an effort in solidarity with

---

[13] Two companies purchased the SICARTSA complex in four parts: a Monterrey-based conglomerate, the Villacero Group, assumed ownership of Etapa I and the mines, and a Bombay-based concern, Caribbean Ispat, bought the yet-uncompleted Etapa II and the factory services unit.

the Zapatistas in Chiapas), and environmental reforms (including the Sector Pesquero, the Comité Ecológico de Lázaro Cárdenas, and fishing cooperatives from La Villita, Petacalco, and Lázaro Cárdenas).

In many ways, the combative campaigns of Local 271 set in motion a mode of politics in which groups would call on local power brokers to resolve disputes, using an available language of proletarian justice, of grass-roots democracy, of anticorruption, and of advancement through con-frontation. The rhythm and character of mobilization changed, however. If mobilization centered around biannual contract negotiations before, now protest had become a perennial presence. With new arrangements that made wage-based protest against private corporations prohibitively costly to would-be labor activists,[14] many ex-workers who had been active in union politics, as well as workers still on the rolls, took up mobilizing in other arenas. This has made the city exceptionally contentious, given to protest and very high levels of left-party activity.[15] A sample of twelve months of one daily newspaper in 1997, *La Opinión de Michoacán*, shows some forty-eight protests by teachers, debtors, neighborhood groups, and several small groups of formal, semiformal, and informal employees demanding intervention of government authorities in particular disputes.

Protesters in the 1990s took modes of protest and lexicon of combat

---

[14] There is growing evidence that new private owners, particularly the new owners of SICARTSA, have used a system of payoffs, threats, blacklists, and selective firing to ward off renewed union militancy. Individuals with close ties to union leadership as early as 1994 privately alleged that they had knowledge that union leaders in Local 271 had taken payoffs from the company to monitor dissident factions in the ranks, and were stealing from union funds. At least some of these allegations were confirmed in early 1997, when it came to light that the outgoing treasurer of the union had stolen over ten million pesos (about $3 million in 1994 pesos) from union funds during his tenure from 1992 to 1996 (*La Opinión de Michoacán* 1997c). This sum, which was stolen gradually from local bank accounts registered to the union, was so substantial that many felt that it could not have been taken without knowledge of the outgoing secretary general of the union, who was charged with conspiracy in the theft but was not convicted. Two events since the scandal erupted suggest company collusion in this scheme. The ex-secretary general now works for management, according to workers, and the ex-treasurer was bailed out of prison for the indefinite future by the company.

[15] In the most recent federal elections in July 1997, the PRD candidate for the lower house of congress won handily against his PRI opponent, with twenty-two thousand votes to fifteen thousand. The PRD is riven with factions, however, and votes sometimes are split between the PRD and runaway factions. In elections in November 1998, for example, one faction of the leftist PRD defected over internal disputes, and the PRI candidate won with approximately 17.5 thousand votes, against the PRD-cum-PT candidate with 6.4 thousand votes and PRD candidate with 13.2 thousand votes (*La Opinión de Michoacán* 1997d, 1998).

from the past, transposing them into campaigns for very specific cash-based settlements or in special cases, small quotas of employment. Protests often had scant relation to one another. If before, the city's shortcomings were symptoms of shortcomings in industrialization and production that could be addressed through a radical labor project, now the city's short-comings were the source and the target of mobilization. Before privatization, informal sector actors stood at times to gain some greater measure of well-being through contract struggles and union largesse. After privatization, it had become the reverse: formal sector actors, even unionized workers, stood to gain more through informal-sector protests than by battling well-guarded and heavily policed private sector corporations.

What is most striking in interviews conducted after privatization in 1994 to 1999 was both the centrality of protest in people's memories of politics in the region, as well as a notable frustration with the local administrative gridlocks that were both a cause and a product of protest. That is to say, interviews suggested one of the only means of gaining assets or even sources of employment (especially in types of work that require licenses of some sort) was through protest, but the manner in which protests were mobilized and brokered inside local political circles tended to devalue in people's minds the language and principles that upheld them. Activists who organized protest complained that authorities routinely colluded with other, more opportunistic protest leaders, speaking of protest as a business, a negocio.

Squatting is the most commonly cited exchange. "You see these people in the municipal buildings?" remarked an ex-steel worker now driving a taxicab, "Some of their leaders are real operators. They take people to protest for land titles, and then they collect four or five lots doing that again and again." He pointed out some of the lots that he said were owned by protest entrepreneurs, which he said were gained by protest and rented out to new settlers. An item in a local newspaper suggests that this is a routine practice. A survey of informal colonias in 1995 revealed that forty-five of ninety-seven lots that had been granted in recent years through pressure were uninhabited (*La Opinión de Michoacán* 1995). Interestingly, the item did not explain much about this but merely alluded to the ubiquity of corruption in the city. To local readers of the paper, the political negocio was so obvious in fact that it needed no explanation. Clearly, protesters who claimed they needed land already had houses and got titles to new lots, which they would sell at a later date, when new migrants inevitably pour in from the parched and violent mountains inland, especially from nearby Guerrero. Despite scarcity in the city, people say, settlers still come because of untenable conditions created by the drug trade, agricultural crisis, military repression, and guerrilla activity.

For many who lament the passing of what they feel were more principled forms of social protest over health care, schools, union democracy, or worker housing, the decline in contentious politics is due to greed or a lack of seriousness on the part of newer activists. Examining protest events over time in the 1990s, the record of protest and resource brokerage suggests, however, that institutional arrangements have made protest intractably a system of one-time exchanges. The exit of federal agencies from an urban space conceived and built entirely through a model of state-led development left a system of liminal jurisdictions and debt-plagued local authorities.[16]

Local government officials who now become involved in dealing the greatest share of protest operate in a pared-down administration that was never designed to administer a city fully. Despite some attempt to generate greater revenues, officials have gained virtually no authority to tax the large private industries that still account for approximately 80 percent of the economic activity in the city. In a region where everything from employment to commerce to public works like electrification and street paving came from government spending on a body of state-owned industries, city authorities never developed the capacity to monitor, much less regulate or challenge, the use of space or natural resources in the area. In the years when federal authorities ran the steel mill and industrial trusts financed and built most of the urban infrastructure, authorities running the municipality largely dealt with the informal and rural groups who fell outside the canopy of industry. Now local government must administer

---

[16] Agencies associated with the industrial and urban planning of the region were phased out, along with the bulk of their budgets. Some of the cuts had to do with the end of direct government involvement in industry in Lázaro Cárdenas, whereas other cuts had to do with general cuts in federal budgets. The Lázaro Cárdenas Trust was dissolved, and its planning and infrastructure-building operations were absorbed by the municipal government by 1993. Also affecting housing policy were budget cuts in the workers' housing agency, INFONAVIT, which ceased to build housing directly and continued as a loan-granting office to workers. Finally, the informalization of the workforce effected by mass layoffs made many of the agencies that still existed in Lázaro Cárdenas irrelevant for many. State institutions that formerly had a broad mandate in Lázaro Cárdenas such as the Instituto Mexicano de Seguro Social (hospital, medical care) and financing agencies such as the National Fund for Workers' Compensation (FONACOT), which provided low-cost financing for workers, and INFONAVIT now served a measurably smaller proportion of the population.

the urban environment almost completely. As a result, municipal authorities can do little but legalize land assets retroactively or broker cash settlements between protesters and targets.

Another significant factor that fragments and compartmentalizes collective action in the region is the expanded use of contract work and day labor by private companies. This has made both work and organizing in the factories less lucrative and more dangerous. At SICARTSA, still the port's largest employer, temporary laborers now make up over half the workforce. Permanent workers report that this phenomenon, in conjunction with corruption in union leadership since privatization, has quietly done more to quell dissent over labor and contract issues than anything else. Although many temporary workers often know permanent workers by name or face – the majority of contract workers are ex-permanent workers fired in 1990 and 1991 – the difference in work status divides them.

According to a local labor lawyer representing temporaries, contract workers take home less for the same jobs as permanent workers and are often forced upon being hired to sign blank pieces of paper that can later be filled in as resignation letters or as liability waivers for injuries sustained during work (Interview A-1 1994). As an implicit warning to permanent workers of the dangers of militance in the factory, temporary workers are often sent to areas where the company suspects worker militance. "They're afraid of us, and we're afraid of them," said a unionized[17] worker, describing contract workers (Interview A-17 1999). "It's the company's signal that they want to get rid of the union altogether," said another, "but you can't say anything, because then you can lose your job" (Interview A-13 1994). In the same interview, workers from a small dissident faction reported that management sent inordinate numbers of contract workers to their areas. The warning was indeed real: three of the four workers interviewed were fired within six months, presumably for political reasons.

Permanent unionized workers, constrained from complaining openly, often force contract workers assigned to their areas to take on the most dangerous or dirty tasks, tasks for which they are often not trained. Although total injury and death rates in the factories are kept quiet, reports that surface from time to time suggest very high casualty rates among con-

---

[17] Technically speaking, temporary workers are represented by Local 271. However, it is significant that rank-and-file workers use the term for "permanent" worker (*de planta*) interchangeably with "unionized" worker (*sindicalizado*). Most contract stipulations and benefits, for example, apply only to permanent workers.

tract workers. In a four-month period in 1996, for example, a newspaper item reported that five contract workers had died in industrial accidents in the steel mills (*La Opinión de Michoacán* 1996). Notably, interviews with contract company owners appear to corroborate unionized workers' allegations that contract companies circulate blacklists of troublemakers, known activists, or individuals with potentially costly health conditions. One contract company owner stated that he would not hire workers without prior records at the factory. As a result, most of his hires are ex-unionized workers let go in 1990 and 1991 (Interview B-1 1994).

In addition to repressive labor practices in the private factories and problems of weak jurisdictions and budget scarcities in local government, changing ideas about economic policy and the role of government have affected patterns of mobilization. As much as it disrupted lives in the region, privatization highlighted the manifold shortcomings of the state-led industrialization in a new and devastating way. Neoliberal language, which spoke of "cleansing" and "balancing" national finances, of "rationalizing," suggested that the corruption that everyone knew about in the factories was an intractable feature of state-led development. This dealt a fatal blow to developmentalist language used by militant workers to demand large reforms or state outlays. The social advances in Lázaro Cárdenas that the government once declared were synonymous with national industrial development now were discursively constructed as an obstacle to Mexico's progress as a nation.

Several ex-workers, fishermen, and journalists have pointed out that privatization as a political process – in which the government sought to legitimize the transformation of ownership and administration in the region – introduced doubts in many people's minds about whether union-based gains and state-led development had ever been worth pursuing. Notably, privatization took place at a time when the national economy appeared to be thriving under Salinas's reforms. Inflation was under control, and by the early 1990s, vast infusions of investment capital from domestic and international markets bolstered the government's claim that the private sector could create far more employment far more efficiently than the state. Inverting the developmentalist language so prominent in the creation of Lázaro Cárdenas, technocrats argued that the private sector could create jobs far more efficiently than the government.

Doubt and sea changes in government discourse help explain why many workers who fought against the downsizing of the workforce in the steel industry eventually fought with one another for the privilege of being fired. Notably, the force used in trying to break the strike was matched by policies that encouraged workers to participate in the privatization process. In a manner similar to the administration's policy shifts in the countryside, the Salinas administration used cash payments and settlements to quell discontent over the termination of industrial subsidies. In an attempt to avert further protest and to soothe tensions in Lázaro Cárdenas, particularly in light of the national attention brought to the conflict during the strike and march on Mexico City, government authorities carried out job terminations of unionized workers[18] in a seemingly legal, even benevolent manner. The *liquidaciones*, or severance payments, were quite substantial, owing in great part to the relatively high wages steel workers earned and in part to the administration's preference that more senior workers leave the plant first. Severance pay amounted to 150 days' pay, plus 50 days' pay per year worked, plus 1.5 percent of that sum (Interview A-1 1994). In addition, as several people recall, the government promised to set up investment funds and credit lines that would enable workers to set up small businesses or return to farming or fishing.

The severance packages were more money at once than most workers had ever seen. "In truth," remarked one ex-worker, "a lot of people wanted to be let go. During the strike, workers had gone for two months without pay, and . . . families didn't have enough to eat. There were a lot of divorces, and a lot of violence between husbands and wives with all the tension of the fight." The ex-worker explained that during the weeks when the company began cutting the labor rolls, many who had fought in the strike movement volunteered to be fired. For a time, "people thought [privatization] would be a good thing, that it would bring prosperity" (Interview A-11 July 14, 1994).

With no prior experience in business, and no clear set of investment options, a great deal of workers' severance moneys disappeared. According to ex-workers' accounts, some men drank their money away. "There wasn't any obvious place to invest," pointed out one ex-worker. "They created a trust fund for small businesses through the Solidarity program, but it was badly managed. . . . A lot of money was lost." Company

---

[18] According to interviews with ex-management workers not represented by Local 271, the severance process for non-union workers was much more corrupt and repressive. There were a number of incidents in which fired employees complained that they were shorted substantial amounts of severance pay, and several other instances in which remaining employees were summarily fired for questioning the salary and benefits offered by the new private owners (Interview A-7 1995).

procurement practices also affected dozens of small and medium-sized businesses. According to accounts of businessmen, workers, and two ex-employees of SICARTSA, the former company quickly terminated supply contracts with local businesses, and commenced buying from its own suppliers in Monterrey. One management employee formerly associated with one of the principal buying departments in the state-owned company, estimated that approximately 90 percent of SICARTSA's outside purchases, amounting to approximately 5 million new pesos per month (about $12 million U.S. per year), were transferred to Monterrey companies (Interview A-10 1995). According to that source and two others, Caribbean Ispat retained considerably more local supply networks, but also began contracts with nonlocal supply companies (Interviews A-10 1995, D-6 1995, C-12 1995).

Corruption and cash payments introduced a spiral of disillusion that made many people feel that malfeasance was ubiquitous in both government *and* social movement organizations. The administration of protest, which almost always involves a combination of official and clandestine transactions, also has introduced a level of public skepticism about protest. While the record would indicate a far more complex scenario, it is significant that most people *assume* that protest leaders gain inordinately from settlements, and that protest leaders make implicit promises to limit demands and cap incipient radicalism. A former worker who had been fired by SICARTSA in 1979, and who still continues organizing in various local groups, remarked that people had actually thought him stupid for not having accepted bribes from authorities. "I could have made a lot of money selling out," he remarked, "and people think that maybe I'm stupid for not doing that."

Conclusion

A decade after privatization of the steel industry, politics are dominated by disputes over the management of the informal economy. In this ambient, however, rights to buy many basic goods, sell products or services, use natural resources, or occupy particular spaces are determined not simply through supply and demand, but also through contention and political bargaining. Privatization transformed the terms of civil politics and how various sectors of the community understood their relationship to one another. As federal institutions receded, and private sector management introduced new schisms among industrial laborers, contention emerged over unprecedented demands among previously quiescent sectors, such as unemployed workers and fishermen in crisis.

In this chapter, I have argued that high levels of protest, and indeed the proclivity of residents in Lázaro Cárdenas City to turn to direct action to address household shortages, owes much to the legacy of the combative labor movement of the 1970s and 1980s. The workers' movement, whose militance and longevity were unanticipated by authorities, drew strength at different times from dispositions of left-leaning elites in the government and from the developmentalist ideology that undergirded the project. It also drew strength from broad discontent over shortages in housing and urban infrastructure, as well as the enclave nature of the city itself in which so many people depended directly and indirectly on the steel industry. However, as I also outline, the changing structure of finance and distribution in Lázaro Cárdenas, the growing population, and the deteriorating quality of the environment introduced many points of social division and antagonism over time. In this manner, privatization and the decline of the workers' movement was a revelatory process as well as a disruptive and divisive one.

These conjuctural factors, however, do not tell us the whole story. Clearly, what they cannot explain is how worker radicalism in Local 271 outlived the political and economic circumstances that incubated it. They also do not show how people reconstructed narratives of protest in the wake of privatization, as beliefs about developmentalist policies and the proper role of the state in the economy shifted. To address this local gap, Chapter 4 takes us back to the Local 271 workers' movement before 1989, and then into accounts of post-privatization movements, showing how they were linked through leadership and opposition party structures, but also how their methods of protest changed in altered political contexts. Delving further into people's accounts of how and why they participated in strike movements and protests, Chapter 4 explores the tools that insurgents have used to maintain movements in the face of threats, institutional retreat, and social fragmentation.

4

Shifting Markets, Shifting Demands in Lázaro Cárdenas

Steel and Protest in the Workers' City

Even now, years after the fact, the visitor to Lázaro Cárdenas will not be in town more than a few hours before someone makes a passing reference to what happened in the city at the end of the 1980s. Perhaps a taxi driver, a hotel clerk, or one of the women selling tortas and fruit from a cart near the bus station will begin to chat with the visitor, often initiating the conversation by asking why she is in town, or where she is headed. If the visitor replies that Lázaro Cárdenas *is* her destination, and that she is there to learn about the city and its inhabitants, conversation is likely to lead to mention of what makes the city distinctive – indeed, why this isolated city exists at all. Then, in a most typical Mexican fashion, the resident may launch into analysis of the region's people – a *como somos* ("what we [in this area] are like") discussion. People from Lázaro Cárdenas City, the resident will explain, are unique because most come from elsewhere. If there is anything beyond a lack of better alternatives that ties them to the place, then, it would have to do with the ties people have to one another, because there is little *arraigo* (attachment to place, or rootedness) that comes of having buried one's dead in a place. Because the city is still young, one major thing that joins people together is their city's history of strife over resources and industrial production.

Conflicts around Lazaro Cárdenas Steelworks (SICARTSA) have marked time in this short-lived city; many, for example, recall a long and bitter strike in 1989 as sort of a division between past and present in Lázaro Cárdenas. In the years leading up to the strike as well as during the strike itself, Local 271 was something of a protecting wall against many of the changes that were happening in the rest of the country. In the years after

DR. CAMDESSUS ■ Helguera

Dr. Camdessus, **by Helguera** Doctor from the IMF to patient: "You're doing great. Now you can go back to your Job!" Patient to doctor: "What job?" From *La Jornada,* May 25, 1995. Reprinted by permission.

the strike, when the union was fairly well purged of its most militant and experienced activists, privatization was accompanied by the firing of half the workforce of some five thousand union employees and hundreds from the rolls of management as well. Local business fell off as local residents had less and less to spend and the new private companies often went to their own subsidiaries for supplies and contract work.

Eventually, the company won through individual settlements and promises of new community investment what it could not win through direct confrontation with the union: a silenced and intimidated workforce, a low wage bill, fewer municipal obligations, and less pressure to adhere to health and safety standards. Such changes made the SICARTSA complex far more attractive to prospective buyers, who purchased the complex in four sections in 1990. That the workers eventually lost out to the pressures of downsizing and privatization needs little explaining; the fifty-nine-day confrontation in 1989 was a gross mismatch of powers. That people risked as much as they did to fight back against a process they saw as unjust, on the other hand, requires a good deal of explaining. A few thousand working people went up against a Secretary of Labor who declared the strike illegal, an army that tried to bring in scabs, a company management that sent around representatives who threatened workers one by one that they would lose their jobs if they persisted in the strike action, a set of labor bosses in Mexico City who threatened the disobedient local with punitive measures, a national steel holding corporation that insisted the union be purged of excessive wage costs in preparation for the industry's privatization, a set of multilateral monetary authorities who insisted that Mexico balance its books better, and a president in Mexico City who insisted that downsizing and privatization were necessary for the well-being of Mexico as a nation.

The reason people say they fought so hard for their jobs, and for the survival of the proletarian movement they had built, was because Local 271 was not like most other unions in Mexico, at least before the 1989 strike. They explain that other unions often do not represent their workers well, being *charrista*,[1] a slang term that translates roughly as coopted. Ex-workers at SICARTSA point out that the workers' local that bears the same name and workers' shield today is not the same union that they belonged to; it is now, they say, like most other unions in Mexico – controlled by labor leaders who ask for little, organize minimally, and aim to please the bosses and not the workers. But Local 271 in the 1970s and 1980s was different, they say, a real *sindicato independiente* – democratic, faithful to the wishes of the workers, and fiercely militant when it mobilized for a strike.

Workers explain that the strike of 1989 was possible because workers had a lot of experience working together and organizing strike movements. "We were educated, experienced at fighting the company," commented a taxi driver who worked for ten years in the factory before being laid off in 1990. "That's why these young fellows can't organize a strike anymore. They don't have anyone in the ranks to teach them. And they don't ask former workers for help, either." Management and businesspeople, on the

---

[1] The term originated during the late 1940s in Mexico. It was originally a reference to the railroad union leader Díaz de León, who often participated in traditional cowboy fiestas.

other hand, explain that the strike of 1989 was a result of the government's having been too permissive with union militants in the past. "They ordered around their bosses!" said one businessman who was once linked with the company's management.

It is telling that people on opposite sides of the struggle offer different explanations for the unusually militant and democratic character of Local 271. Workers, by and large, do not recall their organizing and their long campaigns of fund raising and information gathering between contract talks as responses to prominent political openings. Most, for example, do not note of their own circumstances what industrial relations scholars note of them: that they were, in relative terms, "privileged" workers. Union members recall that yes, they did take home much better than minimum wage, especially when benefits were taken into account. But then again, they note that they were better trained and subjected to higher risk than most workers. In exchange for wages that varied between the equivalent of U.S. $10 and $30 a day,[2] work entailed six days a week in the darkness of a mine or in the 90 to 110 degree heat of a blast furnace area. In most areas, noise levels at 100 decibels deafened workers and caused neurological problems; radiation burned eyes and skin; noxious dust and airborne contaminants complicated respiration; twenty-four-hours-per-day production forced all workers to change shifts frequently – a disorienting and physically fatiguing process.

Nonworkers and outside scholars who argue that workers won what they did in part because of certain special political and economic circumstances, however, are not entirely off-base either. One might note, for example, that workers in dangerous situations, such as silver or copper mines in isolated northern locales, in construction work almost anywhere, or in metal-finishing plants in in-bond border factories work in similar conditions at far lower wages. In addition, when such workers have attempted at various points to win what SICARTSA workers did, they have been swiftly silenced. Both contentions, then, are partly explanatory; the story of Local 271, as located inside the changing political economic environment, shows that external factors and internal strategies affected the mobilizing power of workers in Lázaro Cárdenas up through the end of the 1980s.

[2] Wages as listed in collective contracts, including maximum possible productivity bonuses, divided among ten work categories. Dollar equivalents also vary widely because of unstable exchange rates.

After privatization, as contention over distributive demands shifted from factory to neighborhood and outlying village, groups' strategies of mobilization often reflected a culture of protest developed in the union. This is unsurprising considering the prevalence of ex-worker militants in PRD circles and in various local organizing efforts. However, there were also a great many differences in the way people organized, mobilized public opinion, and made decisions collectively.

Under radically altered bargaining circumstances, groups demanding housing, infrastructure, and compensation for environmental damage encountered different constraints and pathways to bargaining than the union had. On the one hand, they had no legal means to halt production in the region, and attempts to do so resulted in swift repression. On the other hand, they were not bound by formal rules of collective bargaining in which labor authorities or Mexico City union elites could use legal pre-texts to halt protest, or to intervene in internal elections and decision-making processes. After privatization, groups were far smaller than the union had been, and usually more isolated. Solidary support, if it materialized, usually surfaced along lines of demand – that is, fishermen's groups tended to support one another, as did groups pressing for housing and urban services. Notably – echoing shifting national circumstances – environmental protests drew sporadically on domestic and international non-governmental organizations for assistance in publicizing problems and conducting research. The following discussion first provides an overview of the tools of insurgency employed by workers to organize and ride out protracted conflicts; then it turns to successive movements. I argue that the dilemmas inherent in maintaining protest sharpened in the years after privatization, largely due to acute new divisions in the local workforce, to divisions in the local PRD, and to episodes of corruption involving protest leaders.

Strategies of Insurgency in the Workers' Movement

Solidary Support from Groups and Individuals

Labor militants in Local 271 report that, during the 1970s and 1980s, they concentrated the bulk of their organizing efforts on contract negotiations. Until the elections of 1988, when a former Local 271 leader, Rafael Melgoza, ran for federal office on an opposition party ticket, it was

factions and not political parties per se that defined ideological boundaries locally. Factions, which acted like small political parties within the
union – devising political platforms and slates of candidates for union
offices – battled with one another over how the union could best represent workers' interests. As one leader of the leftist faction Coordinadora
de Lucha explained, factions generally went through waves of participation, with periods preceding contract negotiations and union elections
marking high points of activity, and periods in between marking a lull. "All
our time was spent preparing for strikes," he explained. "We spent our
time preparing for the next contract talks, making contacts in the region
and in universities, building for the next contract fight" (Interview A-10
1995).

Veterans of the major strike movements of 1977, 1979, 1985, and 1989
remember those junctures not only in terms of the demands they lodged
at each point, but also, interestingly, in terms of alliances they forged and
material support they secured from individuals and groups outside the
union. For many, preparing for a strike entailed two major forms of organizing: first, talking to other workers in Local 271 about demands and bargaining strategies and prodding reluctant ones to ready for a strike and,
second, visiting with other unions, as well as university groups and other
popular movement organizations. "We had ties to the UCEZ (Emiliano
Zapata Campesino Union), the SUTIN [nuclear workers], and the
Coordinadora Ejidal en Lucha (Ejidal Coalition in Struggle). During
strikes, merchants also gave us food, and women would get together to
support the workers," said one (Interview A-2 1994). Another remembered
help from other unions: "The workers at NKS [Nippon-Kobe Steel] and
Fertimex supported us," he said. "We also got help from [workers
affiliated with] Mass Line in other parts of the country" (Interview A-11
1994). Another recalled that in 1985, there had been help from the *colonias*, from students in Morelia, from farmers, especially the leader Efraín
López of the UCEZ (Interview A-11 1994). Like the first worker, he
also remembered support from the Coordinadora Ejidal en Lucha.
Another remembered how the silver miners' union in Taxco had defied
warnings by the National Mining and Metal Workers' Union (SNTMM-
SRM) national leadership in 1985 and openly supported Local 271 (Interview A-10 1995). Corroborating various workers' contentions that they
were able to cultivate support even among some of their supervisors at
times, an ex-manager and engineer at SICARTSA remembered that he
was often more sympathetic to workers than management. He quietly

collaborated with workers' strike movements by flouting the company's orders to denounce the pickets and threaten workers (Interview A-7 1995). The manager, who had worked closely with union workers in the iron pellet facility, said that he and many other managers were often sympathetic to union demands, particularly those regarding safety equipment and health care.

Notably, while members of all factions (excluding those affiliated most closely with the national leadership, the *Estatutarios*) prominently mention the role of sympathetic groups and individuals in maintaining collective actions and pressuring the state for their demands, members of different factions often enumerate allies in different orders of importance. This is due in great part to the fact that factional militants were the first to begin strategizing about contract negotiations and potential strikes. Ex-militants recalled that in months prior to biannual contract negotiations, they would begin talking with other unions and possible political allies, meeting with them on their own time outside the factory. While official union committees such as the strike committee and the negotiations committee often contained rank-and-file workers of various factional affiliations, the leadership of the factions themselves did not strategize together. As such, political alliances that came into play during strikes generally were due to the preparations and longtime political and social associations of one or another facmion.

The Factions The parallel strategizing that occurred among the factions was reinforced by the way work was organized in the steel mill. Unsurprisingly, in a production environment where a worker could expect to spend his entire career climbing the ranks of a single department among a team of colleagues who often became his best friends, the factions tended to have loyal followings in specific departments. For example, the mines were more conservative, adhering to Mass Line and the Estatutarios; the maintenance crews and Central Shop workers split between Coordinadora de Lucha and Democracia Proletaria; workers in the pellet division were loyal to Democracia Proletaria and Linea de Masas; and workers in the blast furnace were largely sympathetic to Linea de Masas.

The most powerful faction, Linea de Masas, was the more centrist faction among the democratically minded groups in the union. Its earliest roots were in a student-led movement in the 1970s that stressed Maoist principles of grassroots orientation and directional initiative from the rank and file, but the movement in Lázaro Cárdenas evolved into a faction that stressed union-first principles. The fight, as understood by the leadership of Linea de Masas, was first and foremost on behalf of the economic needs of Local 271 workers. Although Linea de Masas occupied prominent positions during Local 271 strike movements, and several were fired for subversive activities on several occasions, leadership of this faction intermittently cultivated allies inside the government and the PRI. Several of the former leaders of Linea de Masas, for example, went on to occupy government positions, including the municipal presidency in 1982.

The other faction that exerted consistent influence inside Local 271 was Democracia Proletaria. Eschewing the more localist orientation of Linea de Masas, Democracia Proletaria espoused an explicitly Leninist-proletarian ideology. Affiliated first with the Mexican Communist Party, later the Unified Socialist Party of Mexico (PSUM) in 1981, the Socialist Party of Mexico (PSM) in 1987, and finally the Cárdenas-led PRD after 1988, the leaders of Democracia Proletaria sought to put union energies into the creation of a national worker front that would oppose the PRI-led government, ideally through a series of general strikes. The position of this faction wavered little over time, certainly less so than Linea de Masas, which rank-and-file workers remember as less radical and more flexible. Democracia Proletaria, which held union leadership posts from 1984 to 1992, and which occupied union committee positions during strikes of 1977, 1979, 1985, and 1989, was adept at cultivating horizontal alliances. These efforts of Democracia Proletaria resulted in the creation of a diverse network of allies; faction members committed to mutual support pacts with the Nuclear Power Workers' Union (SUTIN) and with workers at the National Autonomous University of the state of Guerrero. Proletarian Democracy also organized an annual convention from 1985 to 1989 of some seventy workers' groups (Democracia Proletaria December 8, 1985). The faction also cultivated ties with workers in other state-owned steel plants affiliated with Locals 288 and 147 in Monclova and Locals 67 and 68 in Monterrey. Finally, Democracia Proletaria cultivated ties with peasants through the Union de Campesinos Emiliano Zapata (UCEZ) and the Coordinadora Ejidal en Lucha.

Although Democracia Proletaria and Linea de Masas held the greatest sway over union policy in Local 271, several other smaller corrientes organized in various departments. Notably, the faction Coordinadora de Lucha exerted influence on various strike and negotiation committees through

1987 and in the internal union elections of 1986.[3] This faction lasted only a few years, and by all counts was less influential than Democracia Proletaria or Linea de Masas. Although militant and explicitly leftist in orientation, it differed with Democracia Proletaria in arguing that the needs of local groups of nonworkers ought to occupy a greater part of Local 271 politics. With regard to ties to other unions, Coordinadora functioned in a similar manner to Democracia Proletaria, but members placed greater emphasis on cultivating ties to rank-and-file members. One ex-worker who participated on a Solidarity Committee in 1985 comments on his own experience in the corriente:

Coordinadora was still in its infant stages then, but it did some really crucial things for the effort. The Solidarity Commission, headed by Coordinadora, got a lot of support in the community and in Mexico City. Coordinadora got people to sign on when other Solidarity Committees had been rejected, particularly in the cases of the Mexico City groups and the Taxco [mine] workers . . . [because] its strategy was to go to the rank and file first, and then to the officers. In the past, other corrientes had done the reverse and had not had so much luck (Democracia Proletaria April 21, 1986).

Under the factional leadership of Romualdo García, workers in Coordinadora de Lucha cultivated local alliances by organizing in the *colonias populares*, or squatter settlements. Interestingly, this effort involved the participation of significant numbers of women, who would later come to dominate colono politics in general. Romualdo García's wife, Laura Garabito, along with another colono activist, Altagracia Piñeda, began organizing in the early 1980s for the first local nonworker insurgency in the deeply impoverished Respuesta Social settlement (Interviews A-11 1994, C-12 1995).

While the divisions between the various factions of the union at times became so deep that the Local 271 was unable to sustain collective action, at other crucial strike junctures the various corrientes suspended their differences. In many senses, the submovements differed not over the form of the enemy, but over the appropriate means of confrontation. Each move-

---

[3] Coordinadora de Lucha, originally organized as an internal organ of "political education" of workers, did not seek to participate in union elections when it was formed in the late 1970s. Only later, with the development of cells of adherents in the Taller Central de Ingeniería and departments of maintenance workers, did the corriente seek official influence over union policy. In 1986 union elections, Coordinadora de Lucha received 448 votes, compared with 875 for Democracia Proletaria, 787 for the Estatutarios ("Renovación Sindical") and 1,483 for Linea de Masas (Democracia Proletaria April 21, 1986).

ment, with its own toolbox of strategies, contributed to strikes with a distinct set of allies. Deployed together, collective resistance was difficult to dismantle because support and resources came from dozens of sources at once. For example, strike funds from the Democracia Proletaria network were matched with donations of food and blankets from colonos who sympathized with Coordinadora de Lucha. Businesses, anxious to see the strike end and commerce from workers begin again, also made donations. Campesinos marched in Guerrero and Morelia on behalf of the workers. Linea de Masas's channels to local government from 1982 to 1985 helped defuse potential opposition to Local 271 among local government authorities. Rafael Melgoza, one of the founding members of the union, was Municipal President and took steps to support worker actions and the strike movement of 1985. Meanwhile, Democracia Proletaria and Coordinadora de Lucha allies, including the SUTIN workers and the miners in Guerrero, defied the Secretary of Labor and engaged in solidary actions for the Local 271 workers in 1985 and 1989, despite the fact that sympathy actions were illegal, as were the two strikes themselves.

In these moments, the horizontal alliances with local groups and na-tionally with workers' groups contributed to the creation of temporary ungovernability of SICARTSA and its surroundings. In the cases where factions converged in a fight against a monolithic state enemy, the variety of factional tools, forged through years of painstaking work, may in fact have lent movement insurgency a greater latitude and resiliency than could have been derived from unitary leadership. Significantly, jealousies inside the union tended to ebb during periods in which both major factions – Democracia Proletaria and Linea de Masas – held official posts in the exec-utive leadership of the union. In the strikes of 1985 and 1989, for example, union leadership was shared equally between the factions, with Linea de Masas occupying what was called Group A of the executive board, and Democracia Proletaria occupying Group B (see Table 4.1). The balance between the factions made it so that no single faction would claim exclu-sive credit for having led a successful strike or contract negotiations, or conversely, could be blamed for having compromised the union's interests with a poorly led strike or with substandard bargaining.

As pointed out in the previous section on the impact of the political-economic environment on Local 271, the mutuality of interests of SICARTSA workers and various other sectors in Lázaro Cárdenas fluctu-

Table 4.1. *Union Elections in Local 271: 1984, 1986, 1988*

1984 (group B)**	1986 (group A)**	1988 (group B)**
LM....................976	LM...................1,483	LM...................1,439
DP...................1,467		
21 mayo*..............482	DP......................875	DP...................1,842
1 mayo*................150		USM.................181
annulled.................84	RenSin*..............787	
	CdL.....................448	

* Various versions of what were called *Estatutarios*, or workers who allied with the national leadership of the SNTMMSRM, and generally sought to defuse strike movements.
** The executive leadership of the union was divided into two sets of four-year posts. Every two years, elections were held for one of the two groups.
Abbreviations: LM, Linea de Masas; DP, Democracia Proletaria; CdL, Coordinadora de Lucha; USM, Unificadora Sindical Minera; AdA, Auténtica de Areas; RenSin, Renovación Sindical.

ated over time, beginning with a certain degree of convergence, and becoming more diffuse as the economy diversified. Whether or not this alignment of "real" material interests affected the perceptions of Local 271 activists or altered their strategies of action is difficult to establish with any degree of certainty. However, it is notable, for example, that divisions between Local 271 and various lower income sectors appeared in the mid-1980s where there had previously been mutual support. Interviews with activists in the colonias Respuesta Social and Villahermosa Aeropuerto, for example, reveal that squatters' sympathy for workers in Local 271 ebbed after the 1985 strike due to Local 271's refusal to back a nascent movement of colonos in return. Following a waterborne epidemic in 1983 that killed over forty-two children in the Respuesta colonia, the residents began a series of actions pressuring the government for titles to their settlement plots and the provision of running water (Interview C-11 1994). According to the colonos, a group of them appealed to the workers of Local 271 to speak before the monthly workers' assembly and were refused. Said a colona of this episode, "I had brought the workers food and coffee during their strikes. . . . Then there was a *plantón* that we had one time. It was very hard and we needed help, and they refused. . . . After the strike of 1985, I never helped them again" (Interview C-3 1994).

Forms of Support

Asked what was key to mobilization, one worker answered, "When support came from other groups – economically, physically, and morally" (Interview A-11 1994). Workers' alliances with various groups and other unions, though never unproblematic, were nonetheless crucial during periods of confrontation with the company, the government, and the state-owned enterprise. Beyond the food people provided, the blankets and shelter they gave to workers, the crowds they provided during marches in Morelia and Mexico City, and the legal and medical and professional help they offered, allies lent union members an indispensable moral support as well.

The sense that workers were not isolated and that the demands they were fighting for genuinely mattered to onlookers appears from workers' testimony to have been a particularly important element in Local 271's more ambitious campaigns. The strike of 1985, in which workers struck the company primarily over the issue of workplace safety and health concerns, was such a campaign. Their principal demand – that an epidemiological study be conducted among workers to determine scientifically whether many common illnesses that workers suffered were linked to workplace hazards – met with stiff resistance by labor authorities, who maintained that such a demand was outside the scope of what a union was permitted to include in contract negotiations.

In an effort to pressure authorities to carry out a comprehensive health study of the factory, workers sought the help of professionals in Mexico City to conduct a study of their own. Securing such help was a gamble. It was costly and difficult, and definitive causal links between disease and industrial production among large populations would be difficult to obtain. Militants in Democracia Proletaria who spearheaded the campaign recall that, when they approached various individuals with their proposal for a health study, some professionals were reluctant to extend their services because the steel workers were proposing an expansion of government agencies' standing definition of workplace-related health. According to Asa Cristina Laurell of the Autonomous Metropolitan University of Mexico-Xochimilco, who eventually came to head the professional health study among SICARTSA, workers sought to document the occurrence of chronic illnesses and ailments. Prior to the study, labor authorities acknowledged only industrial accidents that were related to work activities as health problems.

Conducting the sort of comprehensive health study that workers had in mind – including a survey of chronic health problems such as respiratory problems, neurological conditions, and eye and ear damage – involved at least implicit defiance of the government because it bypassed the government agency empowered to document industrial safety, the Joint Committees on Industrial Safety and Health (Laurell 1989b). The company tried to stop the study by firing Guadalupe Corona, a union official placed in charge of it; workers on the union health committee, however, persisted with the issue. The conclusions of the health study that was finally conducted by Laurell and her colleague Mariano Noriega (Laurell and Noriega 1987), with the assistance of a number of public health students, confirmed much of what workers had claimed for some years. Among other findings, the study showed staggering rates of chronic illness among men generally in their twenties and thirties. The study reported respiratory illnesses at 17.3 percent, back and joint problems at 15.2 percent, eye disorders including cataracts and conjunctivitis at 7.1 percent, burns and skin diseases from the heat at 5.5 percent, and noise- and stress-related neuroses at 7.5 percent (Laurell and Noriega 1987: 31). Additionally, the study showed alarming rates of injuries, ranging up to nearly one in three per year in the blast furnace (27.2 percent) and 23.5 percent in the coke-processing plant.

External Audiences

In general, members of Local 271 concentrated relatively little on cultivating audiences through the use of mass media. In part, this may well have been due to the physical isolation of Lázaro Cárdenas – until recently, for example, major newspapers did not arrive daily in the city. Also, more importantly, the local press in Lázaro Cárdenas and in the state capital of Morelia tended to be more subject to Institutional Revolutionary Party (PRI) control. However, the workers' campaign for the health study plowed new ground in the labor movement nationally. It was among only a few such labor campaigns up to that date in Mexico,[4] and its prominence paid off in gaining the union new support from outside groups. "Letters of support arrived from the United States and Germany," recalled a worker (Interview A-10 1995).

---

[4] The Mexican Electricians Union, the Telephone Workers Union, and the miners' union at Real del Monte also made safety and health-related demands in the 1970s and 1980s.

After the 1985 strike succeeded, the health study was published with damning conclusions that workers at SICARTSA suffered significantly higher levels of several chronic conditions than the population at large. The study's findings were widely reported, appearing in international medical journals and the academic press in Mexico City, and, according to workers on the health committee, solicited in other parts of Latin America.[5]

Finally, as previously mentioned, Local 271 benefited from the support of various legal advisors, academics, and national activists. Owing to the more marginal state of the judicial branch in political matters (there are no class action suits in the Mexican system, for example), such professionals performed a motley variety of tasks, often at a moment's notice. Professionals who traveled to Lázaro Cárdenas City also remember participating in many tasks that had little to do with their training. Selva Daville, an academic in Mexico City who worked as a member of Democracia Proletaria and who wrote in the labor press on behalf of Local 271, remembers touring the plant, supporting pickets. She mentioned in her interview about watching works at an improvised proletarian theater. Estela Ríos, a lawyer in Mexico City, recalls that she began working with the union through militants associated with Democracia Proletaria in 1970s, doing both small and large tasks over the years.

I was asked to give advice to Democracia Proletaria . . . but it was minimal in those days. In the 1980s, it was still minimal, until 1985, when there was a problem during the strike. The company wanted a guaranteed number of emergency workers during the strikes. But the number they wanted was too large to be fair. . . . So that demand was won . . . (Interview with María Estela Ríos 1996).

Ríos was also instrumental in the 1989 strike, when there were legal questions about the government's ability to defer a strike that workers had already approved by a wide margin.

Jorge García, an attorney from Mexico City, also offered legal assistance in the strike movement of 1989. Although union members and García later had a falling-out over fees charged to the union, García's support in September 1989, after 30 days of an arduous strike, was reported to have reinvigorated the spirit of striking workers and preserved the unity of the union at that point (Interview A-10 1995).

---

[5] Excerpts and findings from the study appeared as reports of the International Center of Development Studies, Ottawa, and in the *International Journal of Health Services*. See also Rueda Peiro, González Marin, and Alvarez Mosso (1990).

Party Politics

Prior to the opening of multiparty politics in 1988 with the runaway campaign of Cuauhtémoc Cárdenas, there were said to be links between Local 271 and left-leaning groups inside the ruling party. Their precise nature, however, is difficult to establish. Ties to the PRI were a bitter point of contention inside the union. On the one hand, the statutes of the national steel and miners' union (as with all official union centrals) required workers to be members of the ruling party – "a rule that they never managed to enforce," pointed out an ex-worker (Interview A-9 1995). On the other hand, the extensive political base inside Local 271 held by Democracia Proletaria, who openly denounced the government and the PRI, made explicit bargaining with the ruling party a moot enterprise.

Certainly, the 1982 election of former General Secretary of Local 271, Rafael Melgoza, to the municipal presidency indicates that the ruling party sought channels of influence into the SICARTSA workers' union, and recognized the substantial power that they wielded in Lázaro Cárdenas. Melgoza, who changed party affiliation in 1988 and was elected as a federal representative that year, maintains that he was not closely tied to the PRI. He established party membership, he recalled in an interview, only prior to becoming a candidate for the municipal post. His candidacy, he pointed out, was proposed in large part because of his long-standing professional relationship with Cuauhtémoc Cárdenas, who became governor of Michoacán in the same year.

Local 271 began to experiment with open party politics in 1988. The faction Linea de Masas campaigned heavily for the Party of the Democratic Revolution (PRD) candidate Manuel Santamaría, a former union official and member of the same corriente. Santamaría won the municipal presidency, as did the full slate of PRD candidates running for federal and state representative posts that year. The three-year presidency of Santamaría was a controversial one, and members of Linea de Masas split over the issue of party loyalties in the following elections of 1991. Although Democracia Proletaria continued to back the PRD, most of its members and all its old leaders had been purged in the mass firings of 1989 and 1990. Union officials holding office in Local 271 in 1994 and 1995 commented in interviews that the union was now neutral with regard to party politics and did not endorse candidates any more (Interview A-12 1994). Although Local 271 has receded from party politics as a means of bargaining (at least explicitly), Rafael Melgoza commented that workers made up the primary electoral base in the elections of 1994, in which all but one slot went to the PRD. "We [the PRD] have a greater proportion of sectors such as the campesinos and the colonos," he observed, "but the total numbers of worker votes are greater."

Internal Democracy

Prior to the privatization and mass firings of 1989–90, the degree of union democracy and rank-and-file participation was exceptional among Mexican unions. Among the characteristics that distinguish Local 271 from the majority of unions were (and still are, in theory) regular general assemblies of workers, departmental assemblies and delegations, majority votes on strike actions, and participation of rank-and-file members on special committees pertaining to strikes and contract negotiations. As a result, leaders have not held union positions indefinitely, and representation of various factions has fluctuated from year to year.

The existence of union democracy in Local 271 appears to have had three primary effects on collective action and its power of resistance – symbolic, participatory, and political. First, an overwhelming number of workers interviewed expressed pride in this aspect of Local 271. The very existence of channels of expression and participation in the union seemed to make the movement their own, an expression of local will rather than state policy. The contrast between democracy inside the union and a greater authoritarianism in the outside environment also legitimized Local 271's militance. Whatever happened inside Local 271, whatever decisions were taken, there was some sense that a majority of workers as a whole had decided those things. Second, rules that prohibited union officials from simultaneously occupying department delegate positions and/or committee positions broadened the number of individuals participating in union organization at any one time. Rank-and-file members often entered union politics by taking committee positions and learning about organization and union statutes in the process. Finally, the existence of secret votes and regularized rank-and-file participation made it possible for Local 271 to dispute the authority of the central union leadership of the SNT-MMSRM. Statutes that allowed, for example, a local to override the declarations of the National Executive Committee of the union could actually be operationalized in Local 271, where votes were not regularly falsified.

Democracy had its downside as well. The divisions between the various factions became aggravated at various points, and loyalties were sometimes greater to the factions than to the union local as a whole. Indeed, workers today, some having left SICARTSA five or ten years ago, almost invariably identify themselves as having been members of a particular faction. It would appear that as a member of Local 271, one was identified first as a worker, second as a department member, and, if one was active in union politics, third as a faction member. In two of the strike movements – in 1977 and 1981 – the differences between factions damaged the strength of Local 271 actions, as infighting affected the strength of picket lines and strike votes. In the other strike movements of 1977, 1985, and 1989, however, the various factions of Local 271 did not defuse actions. The first General Secretary of Local 271, himself an adherent of Linea de Masas, in fact commented that the presence of opposition factions kept leaders more accountable to members than they otherwise would have been (Interview A-16 1994).

Legacies of Worker Militance, New Forms of Direct Action

The massive downsizing of the permanent workforce in the steel industry rapidly exhausted the insurgent capacity inside Local 271. Most senior workers were dismissed prior to the privatization of the steel mills. According to both workers and contract company bosses, management paid particular attention to eliminating combative leaders from the labor rolls. In various ways, however, energies from the movement persisted. First, the movement left in the city a set of labor leaders with broad popular backing who would come to dominate municipal politics after their exit from the factories. Conspicuously, they brought with them their ideological and personal differences: the factional splits in the factory soon split the local Party of the Democratic Revolution into several warring groups.[6] Second, events in the 1990s strongly suggest that years in the factory left many laborers with some incipient awareness of the links between heavy industry and human health. Although it is difficult to state with any certainty whether a movement effects a shift in public consciousness, it is significant that the workers' movement used a language of industrial liability in

---

[6] A significant number of former leaders and activists in Local 271 now organize in the PRD and in various local groups representing demands of fishermen, unemployed workers, debtors, colonos, campesinos, and citizens in support of the Chiapas uprising. Examples of ex-worker activists who led opinions in the local PRD in the 1990s are Rafael Melgoza, Manuel Santamaría, Manuel Barreras Ibarra, Anastasio Solorio, Sergio Torres, Arturo Nuñez, and José Luis Castellanos.

its struggle. The health campaigns from the 1980s set an example in holding industry publicly responsible for damages. Not coincidentally, in the years after privatization, numerous groups would cite heavy industry for persistent health problems and contamination of air, land, and water.

This public consciousness, combined with a widespread public indignance at the failure of market-oriented changes to generate employment and greater prosperity in the region, led to a rapid development of both health-linked and environmentally linked contention in the years after privatization. In addition to ubiquitous struggles of squatters for housing, land titles, and infrastructure, an unusual number of protests named environmental problems as a part of their struggles or even the focus of them. Protests spearheaded by loose alliances of campesinos, fishermen, and neighborhood groups targeted private industry via petitions and confrontations with government agencies, calling for the state to broker settlements with the private sector over toxic dumping and decimation of fisheries and farmland.

In the ongoing struggle over resources in Lázaro Cárdenas City, it is worth examining what tools of insurgency activists now employed outside the factory and how the use of those tools both expanded and limited the possibilities of contention. On the one hand, environmentally based demands for resources or alternative sources of employment were potentially more unifying than union struggles had been.[7] This was reflected in a brief storm of protests in the early 1990s in which peasants and fishermen managed to gain audiences with management representatives of virtually all the port's major enterprises, as well as with half a dozen federal agencies. Where developmentalist demands for greater employment or expanded government spending in service of social goals no longer had obvious pull, a language of industrial liability appeared to provide some means of reacquiring some community voice and power vis-à-vis large industry.

At the same time, however, contention after privatization was institutionally unmoored. Insofar as it remained perennially unclear after priva-

---

[7] Ostensibly, campaigns based on claims that private industry or the state-owed residents compensation for destruction of public goods such as land, air, or water would be limited not by union membership or labor statutes, but instead only by people's ability to claim that they were affected by industrial practices. This was bolstered by the presence of thousands of ex-workers in the city with insider knowledge of industry practices. Although none had any expert credentials to back claims in tribunals, knowledge based on workers' observations of production practices made for sufficiently reasonable conjectures to make initial demands.

tization who was responsible for two decades of environmental destruction, and who had the authority to deal with protest under what set of juridical and institutional norms, protest hovered between attempts to unify demands over long-term goals and frantic campaigns to secure one-time monetary or infrastructure settlements for desperate residents now eking out livings in mixtures of informal commerce, fishing, and farming. For this reason, mobilizing and maintaining protest brought new contradictions and divisions to organizing. Despite the fact that environmental groups' demands for cleanups – if fulfilled – would have benefitted the public at large, by the mid-1990s, many saw campaigns for environmental justice as struggles for particularistic ends (e.g., cash settlements) rather than public goods (e.g., cleanups).

From Factory to Farming and Fishing

In the migration of contentious demands from factory to municipality, and from wage-based demands to urban demands over housing as infrastructure, narratives of environmental justice appeared to many activists to be viable means of connecting various social demands and of establishing new channels of negotiation over resources. Following the emergence of protests by fishermen, campesinos, and colonos over industrial contamination, activists linked to the PRD, for example, formed the Ecological Committee in hopes of linking the former groups' demands to other groups' demands for employment, legal representation, and urban services (Interviews C-7 1994, C-10 1994). Notably, Lázaro Cárdenas City had never become a consolidated city space but instead remained an idiosyncratic mixture of heavy industry set among unplanned coastal and riverine settlements of workers. As earlier remarked, significant numbers of workers laboring in heavy industry had migrated from rural areas, and many households had continued to supplement wages with small-scale horticulture or fishing. Many colonos, for example, tended small crops of corn, beans, squash, and mango on plots next to their homes.

Protest over land and water had much to do with changing livelihoods. When labor rolls in construction and heavy industry plummeted, many had returned to primary sector activities such as fishing and farming. Significant numbers of workers with severance pay bought fishing equipment or trucks and machinery in hopes of establishing new careers working full-time at sea or on small ranches.

Fishing and farming, however, were no longer viable enterprises for many people living within the vicinity of the heavy industry. Heavy metal salts had made land sterile in some places. In other areas, ash from smoke-stacks singed leaves and grasses, destroying farmers' crops. In the coastal waters off Lázaro Cárdenas and in the Balsas River delta, commercial species had begun to disappear. Fishermen in interviews noted that where one once could catch barbel, chancleta, striper-fish, parrot-fish, sea bass, and clams, there was only mojarra fish, carp, and charal fish. As pointed out by a fisherman and activist who lived in Lázaro Cárdenas, "Produc-tion [in the riverine fishing] had been down for a long time. . . . Fisher-men had complained about oil spills in the late 1980s, but we never got a hearing." He continued, saying that such demands had little support at that time from a municipal government led by an ex-labor leader who derived his support from Local 271 or from neighbors on the island who later returned to fishing as a primary occupation. "Most people here worked in construction, or in the factories at least half time, so they didn't see [river contamination] as such a problem," he recalled (Interview C-8 1994).

Accounts of environmental protest in the mid-1990s place the first major confrontation in late 1991. The juncture was a crucial one for mobilization because of the imminent turnover of industry from public to private hands, and the pending legal dissolution of SICARTSA as a federally-owned entity. Ejidatarios with land titles in the nearby villages of Acalpican and Playa Azul mobilized three blockades of the power instal-lations feeding the SICARTSA iron mines, demanding compensation for lands rendered sterile by heavy metals. This mobilization, which ended in a settlement with the government for three million pesos, set the stage for similar local protests linking destroyed livelihoods to industrial contami-nation. However, the settlement also provoked jealousy and accusations of opportunism. Observers accused protesters and government officials of having negotiated "very quickly and in the dark." Beyond the hasty set-tlement itself, there was no official admission of guilt for industrial con-tamination. The exiting manager of the parastatal was careful to declare the settlement a "final benefit"offered by the state-owned company and offered the settlement in exchange for promises on the part of campesinos to retire a pending civil case they had filed against the government enter-prise (Méndez, 1992).

Subsequent protests by different groups surfaced within months, growing in combativeness and sophistication. In early 1992, fishermen formed the *Sector Pesquero* (Fishing Sector) and allied briefly with campesinos and neighborhood groups in an attempt to shed light on environmental damage to fisheries and farmland. Having petitioned the government in the previous year for a study of river and coastal health to little avail, they began mobilizing direct actions in an attempt to gain access to data and information that would help them make a case for industrial reforms and direct compensation. Fishermen took the lead in protest and ad hoc negotiations with various government intermediaries. Fishermen also began organizing forums demanding larger and more involved settlements, this time targeting both federal authorities and private companies. Nationally, they sought the help of several nongovernmental organizations and progressive activists involved in similar grassroots social and environmental causes. These organizations and individuals, as the Support Group for Riverine Fishermen, assisted lateral communication and a national conference among activists from fishing cooperatives from nine states involved in various production and environmental struggles (Grupo de Apoyo a Pescadores 1993, unpublished).

Using threats to disrupt production at a key juncture in the delicate privatization process, fishermen called for negotiations with a host of actors, including the new private owners of the steel industry, the heads of soon-to-be-privatized Fertimex, the federally owned PEMEX, the Secretary of the Environment, the Secretary of Fishing, and the Federal Attorney General of Environmental Protection (Torres Oseguera 1992). Notably, the fishermen's protests compelled the involvement of representatives of one of the federal government's most powerful agencies, the Attorney General of the Republic. Without clear civil laws regarding liability for environmental damage, fishermen had begun filing criminal cases against the municipal government and several port industries (Interviews with Casto García 1994, Hilda Salazar 1994).

The fishermen's actions were costly. Within weeks after a public forum in which fishermen cited industry and the municipal government for criminal failure to clean up known sources of organic and industrial contamination to fisheries, gunmen ambushed and killed José Luis Valdovinos, a legal and political advisor to the group. Police investigating the murder maintained that the killing was the result of a drunken brawl; fishermen maintained that it was a planned reprisal by judicial police. Subsequent to the shooting, fishermen blockaded the highway and port entrances to industrial installations, citing Fertimex, NKS, and the various steel industries. Editorials sent to the left-leaning Mexico City daily, *La*

Jornada, accused Fertimex of having ordered Valdovinos' murder (*La Jornada* 1992).

Again, a cycle of accusations and reprisals brought government officials to the table, but also created fissures and new costs that eroded the ability of protesters to organize broad support. Several hundred fishermen and campesinos mounted a blockade of the land and water entrances to the port; heavy industries, meanwhile, docked workers' pay for the eight days while production was suspended. As a result, many workers viewed fishermen as a threat to their livelihoods, renewing public accusations of opportunism on the part of fishermen. Notably, three years after the blockade, divisions of opinion persisted. A number of militant workers and ex-workers – certainly no friends to port industries – remembered the blockade without sympathy. Despite the fact that the protesting fishermen were mostly ex-workers, and many residents of farms and urban settlements suffered what they believed were environmentally related gastrointestinal and eye problems, workers condemned the fishermen's protest in interviews. When asked about the blockade, two ex-union militants cited authorities and protesters with equal venality. "They should concern themselves more for the benefit of society," an ex-worker remarked. "Both the ecologistas and the authorities manipulate people" (Interview 11-A 1994).

In ensuing years, rounds of confrontation and negotiation continued. The port blockade was followed with one explosive round of protests in 1993 after a scandalous incident in which a poorly maintained Norwegian frigate, the *Betula,* began leaking its cargo of five thousand tons of sulfuric acid into coastal waters. Reaction to the incident was particularly contentious because it occurred in the midst of ongoing protests over the environment. The reaction of federal authorities also bolstered claims of protesters that the government did not enforce environmental laws, protected industry at the expense of the public, and silenced dissent on such matters. Although authorities ordered the indefinite suspension of all fishing activities, they also attempted to hide the acid spill by towing the barge seven miles north of the port.[8] In response to a blockade of port industries similar to the blockade in 1992, government response was unequivocal. State and federal police authorities arrested 24 fishermen, and placed arrest warrants on another 525 (Greenpeace 1993, unpublished).

---

[8] They were then further embarrassed when a hurricane grounded the barge and spilled the remaining hazardous chemicals and oil into coastal waters.

144

The struggle over the *Betula* marked a high point of environmental contention in Lázaro Cárdenas. Protest leaders focused energies on developing vertical links with national and international nongovernmental organizations, notably Greenpeace-Mexico and Greenpeace International. For several months, Greenpeace staged protests in Mexico City, and pressured Dutch and Norwegian authorities for information regarding the boat. Meanwhile, authorities evaded charges of negligence in admitting vessels known to have been banned from other countries (Moyssen 1993).

With respect to contentious politics in Lázaro Cárdenas, protest over the *Betula* spill merits attention for what did and did not result from it politically and organizationally. As public as the incident was, generating communiques and letters of support from environmental groups in India, Canada, the United States, the Philippines, and Chile (Greenpeace 1993), the incident at the same time generated little additional local backing for environmental protests. This was crucial, for despite the national coverage the incident received, protesters had little means to maintain direct actions during months of alternating police actions and negotiations. Nongovernmental organizations 14 hours away in Mexico City could provide publicity, which created some pressure on authorities to reach a settlement with fishermen (Interview with Casto García 1994). However, carrying out protests locally involved mobilizing costly actions over and over, battling police authorities, and bailing leaders out of jail, among other things. This required harnessing material resources nearby and convincing the local public of their side of the issues.

Here, the dilemmas of maintaining protest locally and drawing on external resources were exacerbated by clear voids in governmental capacity. The chaotic state of jurisdiction over the matter and the isolated location of the port city made negotiations ad hoc and dependent on continuous direct action. Although nongovernmental authorities called on port authorities for answers about the boat's presence in Mexican waters, port authorities called for federal judicial authorities to negotiate with protesters; meanwhile, fishermen called on human rights authorities to intervene in any negotiations that would take place, while demanding meetings with the Attorney General on Environmental Protection, the Secretary of the Interior, the Secretary of Fishing, and the Secretary of Social Development (Rudiño 1993).

Fishermen's and campesinos' demands in Lázaro Cárdenas suffered in ensuing years from a surfeit of environmental culprits and a paucity of legal help and available data on the environment.[9] On the one hand, fishermen's accounts of production over time suggested a decline of 70 to 80 percent of production since the early 1980s (Secretary of Fishing figures, cited in Méndez 1992). On the other hand, no study could pinpoint exact causes of the decline. For example, workers and fishermen knew that the discharge pipe for Fertimex had ruptured in the 1985 earthquake and had been leaking phosporous and gypsum into waters along the coast. At the same time, however, canals from urban settlements also poured raw sewage into the sea. Fishermen alleged that massive waves of heated water coming from the new thermoelectric plant fifteen miles to the south of the city were also affecting fisheries. Finally, industrial contamination and landfills in mangroves and lagoons had destroyed fish habitat and hatcheries for many species. Each set of authorities was quick to point out that they could not be held singly accountable for long-term declines in coastal fisheries. Confronting one set of authorities or one company, then, often meant confronting them all – a near impossibility with very scarce resources.

Devastated financially from months of lost production in 1993, and facing threats from outstanding arrest warrants issued during confrontations, fishermen alternated between calls for new practices and alternative fishing projects and direct pressure for settlements. Generally, these rounds of contention produced impasse on negotiations regarding long-term cleanups of fisheries. Casto García, a leader of the Sector Pesquero, lamented in an interview the difficulties of establishing enforceable accords with authorities. After fishermen secured the release of an environmental study commissioned by the Profepa, consultations about how the report's findings could be used were disputed among half a dozen agencies with differing political agendas, including the federal Attorney General, the Secretary of Fishing, the Secretary of Agriculture, and the Secretary of Social Development (Interview with Casto García 1994). Agreements reached with these agencies or their successor agencies[10] at best provided

[9] A year after the *Betula* incident, activists with the fishermen's movement said that they no longer had available legal assistance (Interview C-7 1994). They also had scant access to the environmental data that presumably informed government policy. Fishermen had to stage repeated protests to gain access to an environmental study commissioned by the government in 1992. Ironically, the study itself was commissioned as a result of protests by fishermen and campesinos for a baseline environmental study (Interview with Hilda Salazar 1994).

[10] During the 1990s, several federal agencies dealing with the environment or with rural production were condensed, eliminated, or renamed, which further complicated negotiations. The Secretary of Agriculture and Hydraulic Resources became the Secretary of Agricul-

fishermen with settlements of a few thousand pesos apiece and subsidized lines of credit for equipment that would enable fishermen to work farther out at sea.

From Farming and Fishing to Neighborhood Settlements

The devolution of urban and environmental protest into quarreling small groups demonstrates the immanent tensions in mobilizing around distributive demands. Particularly after already weak governmental jurisdictions receded, many became skeptical of the terms of ad hoc legal agreements and one-time settlements that were reached with protesting groups. As in Local 271, where factions were sharply divided over questions of whether shorter or longer term issues should lead demands and whether the union ought to mobilize broader or narrower sectors of the urban population, movements after privatization struggled with similar questions. However, the tensions inherent in organizing durable cross-sectoral coalitions became more pronounced. Not only did groups with grievances have to use direct action to get a hearing with authorities, and then to negotiate agreements with authorities, in most cases, groups had to use direct action to compel authorities to comply with them. Clearly, small protest groups, with extraordinarily scant resources, had an immediate interest in taking one-time settlements when and if they were available. However, cash or in-kind settlements at the same time eroded the larger ideological claims that made broader coalitions and more durable protest feasible for people who had little to their names.

Notably, fishermen's protests had parallels in urban struggles for services. In much the same manner that fishermen continued protesting the failure of authorities to comply with agreements signed years ago in 1993 and 1994,[11] protests among colonos, ex-workers, and taxi and bus drivers

ture, Cattle, and Rural Development. The Secretary of Fishing was dissolved and replaced by the Secretary of Environment, Fishing, and Natural Resources. The Secretary of Urban Development and Ecology was dissolved and replaced by the Secretary of Social Development. The systemic impact of these changes is complex, and beyond the scope of the discussion here.

[11] Protests of fishermen claiming lack of compliance on legal agreements in the fishing sector continue to date. Fishermen in 1996, 1997, 1998, and 1999, for example, claimed that authorities failed to prevent industries from filling in coastal lagoons and swamps, and from dumping oil and heavy metals in river waters (Servicio Universal de Noticias 1996a, 1996b, 1998; La Opinión de Michoacán 1997b). In several protests, fishermen also protested authorities' failure to establish promised alternative fishing projects, including aquiculture.

suggest similar patterns. Collective campaigns for even very straightforward regulation had little chance of success, thus prompting movements to demand cash settlements or selective subsidies instead. An example is a recent struggle over the price of tortillas. In that campaign, one of the city's most powerful colono leaders – known for prior campaigns that had gained hundreds of people titles to urban land and services – led a campaign calling for the government to enforce nationally set price guarantees on tortillas. Despite unequivocal laws in his favor and clear agency jurisdiction over the matter by the Attorney General for Consumer Protection, protests over the matter continued for over two years. Facing counterprotests by tortilla makers who claimed that they could not make a profit at government prices, the agency was unable to muster sufficient power to resolve the conflict. The protests were solved not by enforcing price guarantees, but instead through a selective, ad hoc agreement in which the local government began dispensing tortilla coupons to protesting residents.[12]

There is little question that greater numbers of people have become willing to openly express discontent and to denounce authorities and the private sector for malfeasance and corruption. Significantly, however, a great deal of protest is aimed at municipal government in hopes that officials will broker demands with a tangled array of state and federal authorities. As a result, contention often remains mired in local intrigues and fruitless negotiations.

In some ways, elected officials and their appointees hold broader legal capacity than ever to broker settlements between warring groups, which renders local party politics more significant in distributive disputes. It is significant, however, that their powers of arbitration exist on a case-by-case basis. In most instances, local and state officials can release temporary resources but are powerless to reverse larger processes. An engineer who worked in housing in the city government of Lázaro Cárdenas explained very aptly why large groups of people came *every day* to sit in apparent protest in municipal government offices and why there had been twenty-three separate takeovers of the municipal government

---

[12] Accounts of the protest campaign were taken from *La Opinión de Michoacán*, which began reporting the conflict in February of 1997 (1997a). Protests continued through that year and 1998, and in 1999, the local government brokered a deal in which several thousand tortilla coupons would be dispensed to urban residents. Notably, sporadic protests continued because demand for the tortilla coupons exceeded the supply (*La Opinión de Michoacán* 1999).

building in twelve months' time. I asked the engineer how the municipality tried to budget money for housing and services. "In truth," he said, taking a long draw on his cigarette, "there is no plan." I asked him how a typical community went about procuring his services in getting a wastewater system. He explained that the colonia would go initially to the mayor and ask for what they wanted. Of course, it would be unlikely that such people would have title to the lands they occupy, so they would be sent to the Comision Regularizadora de Terrenos. Now, they should have the title, he explained, but they often do not. The process takes a long time, and while the process is in *tramite* (in the bureaucracy), the settlers will likely carry on their protests and petitioning for services with a convenio in hand. The *convenio*, or loose legal agreement, likely promises titles at some later date and may hold the colonia to certain promises not to invade more land. Each step of the way, the engineer said, requires collective pressure, meaning groups of people, constantly present in the offices of government. *"Hay presion para que les autoridades les haga caso"* (They pressure the authorities to attend to them), he explained (Interview D-2 1995).

In light of the ongoing economic crisis among working-class Mexicans and the specific environmental and infrastructural problems in Lázaro Cárdenas, what will follow in terms of social movements in Lázaro Cárdenas is an open question. What may be very significant is a reconvergence of interests owing to an acute failure of privatization to generate new employment and commerce. As in much of the country, small and medium-sized enterprises complain that their debt loads are unmanageable and, furthermore, that much of their wholesale business formerly associated with the state-owned companies has been absorbed by vertically integrated companies with bases elsewhere. Unemployed workers complain that they do not have the option to earn a wage or to make a living from informal commerce. "No one is buying. Everyone is broke," commented a merchant selling items on the sidewalk.

Beyond even material structures, however, the unescapable reality in Lázaro Cárdenas is that it continues to be a city that the state built, in concrete and consciousness. Despite the contempt with which many speak of the government, the state is also viewed as the source of solutions to problems of development. And despite the apparent inability of urban architects to accommodate the needs of the population, many stay on in the region. Lázaro Cárdenas, once a city of strangers with no common history, is now a place where people have come to know one another, where they have married and had children, and where they have begun to bury their dead. As one company manager who came to live in Lázaro two decades ago mused, "This is our Macondo, our one hundred years. . . . We are from here. We thought about leaving, but now the children are from here. We're going to stay."

5

The Rise of the Barzón Farmers' Movement in Zacatecas

Few would have predicted even two years ago that a major front of political protest comprised of tens of thousands of shopkeepers, mortgage holders, pushcart vendors, industrialists, farmers, and even taxi drivers would rise from a small rural movement in the dusty north-central state Zacatecas. With livings culled mostly from dryland agriculture and a handful of petty urban industries, Zacatecas is one of the poorest states in Mexico. In addition to its reputation as provincial outpost of humble corn and bean farmers, Zacatecas has also been regarded as one of the most politically quiescent regions in Mexico, where until 1995 the ruling party was always assured of across-the-board victories in local, state, and national elections.

If the industrial city of Lázaro Cárdenas represented what national leaders once believed was the wave of the future, Zacatecas signified the past that they sought to leave behind. Relatively little public investment ever arrived in Zacatecas, for agricultural or urban development. Roads are poor, and 90 percent of the farmland remains nonirrigated. With an average of only 400 millimeters of rain a year, only drought-resistant grains and legumes thrive on most of the lands. Intense monocropping has depleted soils over time, and farmers in some areas see average yields at as little as one-half of what they did in the 1970s (Rudiño 1995a; Interview with Efrén Bañuelos 1995). Today's harvest per acre in Zacatecas is about one fifth of U.S. farm averages.

The austerity of life in Zacatecas makes it all the more striking that six or seven years ago farmers began to murmur that things were worse than they'd ever been. Although nearly every farmer in Zacatecas had seen drought, plague, and scarcity, the word now was that a farmer couldn't operate in the black even with a good crop anymore. With low commod-

151

1995 ■ Helguera

NO HAN LLEGADO LOS RECURSOS DE PROCAMPO

ES QUE NO HAY ELECCIONES HASTA EL AÑO 2000

1995, **by Helguera** Peasant on the left: "The Procampo subsidies haven't arrived yet." Peasant on the right: "It's because elections aren't until the year 2000." From *La Jornada*, May 19, 1995. Reprinted by permission.

ity prices and deteriorating credit terms, in addition to subsidies cut off by the government in Mexico City, a consensus emerged that agriculture was lurching from perennial difficulty toward permanent ruin in this arid region.

It was impending bankruptcy that prompted a group of seven farmers and ranchers to organize a protest in October of 1993 in Fresnillo, a small, mostly agribusiness city in the center of the state. The plan, as they recalled two years later, was to organize an occupation of the central plaza with heavy machinery, in a similar fashion to a much-talked-about farm protest in Guadalajara that was going on at that moment (Interview with Manuel Ortega 1995). Upon arriving in Fresnillo, the ranchers issued a public invitation to any farmer and rancher who had similar problems of debt and falling profit margins to join their occupation. Within days, the seven ranchers were joined by dozens, and then hundreds of farmers with debts they couldn't service. Although the newspapers did carry coverage of the occupation, most farmers who report that they joined the protest say they heard of the protest by word of mouth, or learned of it while passing through town. Contrary to past protests in Zacatecas, the protest was comprised not of farmers from one *ejido* (collective farm) in particular, or a union of ejidos, or a cooperative of private farmers or ranchers. Accounts of the protest indicate that the individuals at the protest were from a variety of ejidos and villages, but that the leaders of the protest had not managed to garner the support of any ejidos or cooperatives in their entirety.[1] The farmers who came were in many cases friends of friends of the initiators, or friends of cousins – somehow known to those who joined the occupation. Some were large farmers on private lands; others owned only small plots on nearby ejidos.

By the third of October 1993, the paper reported that five hundred farmers were in the city of Fresnillo occupying the central square, complaining that repossessions, decapitalization, high interest rates, and loss of production supports were threatening their livelihoods. Camped out with tractors and trucks, they had driven into town and jammed up next to the white gazebo in the central plaza in front of the cathedral; the farmers were a rare spectacle. Farmers say that passersby in Fresnillo were by and large sympathetic, occasionally bringing out food, water, or blankets or letting farmers into their houses or businesses to wash up. Initially the farmers denied any linkage to political parties or organizations, including the organization of farmers calling itself the Barzón in the next-door state of Jalisco (*Imagen de Zacatecas* 1993a). Days later, however, leaders of the Fresnillo occupation met with visitors from Jalisco and announced that they would become a Barzón chapter of their own (*Imagen de Zacatecas* 1993c) but still would make no private deals with parties or government officials.

In unifying such an embarrassingly large group, the protest superseded even the expectations of its initiators. Similar to the workers' Local 271 in Lázaro Cárdenas, which fought the labor authorities and the management of a state-owned plant, and subsequent small movements that battled private enterprise and local and federal authorities over contamination and urban shortages, the Barzón movement mobilized against dual opponents: in this case, the government and Mexico's most powerful industry, the

[1] Accounts drawn from interviews with growers in Ejido Rancho Grande and Ejido Chapa Rosa, Villa de Cos, May 1995.

newly privatized banks. Unlike the workers' movement in Lázaro Cárdenas, however, it expanded over several years from a local, sectoral protest into a mass multiclass, multisectoral organization.[2]

This chapter and the next examine the El Barzón mobilization from the time it appeared on the map as a provincial movement of ranchers and grain farmers in Zacatecas to the point where it began replicating its form, posting chapters in nearly every state of the country during the depression year of 1995. The analysis seeks to explain first, what structural and ideational factors enabled the movement to emerge when it did, and second, what organizational practices prolonged its insurgency, expanded its constituency from farmers to urban consumer and business groups.

In the case of the workers in Lázaro Cárdenas, I argued that the factors that shaped contention over time had to do with regional residents' relationship to central industries, with their relationships to government agencies, and with associated narratives of distributive justice that they could summon at different points. Facilitating the initial mobilization of an insurgent workers' movement with broad cross-sectoral support were national networks of insurgent workers pressing for union democracy, plus a confluence of urban interests around the workers' contract demands. Subsequent to privatization of the port's enterprises, however, contention splintered among numerous small groups who had very limited power to challenge distributive policies of the state. Workers' power to demand goods and services for residents of Lázaro Cárdenas declined, and unifying narratives of developmentalist justice broke down in the face of declining formal-sector employment and dwindling government stewardship in the region.

In central Zacatecas, the factors that prompted shifts in contentious politics over distributive issues in the 1990s were also a mixture of economic, institutional, and ideational factors. First, I argue that national government policy under President Salinas de Gortari altered the administration of agriculture such that farmers of different size and property status began to use many more financial institutions and production programs in common than before. Second, and associated with these policy alterations, new debt crises in the agricultural sector prompted a convergence of griev-

---

[2] The case study presented here is in no way a comprehensive account of the national Barzón movement in Mexico. The purpose here is to demonstrate how a movement begins, and how it may gain momentum in the context of national economic change. For an examination of the Barzón movement as a national phenomenon, see Williams (1996, 1999a), Senzek (1997), and Charnas (1999).

ances among formerly antagonistic groups of large and small farmers. Third, the centrality of ideas about land and the inviolability of household patrimony – or one's means of making a living – provoked vociferous protest over attempts by banks and other lenders to repossess properties and businesses.

As I will discuss in this chapter and the next, market-oriented policies had made marked but contradictory impacts on contentious politics in Zacatecas. Rapidly accumulating debt and decapitalization provoked new means of aggregating social demands behind common anti-neoliberal campaigns, but also introduced new dilemmas for activists seeking to leverage protest for state brokerage of demands. On the one hand, the new vulnerability of farm and urban residents to shifts in monetary and trade policy provided activists with new means of unifying disparate social demands behind broad calls for debt relief, subsidies, and low-interest credit lines. On the other hand – similar to contentious politics of recent years in Lázaro Cárdenas – the unmoored nature of protest made it difficult for activists to persist in long-term campaigns for policy reforms, while also securing short-term settlements for individuals participating in direct actions.

The Rise of the Zacatecas Barzón

Most farmers in the original Fresnillo occupation came from a wide swath of agricultural land that cuts through the middle of the state, extending from San Luis Potosí on the east to Durango on the west. Leaders made no formal list of the farmers who came to Fresnillo, but media reports and interviews suggest that the farmers were drawn principally from the municipalities of Río Grande, Jerez, Zacatecas, Juan Aldama, Miguel Auza, Sombrerete, and Fresnillo itself (see Figure 5.1).

Together the farmers were a heterogeneous group of large and small growers, some of them growers of chile and peaches and others strictly producers of corn and beans. The farmers and ranchers who initiated the protest (later called the San Tadeo group after the ranch where they held their first meeting in September 1993) were wealthy by Zacatecas standards. Two of the organizers were cousins who split duties on a 700-hectare farm close to Fresnillo. Another three of the organizers, Juan José Quirino, Manuel Ortega, and Alfonso Ramírez Cuellar, were part-time ranchers who had met in their college years in Mexico City. They were also long-time political activists who had participated in Cuauhtémoc Cárdenas'

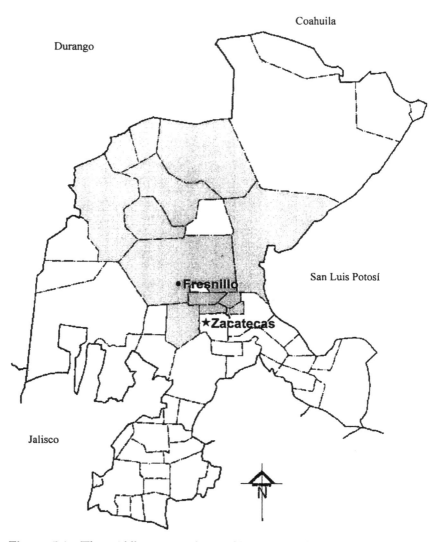

Figure 5.1 The middle municipalities of Zacatecas. The shaded areas denote municipalities with participants in the Fresnillo occupation.

opposition party (the Party of the Democratic Revolution, PRD) since 1988 and in various leftist student and labor movements. The small farmers and ejidatarios occupying the square with them, for the most part, were of much more humble means, although they, in turn, were better off than much of the rural population in Zacatecas. Their lands, though about average for rain-fed farms on a national scale, were more productive than the areas in the southern canyons bordering Jalisco or the northern deserts stretching up to Coahuila. They were also, notably, market farmers, not subsistence producers or sometime day-laborers, like many of the campesinos north and south of them.[3]

As grain prices were lowered in the 1990s to match prices of imports from the north, farmers' relative status as cash-and-credit growers in the middle municipalities had become a curse. Ironically, poorer farmers in the outlying regions routinely adjusted to falling prices by consuming most or all of their food crops in place of selling them and by migrating seasonally to the United States (Zacatecas State Government 1991, unpublished policy paper), but farmers who worked on credit simply saw lower profit margins as real prices of food crops fell in the late 1980s. Interest on yearly loans then took up an increasing proportion of their gross income, and squeezed net income in the process. Discontent among market farmers in rural Zacatecas came to a head in the summer and fall of 1993, as low prices and lingering debt combined with a number of ongoing personal disputes between particular farmers and the state government.

In hindsight, what grabs the attention of the observer is that the San Tadeo ranchers were able to initiate such an aggressive first protest of such a novel mix of farmers with so little prior organization. Farmers claim that acute strain in their financial situations was a principal factor in prompting them to participate in the Fresnillo action. Market farmers in Zacatecas felt the crisis most immediately in the form of profit margins below the level necessary to pay their yearly creditors. Testifying as to why they joined the Barzón protest, farmers said, simply, "I had no choice," or "I had nowhere else to turn." Some were in hot water with the banks, others with the shops that sold them farm implements on time, and others with the government's Bank of Rural Credit.

---

[3] Predominance of a cash economy in the middle municipalities, even in drought-stricken, nitrogen-poor microclimates, may be attributed to a number of factors. First, subsistence farming in the central region is associated with poverty and is considered low status. Second, farming practices tie farmers into a cash-and-credit cycle. Few farmers plant, fertilize, or harvest without some use of tractors, although these may be bought communally. A single machine may cost the equivalent of two to ten years' income, thereby prohibiting most farmers from buying equipment outright. Once in debt, the cycle of borrowing, planting, harvesting, and servicing becomes routine.

Farmers describe the crisis that emerged in the early 1990s as a result of crooked bankers and bought-off politicians, but a more distanced technocrat would likely describe the farm crisis in Zacatecas as a regrettable consequence of grain market liberalization. Despite some planned research and development programs designed to transform agriculture to new commercial conditions (Zacatecas Governor's Office 1992), production adjustment never occurred on a measurable scale. With climate and poor soils limiting the choice of what almost any farmer can grow in Zacatecas, farmers will attest that even the best-trained among them have limited capacity to convert from food grains to products that bring a better price. Whether or not this is so, beans and corn cover the fields today still, interrupted only occasionally by fields of higher-value crops such as peaches, apples, and chile.[4] Of these, only chile has been planted for much time and, subsequently, has an assured market in an elaborated processing and transport network.

Notably, if 1993–4 data furnished by the government-run Bank of Rural Credit is correct, the farmers in Zacatecas who experienced the largest relative drop in profits as a result of Mexico's market liberalization were, in fact, the wealthiest farmers. Mid-size and larger farmers with some irrigation – whose fortunes normally were divorced from those of hard-scrambling campesinos with five to fifteen hectares of rainfed land – found themselves in a position where their profit margins had fallen to a level *below* that of small farmers on more marginal lands. Whereas small market farmers had seen cycles of government policies that had threatened real household income from farming, it was a more singular phenomenon for large farmers as a group to face a rapid fall in profits. Three changes in the early 1990s were key to the fall in real incomes for large and small farmers: the end of guaranteed prices for all crops except corn and beans, the drop in real prices on the still-guaranteed corn and beans, and the termination of input subsidies.

As prices for beans, for example, dropped by 25 to 50 percent, most farmers found themselves unable to sell their crops at a price that covered their production costs. Relative to planting costs, corn prices were even worse. The Bank of Rural Credit (Banrural), for example, by 1992 no

---

[4] Apples and peaches are generally grown by wealthier farmers because they are able to finance the lag years between planting and first harvest when the fields bring in no income. Although fruit trees can be grown on rain-fed land, they also require extensive capital investment. Chile may in certain cases be grown by small farmers, but it does require irrigation.

longer included rain-fed corn in its production books in Zacatecas, presumably because the ratio of benefit to cost was below 1.0 (Interview with Faustino López 1995). An article by an agronomist in a Zacatecan weekly put the cost per hectare (not including interest on loans) of planting corn on rain-fed land at 1,120 pesos in 1994, with yields of up to two tons per hectare (*Horizonte* 1995). With corn prices regionally hovering at around 700 pesos per ton, a corn farmer on nonirrigated soil could hope, at best, to clear an average of about 520 pesos in profit, or about U.S. $160 per hectare for the year's harvest. If the farmer borrowed from a local lender at 50 percent (based on going *agio*, or loan shark rates of 100 percent annual fees), the net profit was, in fact, around zero.

A key area where federal government policy had created an unforeseen convergence of demands among large and small farmers was in finance. President Salinas, who sought to control inflation and attract foreign portfolio investment, did two things that rendered grain production less profitable. First, the treasury's policy of overvaluing the peso against the dollar while keeping the money supply fairly tight successfully controlled inflation by giving urban consumers access to artificially cheap imports. However, it also put downward pressure on the government buying agency's price for grains. This agency, the National Company for Popular Subsistence (CONASUPO), was operating under a free-trade ethos of "market price," paying Mexican farmers a peso price per unit equivalent to the price of U.S. grain sold in international commodity markets. As a result, the inflated peso resulted in Mexican grain being bought and sold at an artificially low price. This was good for urban food consumers and good for tempering inflation, but bad for Mexican farmers. In addition to low prices, farmers were troubled by the high cost of capital, which ranged from 20 to 31 percent annually at commercial banks. Due to insufficient national savings, government bond issues on the international market generated a substantial portion of domestic capital. The high interest rates paid to international bondholders put upward pressure on consumer interest rates. As a result, farm credit in Mexico was two to five times[5] as expensive as it was in grain-exporting countries who traded with Mexico.

At this juncture, private bankers saw little viability in farming, and preferred in many cases not to lend money to basic grain growers, particu-

---

[5] The official annual rate charged by BANRURAL in western Zacatecas was 12 percent (Interview with Efrén Bañuelos 1995), compared with U.S. rates, which ran about 5 to 6 percent.

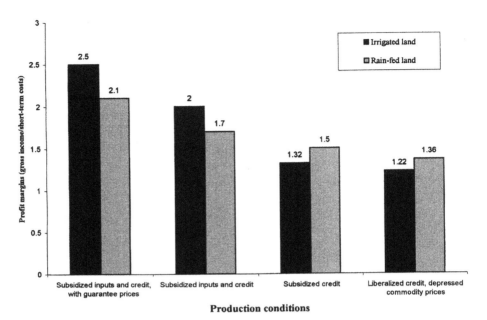

Figure 5.2 Profit margins under changing production conditions.
Source: Banco de Crédito Rural del Centro Nortel 1994

larly smaller scale producers. Inputs were expensive, and prices were low; therefore, marginal profits were nearly nonexistent, even if there were no losses to drought or plague. Farmers who normally guaranteed their loans with the crops they expected to harvest at the end of the year faced a situation where even the price they received for a good year's crop might not cover the cost of the credit alone.

The following figure demonstrates the effect of progressive market opening on the principal crop in Zacatecas, black beans. Figure 5.2 shows the progressive decline of profits following price adjustment, then following termination of input subsidies, and then following rationalization of the credit mechanism. It compares relative losses for farmers with irrigated land as opposed to farmers on rain-fed land – a rough rendering of the differential between wealthier farmers with better land and low-income farmers with more marginal land. Irrigated land in the middle municipalities of Zacatecas, according to the Rural Bank's survey, yields on average 1.8 tons per hectare; the rainfed lands average 0.6 tons per hectare. The figures on the far left represent expected benefit-to-cost ratios when farmers had access to input subsidies and a higher relative price on their crop. The second set of figures, reflecting losses sustained when prices fell, shows where profit margins would lie after a 25 percent drop in real prices in the bean market.[6] The third set of figures shows the profit margins after input subsidies are ended. In this case, irrigated farms show the sharpest decline in profitability owing to their greater relative reliance on subsidies (higher item costs in labor, pesticide, electricity). In the final set of figures, the profit margins are even lower due to rationalization of the credit mechanism. When profit margins are too low for the Rural Bank to risk investment, farmers turn to commercial banks (whose relative inexperience in grain agriculture has prompted those in Zacatecas to lend unwisely to farmers with low profit margins) or private lenders. In this last set of figures, irrigated farmers actually fare *worse* than rain-fed farmers because they must borrow more money per ton of crop (due to greater relative use of inputs).

If, as Figure 5.2 suggests, the spark that set off the protest in Fresnillo may have been the more sudden drop in profits for the wealthier farmers in Zacatecas; interestingly, small and large farmers interviewed in 1995 recall that farming crashed in the same way for everybody at the same time. One small farmer said, "Back two or three years, things were alright. You could work hard and make a profit." Despite price/cost indices that indicate that the small farmers' plight predated the market liberalization and that subsidies were disproportionately geared toward more capital-intensive enterprises, most assert today that small and large farmers' problems are, in fact, the same problems demanding the same solutions.[7]

As much as it was a reaction to the encroachment of international markets on local production livelihoods, the Fresnillo occupation also revealed a new set of dilemmas facing the Institutional Revolutionary Party (PRI)-controlled state government. When farmers occupied the plaza in

---

[6] Although beans and corn still carry what the government calls "guarantee prices," or price floors, the amount paid per kilogram has declined in real terms since the late 1980s. The policy under President Salinas was to pay guarantee prices that reflected the price of given commodities on the international market.

[7] Interestingly, in the Barzón occupation in nearby Jalisco, large farmers (with fifty-plus hectares of land) had one demand in particular that indicates their belief that changes in agricultural policy had qualitatively altered their status as producers. They demanded that the government reclassify them as "small farmers," presumably to qualify for certain programs or tax exemptions (although media accounts are murky about the specific goal). For an account of the early stages of the Barzón movement in Jalisco, see Rodríguey Gómez, and Torres (1994).

Fresnillo and declared that they would not leave until the government negotiated with them, the response of authorities was mixed and lacked a finality consistent with the autocratic power normally wielded by the state government. In twenty years of relative quiescence in Zacatecas, governors and their men normally had done one of two things when occasional groups formed public protesters: they had either invited the protest leaders to negotiate a settlement with an appropriate agency or sent the police to evict the protesters.

This time, no clear action was taken. The governor of the state waited for the protest to dissolve. Dismissing any notion that the problem of farm debt and repossession was serious, he carried on business as usual. His action was reinforced by the central government's announcement of a new cash-subsidy program for agriculture called Procampo, which, the governor promised in a press conference, would bring 615 million pesos to Zacatecan farmers. The press coverage of the Barzón movement subsided for several days as the governor arranged a mass sign-up ceremony for the Procampo program, summoning twelve thousand farmers to the state offices of the National Campesino Confederation (CNC) to register in person, and using the occasion to denounce the antics of "pseudo-leaders" stirring up antipathies nearby (*Imagen de Zacatecas* 1993i).

When the news passed, though, the public found the farmers still in the middle of Fresnillo with their tractors. Calling the government's program a hoax and reiterating that their debts weren't going away, they demanded lines of credit for the next planting season (regardless of whether a farmer was already in debt or not), a temporary halt to bank repossessions, a study of the impact of imports on the grain and bean markets, and better government planning in agriculture (*Imagen de Zacatecas* 1993c). The governor stayed in the state government building, meeting only once in private with Barzón leaders and reaching no resolution. The banks and ministries bided their time, waiting for signals from the governor.

In part, the standoff was due to changing federal policies, which limited the power of the state government to negotiate farm finance issues directly with the protesters. Interviews also suggest, however, that the resonance of farmers' demands was also bolstered by broad antagonism to the governor of the time, Arturo Romo. Perceived as an outsider in the state, imposed through intrigues of elites in Mexico City, Romo had little stake in his personal popularity in Zacatecas. Romo, a longtime party official in Mexico City and protégé of labor leader Fidel Velásquez in Mexico City, was rumored to have received the governorship as a consolation prize after losing a congressional race in Mexico City in 1988. Residents of the capital city, Zacatecas, remarked that the governor was distant and not well liked, precisely because he eschewed public contact with citizen groups of petitioners. *"No es de la gente"* [He is not from the people], said one shopkeeper in passing. Another individual commented that in comparison to his predecessor, Governor Romo was seen as cold, and that there was no *"confianza"* [trust] between the governor and the people. *"Nunca sale del palacio como el gobernador de antes"* [He never leaves the government building like the last governor], the informant commented. *"Aquel era corrupto como todos los otros, pero la gente lo quería mucho . . . porque andaba mucho en público"* [That guy (the last governor) was as corrupt as all the others, but the people loved him . . . because he went out a lot in public].

The Barzón demonstration brought into relief this public malaise with the state executive, a mistrust that reached even into high-ranking ruling party circles. After the Barzón began to organize, PRI officials at the helm of official farm organizations made statements to the press about their sympathy with the Barzón demands, adding safely that they felt the Barzón's tactics were uncalled for (*Imagen de Zacatecas* 1993a, 1993b, 1993e, 1993g). Although such statements are often made by party officials in order to draw away members from a protesting organization or to coax leaders into negotiations with the government, state party officials loyal to the governor interpreted such comments this time as disobedience in the ranks. One prominent PRI official who made repeated comments to the press criticizing government agricultural policy was purged from his position at the head of the CNC, denied a candidacy in the upcoming 1994 elections, and placed at the helm of a lesser party organization.[8]

Political Control of Agriculture

Key to the success of the PRI in a farming state such as Zacatecas had been the party's role in the administration of agriculture. The Barzón demonstration, including the large ranchers and better-off ejidatarios who had

---

[8] The sequence of cause and effect in party careers is difficult to describe with any certainty. This information is speculative, drawing on comments by the same official in an interview in June 1995, where he complained that he had been persecuted by members of the party who were hostile to farming. He also remarked that federal trade policy that had opened basic grains to foreign competition could never have been formulated by "true" party members. Free trade architects Jaime Serra Puche and Pedro Aspe (the trade and finance ministers under Salinas), he remarked, were interlopers. See *Imagen de Zacatecas* (1994f, 1994i).

been a bulwark of PRI support in Zacatecas, capitalized on the party's declining ability to maintain even the modest production levels of Zacatecan farms. The leaders of the demonstration sensed accurately that the market adjustments had transformed productive arrangements such that significant numbers of normally quiescent, party-loyal landed farmers in Zacatecas were disposed to join a combative public protest of government policy.

The most powerful party organizations in the state, including the PRI-sponsored National Peasant Confederation, the National Cattlemen's Association, and the State Federation of Small Property Holders, typically held control over political and business channels in farming. And owing to the centrality of farming in Zacatecas, routine committee votes and everyday activities of those organizations captured front-page news in the capital city's daily newspapers. Programs channeled through PRI organizations injected substantial amounts of capital or infrastructure into the state. In addition, various government agricultural agencies played an important role in the maintenance of production and market structure. The FIRA-BANRURAL (National Trust Related to Agriculture/Rural Bank) system provided much of farmers' capital for seed, fertilizer, machinery, and repairs; the CONASUPO (National Company for Popular Subsistence) provided a market for grains; the CFE (Federal Electricity Commission) provided irrigation service and constructed new wells; and the Secretary of Agriculture was responsible for various production needs, such as extension services, phytotechnology, seed and fertilizer distribution, and administration of funds for cooperative purchase of machinery.

Notably, although the party organizations representing PRI farmers and the government organizations that technically served *all* farmers were separate, the two were, in fact, closely linked. Loyal ejido unions, particularly prominent ones in important municipalities, were the most likely to receive services from government agencies. Typically, visits by national party dignitaries were punctuated by ceremonies where thousands of CNC members would file past the dignitary to sign up for the newest production support program offered by the Ministry of Agriculture or would cheer as the dignitary cut ribbons or broke the ground of the sites of new silos or processing centers. Without such open support, it was unlikely that the program would actually deliver the checks, or that the silo or processing center would actually be built. In addition, the tie between the ruling party and agricultural administration in Zacatecas CNC and other party officials was reflected in the degree to which party leaders switched back and forth from party and agricultural administration posts. Officials interviewed reported an employment history in which they typically went from government administration to party positions, and drew on fluid networks of contacts in government and party circles in order to drum up support for their initiatives.

The power of the party's farmer organizations lay in their ability to deliver goods of production to the loyal, and concomitantly in their ability to block access to capital and markets when farmers were seen as being politically disloyal. PRI officials themselves in Zacatecas, now floundering somewhat in their positions as agricultural administrators because traditional pools of public money for agriculture had dried up, similarly pointed out that when public resources had been more plentiful, unnamed *others* among their peers had made distributive decisions according to a crass political calculus. For that, they lamented, the countryside remained backward and underproductive. Votes, not yields, had been the bottom line for traditional agricultural organizations affiliated with the PRI, confided one twenty-year veteran of CNC administration.

Perversely, when the national government got out of the business of subsidizing agricultural production as an industry[9] and aggregate public spending in agriculture declined through the 1980s, dissenting farmers had less to lose by pointing out growing misery in the farm sector.[10] The Barzón of Zacatecas, whose first protest was inspired by the "Barzón" farmers of Guadalajara who had taken over the main plaza there in August of 1993, heard echoes of their complaints in protests that broke out in various other localities at that time. Affiliated mostly in name with the growers calling themselves the "Barzón" in Jalisco, the protesters in Fresnillo emphasized to farmers that they were not alone in their problems. North of them in Chihuahua, grain farmers with the Confederation of

---

[9] Public investment in agriculture declined 80 percent in real terms from 1980 to 1989. Subsidies went from between 2 and 3 percent of the gross domestic product in 1982–6, to less than 0.07 percent in 1991 (Cruz Hernández 1994, unpublished paper).

[10] The Barzón protest, in fact, was not the first sign of restiveness among landed farmers. A sign of growing discontent with the PRI's declining appeal among farmers appeared when organizers from the leftist campesino organization, the UNORCA (National Union of Regional Campesino Organizations), managed to gain a majority in the administration of one of the state's most powerful ejido unions. The Unión de Ejidos Guillermo Aguilera, which represents several thousand farmers in the vicinity of Fresnillo, elected a leadership slate from the UNORCA-affiliated group Alianza Campesina in 1989. The group encountered stiff resistance from state authorities, and PRI forces regained control of the ejido union in the next elections.

Chihuahua Campesinos (CCC) blocked international bridges to protest grain imports and falling prices. West of them in Colima and coastal Michoacán, produce and grain farmers warned that they would form Barzón chapters if something were not done to address rising debt loads. South of them in Guanajuato, dairy farmers spilled containers of milk into the streets to emphasize the falling value of their product. Further south still, the Democratic Union of Campesinos marched on Mexico City and occupied the central plaza of Mexico City (the *Zócalo*), demanding subsidies, tax relief, and a solution to farm debt.

The Barzón in Zacatecas carried on their local protest against state authorities in a circuitous battle against what they recognized was a set of national problems. After three weeks, the occupation had spilled over into the offices of the Rural Bank, and no agreements had been reached. Attempting to escalate their action further, the Barzonistas began marching toward the highway in an effort to block motor passage from Fresnillo to the state capital. The action provoked a confrontation with the state judicial police, in which substantial threats were lobbed toward the protestors.[11] The police, however, took no one into custody, despite what could have been made into the legal equivalent of felony charges for blocking a federal highway.

Clearly, despite the state government's reluctance to deal with the protesters directly, there was also some apprehension about dissolving an extensive movement that included local elites through the use of force. Meanwhile, public and private firms that financed farmers quietly made deals with the Barzonistas to restructure individuals clients' loan-servicing schedules. The papers reported that the leaders of the Barzón had extracted verbal commitments from the BANRURAL, the Ford dealership, and Bancomer (a private bank) by the beginning of November, some 30 days after the farmers first occupied the Fresnillo plaza. It would appear that the Barzón was too visible to repress but, at the same time, too weak to prevail upon the government for direct and thorough conciliation.

Embarrassed and miffed by the protest, party officials worked quickly to make it clear that it would be the PRI, and not the Barzón organization, who would make debt restructuring possible for farmers in the middle municipalities. Public money for bailouts appeared where none had been before. Farmers on ejidos or in organizations that had remained loyal to

[11] This is a claim that is difficult either to corroborate or disprove. One of the movement leaders filed a formal complaint to the National Human Rights Commission about police abuses during a march on October 20 (*Imagen de Zacatecas* 1993e).

the party were rewarded with what the Barzonistas had demanded; the disloyal Barzonistas, meanwhile, were granted only more inconclusive meetings with mid-level bureaucrats. The same day that Barzón leaders announced pending negotiations with banks and government agencies, PRI officials announced that twelve hundred farmers affiliated with the ruling party-affiliated Guillermo Aguilera Ejido Union, the State Federation of Small Private Farmers, and the Federation of Agrarian Settlements would be eligible for a restructuring plan that would enable debtors from those organizations to reschedule their debt service with the government-owned Rural Bank (*Imagen de Zacatecas* 1993b).

Despite the course of events, the Barzón protest actually expanded rather than weakened. Daily, the government and the Barzonistas tenuously tested the limits of the other's resolve, sending simultaneous messages of willingness to deal with the other and of willingness to sever negotiations. On the one hand, the Barzónistas accepted the invitation of the government to join the "Concertation Table," a forum in which various farm groups (in this case, all organized by the ruling party) were supposed to have access to channels of agricultural administration. On the other hand, the Barzón leaders announced that they would not leave the plaza until they got written and binding agreements on farmers' debts. The PRI also sent mixed messages, calling the Barzón's demands just, on the one hand, and then expelling the Barzón representatives from the Concertation Table for comments that showed "lack of respect" for the government (*Imagen de Zacatecas* 1993h).

A cycle was established: one side or the other would win a small moral victory but then might misjudge the power of its opponent to counter its moves effectively. For example, in November, the government expelled the Barzón from negotiations, only to have farmers grow angrier and more numerous in the protest.[12] The Barzón leaders, emboldened, marched on the capital city, only to find their entrance to the city blocked by taxi drivers (*Imagen de Zacatecas* 1993f). The retreat appeared to be a popular rebuff to the organization until it was leaked that the taxi drivers had been "encouraged" by the PRI-controlled union to use their powers to block the protest, and also were paid 100 pesos and given a free tank of gas for their loyalty. As national newspapers began to pick up on the payoff scandal, an indignant Barzón was permitted to march on Zacatecas, with no taxis blocking their way, parking their tractors in the plaza in front of the governor's office.

---

[12] The occupation was, on average, six hundred farmers at a time (*Imagen de Zacatecas* 1993d).

After closed-door meetings with the governor's second-in-command, José Zúñiga, the Barzonistas conceded in moving their occupation from the central plaza to the law school in exchange for the governor's word that he would, in fact, address the farmers' demands seriously.

The Barzón protest, for the moment, had reached something of an impasse. It had gained some new bargaining power through a convergence of grievances among large and small landholders but still floundered as a movement capable of representing collective demands effectively. Similar to fishermen's and campesinos' protests in Lázaro Cárdenas after privatization, farm debtors' demands fell in uncharted institutional territory where governmental jurisdictions were vague, and where agreements reached with governmental brokers were dubiously enforceable.

On the one hand, the Barzón had chipped away at the veneer of invulnerability of the ruling party, radicalizing several hundred market farmers, making a credible claim to have the tacit support of several thousand more, and demonstrating that it could garner sympathy among journalists and townspeople. On the other hand, the state government had maintained loyalty among key cells of farmers in the middle municipalities, notably among the ejido unions. The windfall Procampo subsidy program, combined with the commitments extracted from the government Rural bank, insulated the government from a more extensive mobilization. Despite the fact that it could not reverse certain fundamental threats to farm production presented by market reforms on a national basis, the state had managed to come up with short-term solutions for landed farmers, thereby revitalizing for a time its image as a good steward of agricultural production.

As winter set in, the Barzón occupation continued, but the movement's momentum slowed. Those farmers in immediate danger of repossession were already in the protest; other farmers were in a position to wait until spring to find out what funding they could get for May planting. The Procampo program, some felt, would cover a portion of their expenses in the springtime. Protest, some undoubtedly felt, might well jeopardize their accounts in the program. At any rate, the Barzón occupation lingered but did not grow in Zacatecas.

Protest and Narratives of Justice

A less clear-cut, nonetheless important, component of opportunity lay in the way President Salinas's market project interacted with historical-legal notions of farming and finance in Zacatecas. The Barzón movement that swept farmers into city centers with virtually no prior organization unquestionably touched upon a widespread belief that the government, the banks, and/or the official party had violated a covenant of sorts. Despite the fact that farmers claimed that corruption and graft were present in the system for as long as anyone could remember, the credit crisis of the early 1990s brought these individuals out in a different fashion than ever before.

Although difficult to measure or test, it is quite possible that the Zacatecas Barzón was able to unify large and small farmers in protest in a way that would not have been possible in other regions of Mexico that have been characterized by chronic confrontation between large and small farmers, private and ejidal farmers, or Spanish-speaking Mestizos and Indian communities. One may also hypothesize that a particular mode of land distribution and property management inscribed in Zacatecan law and practice in the 1920s following the Revolution conditioned farmers' expectations of banks and government in particular ways.

The model of ejidal farming in Zacatecas is quite different from ejidal farming in the south, where settled agriculture pre-dates the conquest. Zacatecas matches more closely a U.S. model of settlement, in which indigenous residents of the land were expelled from lands and forced into labor in colonial silver mines, while mestizo settlers occupied lands granted by the crown. While official census figures on land tenure list property according to basic categories – private versus community-held land – one prominent form of land occupation in Zacatecas is the rural *fraccionamiento*, distinguishable from either the rural community (*communidad*) or the ejido. Established as a legal category in the original Article 27 of the 1917 constitution[13] and promoted by revolutionary-era governor General Enrique Estrada, a liberal who opposed the ejido system and sought to create a system of independent capitalist growers, the fraccionamiento is actually a hybrid between public and private land (Arteaga Domínguez 1993).

The five municipalities with the greatest numbers of fraccionistas are also five early strongholds of the Barzón movement. Interestingly, many of the reformist demands made by the Barzón movement echo notions

---

[13] Interestingly, the reforms to Article 27 left intact several key components of the fraccionamiento, including the definition of family patrimony, which preserved the inalienable character of the land. De facto, many fraccionamiento lands previously were locked in property struggles because the cost of transferring them, though it could be done, was expensive. Fathers often passed land on to sons or relatives, or even outside buyers, by oral contract.

about property and the role of the state contained in the fraccionamiento laws. For example, the fraccionamiento law required that land grantees pay for their land, but guaranteed buyers mortgages of no less than twenty years, with annual interest rates not exceeding 5 percent. In a parallel fashion, the Barzón movement called not for direct distribution of goods to alleviate the farm crisis, but instead for guarantees of long-term loans, with fixed limits on the amount of interest that banks could charge clients. In the fraccionamiento system, lands could be sold or rented by their owners but, at the same time, could not be regarded by banks as collateral. Likewise, the Barzón movement in 1995 called for immunity of productive goods or family necessities from the threat of repossession by banks or loan sharks. Goods that the Barzonistas felt should be inalienable included land, tractors, and homes, as well as household items such as stoves, refrigerators, and pots and pans.

The fraccionamiento system called for the government to set limits on maximum size of land holdings. If large landowners refused to cede to state land reform initiatives, lands were to be expropriated. The Barzón also called for the state to intervene in the economy in order to limit excessive accumulation of capital, create jobs, and promote greater economic equality.

Finally, the Zacatecan state constitution mandated that municipalities enact local laws to establish principles of "family patrimony" (*patrimonio de familia*). These were to limit the reach of the market to a sphere outside basic household and farm goods. That is, a bad or unlucky farmer might lose luxury goods, cash, a bank account, or a cow, according to the law, but not that which allowed him to provide for his family. Again, Barzonista ideas echo the fraccionamiento code. The Barzón justified many of their demands and local vigilante actions in the assertion that they were acting to defend something called the *family patrimony*. Broadly conceived, the contemporary notion of *patrimonio familiar* is that which supports one's family, and, eventually, that which is one's children to inherit for the support of their own families. It often refers to family land, a house, and perhaps one's rights to a water source. For the wealthier, a university education afforded by one's parents, or a shop or business, would also be called one's family patrimony. The premise, of course, is that such things are not readily traded or sold by the owners – as much as they provide necessities for the holder – they also may act as a raison d'etre of sorts. Typically, such a notion stems from traditional expectations that trades would be passed down through the generations.

Renewal: Debtors and the Electoral Season of 1994

The Zacatecas Barzón came to a dangerous standstill in December of 1993. Manuel Ortega, the movement's state leader, and others describe the time occupying the law school as a bleak episode in the movement's course. Leaders later commented that their it was a mistake to have agreed to transfer their occupation to the law school from the center of the city. The strategy of focusing almost exclusively on formal debt in December of 1993 may in fact had reached certain limits by that point. The movement needed either a reformist message that stirred a wider constituency or a more spectacular record of victories on behalf of its members.

The Barzón might have faded away in the winter of 1993 had it not been for a combination of recruitment innovations by leaders as well as a set of events that reopened the field of political opportunity. In the same manner that the Procampo program had arrived from Mexico City as a political windfall for the state government, the Chiapas uprising on New Year's Day 1994 gave the Barzón a tremendous opening to renew actions and to amplify the combativeness of its rhetoric. As an armed guerrilla movement took over San Cristóbal de las Casas eight hundred miles away, the Barzón utilized the wave of public sympathy for the Zapatistas to move further forward in their own distributive campaign.

In the days after the initial Zapatista offensive, wild rumors circulated of impending insurrections in Michoacán, Puebla, Oaxaca, Zacatecas, and Mexico City. The Barzón, with its impudent but peaceful occupations, looked moderate by comparison with what was feared might exist in the poverty-wracked mountain- or canyonlands. El Barzón leaders seized the moment, escalating the stakes of their confrontation by declaring their sympathy for the movement in Chiapas and pointing out that their protest paralleled the Zapatistas' anti-free-market campaign. The Barzonistas were prominent participants in spontaneous protests of students and opposition-party members that occurred in the capital city.

The Barzón, in early 1994, began expanding the scope of the organizations by decrying not just debt, but now a set of municipal-level conflicts with the government buying agency, CONASUPO. While one flank of the organization stayed in the occupation in Zacatecas, 100 growers in the north-central municipality of Juan Aldama took over the municipal government offices, complaining that CONASUPO had refused to buy many growers' bean crops there, as well as in Miguel Auza, Río Grande, and Francisco R. Murguía because of stains on the beans caused by late rains the previous harvest season. Eight days after the Chiapas uprising, the Barzonistas were barging into the CONASUPO offices yelling "The north will boil!" and "They want what happened in Chiapas to happen here!" (*Imagen de Zacatecas* 1994c). Farmers declared to the press that they would plant their acreage with corn and beans and send a portion to the Zapatista army instead of to the government buying agencies (Interview with Juan Figueroa, 1995).

The Barzón also began to address the issue of loan sharking in a more serious fashion, an act that later would delimit its class constituency in Zacatecas in an important manner.[14] The choice to press the government to annul contracts between debtors and loan sharks, in fact, represented a decision to include farmers in a mid-to-low income bracket in the movement. This also meant alienating rather than enlisting the help of informal moneylenders in the movement, individuals who were often, in fact, wealthy farmers who borrowed from the commercial banks for bogus projects and then lent out the capital in minimal sums at exorbitant rates to small farmers. Presumably, the Barzón, as an organization that defended debtors, might have attracted loan sharks who had speculated unsuccessfully on small bean farmers' enterprises and then couldn't pay back steep commercial interest rates.

A final boost to the Barzón movement came in the planting season of 1994 when Procampo checks were due to arrive. Farmers who had anticipated the reestablishment of subsidies that supported their production schedule found that no money would arrive to help fund inputs and seed purchases in April and May. When still no Procampo funds had arrived for most farmers by the middle of June, aggressive protests broke out in various parts of the state. Normally quiescent Labor Party affiliates occupied government buildings in the canyonlands of Noria de San Juan.[15] Farmers from various ejidos invaded municipal presidents' offices in Río Grande, Nieves, Juan Aldama, Miguel Auza, Saín Alto, and Sombrerete. Angry farmers lined the route of Secretary of Agriculture Hank González

---

[14] The first mention of demands with respect to the practice of loan sharking is in February 1994, when the Barzón leaders claimed that 715 of their members had problems with loan sharks (*Imagen de Zacatecas* 1994d). The Barzón also occupied the central plaza in the western farm town of Sombrerete, denouncing the "conspiracy" that existed between loan sharks and judges (who presumably ruled on repossession schedules and amounts) (*Imagen de Zacatecas* 1994j).

[15] *Imagen de Zacatecas* (1994g) reported that a group of farmers affiliated with the Frente Popular de Lucha Zacatecano (an arm of the PT, or Labor Party) occupied government buildings demanding free seed and Procampo checks.

172

when he visited the state in mid-July, denouncing the program as a bid to control votes in the upcoming elections (*Imagen de Zacatecas* 1994a). In August, 250 farmers took over Ministry of Agriculture offices in Río Grande and Sombrerete, while nine farmers simultaneously began a hunger strike in the government offices of Guadalupe, a city adjoining Zacatecas (*Imagen de Zacatecas* 1994e).

The same Procampo program whose announcement had served the government so well in quieting restive farmers a few months earlier had become a political minefield for the government. As one of the only sources of early-season liquidity left for small and large farmers, discontent over the Procampo program was ubiquitous. Everybody who had land and who farmed basic grains in Zacatecas had at least one demand in common: *Procampo funds now*. The Barzón, as one of the few organized bodies outside the official party, was able to capture protest and recruit new participants by championing farmers' demands for the Procampo subsidies.

When conceived the fall before, the Procampo program had worked ideally within the rubric of a market-oriented program, relieving rising political pressure from farmers angry over rising grain imports and falling subsidies without offending overseas agribusiness at a crucial negotiating period for the North American Free Trade Agreement (NAFTA). As a compensatory program[16] for grain producers who were not projected to continue operating in great numbers for much longer, the program created a liability for the ruling party once in practice. Growers, unaware that they were supposed to use the money to phase themselves *out* of basic grain farming, interpreted the nonappearance of cash subsidies as a betrayal of the government's constitutional obligation to food production in the countryside.

Meanwhile, the state PRI was trying to administer Procampo funds in the same way that they had administered a more segmented fiscal budget before, conditioning the distribution of funds in the municipalities on

---

[16] The Procampo program was an example of what is known in General Agreement on Tariffs and Trade (GATT) circles as a "green" subsidy, as opposed to a "red" or "yellow" subsidy. The colors are a metaphor referring to a stoplight, with red and yellow subsidies being, respectively, unacceptable and borderline-unacceptable policies with respect to international trade agreements. Examples are price guarantees, or subsidies on seeds or inputs. Generally, such subsidies directly affect market prices and therefore affect imports negatively. Green subsidies, on the other hand, are subsidies which do not directly affect market prices. Instead, these support consumption. Pensions, food coupons, cash payments, insurance, or services are examples of green subsidies.

votes for PRI candidates. Ironically, they found instead that it was harder to manipulate votes discreetly with cash payments that were to be administered directly to growers. Although farmers may be very aware that, with heterogeneous local production programs, some communities receive more resources than others, the differences are often difficult to quantify. With flat payments per hectare of land due to be paid to farmers on a yearly basis, officials could not come up with plausible explanations for why some communities got payments and others did not. In an environment in which at least the language of multiparty pluralism was starting to take hold, blatant conditioning of cash for votes marred ruling party-linked officials' reputations.

The Growth of a Multisectoral Organization

What form the Barzón movement would take as a social movement organization was unclear for some months. Signals from leaders were mixed. In a meeting of Barzonista leaders from the Bajío states of the middle-northwest in February 1994, leaders announced to the press that Barzonistas would not vote for the PRI, and confirmed that they intended to form themselves into an "authentic agricultural party" (Hernández and Amador 1994). Several days before the meeting, however, it looked as if the organization would go in an entirely different direction. Manuel Ortega and Alfonso Ramírez Cuellar formally invited businessmen to join the movement, declaring that economic crisis was affecting not only agriculture but also small businessmen and consumers who utilized commercial credit (*Imagen de Zacatecas* 1994h).

As would become clear in the fall of 1994, when the Barzón leaders in Zacatecas and Jalisco would publicly break with one another, that substantial disagreement was surfacing as to what actions the Barzón would engage in, and who would be included in the Barzón organizations. There was the option of solidifying a single organization of Barzonistas, encompassing more diffuse local efforts of the same name (in most cases, just a few organizers hoping to form coherent movements of the rising number of indebted farmers in their states) in Guanajuato, Chiahuahua, Colima, Hidalgo, Nuevo León, San Luis Potosí, Durango, Sinalóa, and Michoacán. However, mistrust between Maximiano Barbosa in Jalisco and the three Zacatecas leaders probably stood as a primary obstacle preventing any serious moves toward centralized organization.

When Barbosa – a longtime member of the PRI – declared that the Barzón might become an agricultural party, he was essentially making a public threat to defect from the official party if farmers' demands were not met. When Juan José Quirino, Manuel Ortega, and Alfonso Ramírez-Cuellar – all six-year veterans of the PRD – made the same declaration, they were essentially making a public threat to incorporate the Barzón in the already organized opposition force represented by Cardenas' party. Barbosa was advocating an organization that fell closer to traditional lines of corporatist political structure. The Zacatecas trio was advocating an organization that worked in tandem with the enemies of the official party, including independent labor, business, and neighborhood movements. Barbosa's vision for the movement was an aggressive but focused farmers-only lobby that could negotiate with federal agencies for more favorable production conditions inside a free market system. The Zacatecan trio's vision for the movement was a broad front of producers and citizens that would work to defeat the official party and the neoliberal paradigm themselves.

After the spring meeting, the leaders' divergent intentions became clear in their respective state campaigns. Maximiano Barbosa accepted a candidacy for the official party in Jalisco, while Manuel Ortega became a PRD candidate for Federal Deputy,[17] and Alfonso Ramírez Cuellar became a PRD candidate for the national Senate in Zacatecas.

Ironically, all the leaders lost in their respective state elections. In addition to two state leaderships' antagonism toward one another, there was a deep disillusion all around with political parties as vehicles for the Barzón movements. However, the latter bad feeling did not cancel out the former, and recriminations of leader against leader began shortly after the elections. Each set of leaders sought to paint themselves as independent and the others as puppets of a political party. Just prior to an interstate meeting of Barzonistas, Barbosa declared that he would expel the Zacatecas leadership from national assemblies for "having proselytized in favor of the PRD" (*La Jornada* 1994). At the meeting itself, Juan José Quirino announced that he would break with the Jalisco group and form a separate interstate faction because Barbosa had made deals with the PRI (*La Jornada* 1994).

---

[17] A member of the Cámara de Diputados, something akin to a congressman in the U.S. House of Representatives.

The Zacatecas leaders' strategy of broad front politics continued after the elections. The Barzón began in earnest to recruit businesspeople in urban areas who were facing bankruptcy. The first sizable urban contingent of the organization, 175 fruit and vegetable sellers in the Jeréz city market, joined the organization in mid-July, a month before the elections. In addition to debts from high interest rates, various vendors later interviewed reported that they were furious with the PRI, claiming that they had long been bullied by corrupt officials. As very small entrepreneurs without elite representatives in governing circles, they were easily bilked, they said, for protection money by roving functionaries and policemen.

Notably, the areas where the Barzón had enjoyed the greatest sympathy were in urban areas in which agribusiness and retail industries monopolized commerce. Despite the fact that the Barzón began as an organization geared toward gaining a selective settlement for members, participants in the group's first urban occupation recall that residents of Fresnillo, and small businessmen in particular, were sympathetic to the Barzonistas. The protesters in the central square were customers of businesses (many of them farm-linked), so financial relief for farmers may well have been judged by residents to be worth the inconvenience of noise, blocked streets, and heavy police presence in the center of the city.

Conversely, when the Barzón moved to the capital city of Zacatecas, it had encountered considerable opposition from the citizenry. There, in addition to agriculture-related activities, people drew incomes from the tourist industry and the government. Students and shopkeepers in the capital city reported in interviews that they were initially upset about the Barzón occupation and were incensed at their actions. "I didn't know who these people were, or why they were blocking the banks. . . . I was mainly mad that I couldn't use the bank on the days when they did their protests," commented a student whose parent is an attorney for the state government. Others complained about the traffic and parking problems caused by the protest. In the case of Zacatecas (city), residents were likely to see the Barzón protest as a zero-sum situation. Their fortunes were not so directly tied to agriculture; furthermore, if the Barzón maintained an unsightly protest in the middle of the city, people who drew tourist dollars might well lose income.

The degree to which urban residents were linked to the farm economy explains some, but not all, of the fault lines that existed. If all the citizens whose livelihoods came from agriculture in the state's central valleys had joined the protests, certainly the Barzón would have enjoyed support from agroindustrialists, including seed and fertilizer suppliers, and truck drivers who also depended on income from the farm sector. However, it appears that it was not until after the devaluation crisis of 1994 that the Barzón drew any support from these sectors.

From Farm to City, State to Nation: The Barzón and the Error de diciembre

The Barzon's power to expand its constituency undoubtedly would have remained considerably more limited if interest rates and economic growth had remained stable. However, a disastrous series of events catapulted Mexico into what is now known simply as "The Crisis."[18] A set of government adjustments meant to ease pressure on an overvalued peso set off a financial panic, and the currency fell by over 50 percent in a matter of weeks. As investors fled the nation's financial markets, commerce and industry suffered from the sudden dearth of capital. Floating interest rates on consumer loans, already high, soared to three times their previous rate. Imported goods doubled in price, and national consumer buying power dropped by nearly 40 percent.

The problems that the crisis caused for urban lower and middle classes were very similar to those already existing for grain farmers. For industrialists and businessmen, the crisis was a problem of rising factor costs (credit and inputs) and falling sales.[19] For people on salary or wage, the crisis' greatest threat was unemployment: two million workers lost their jobs in the first eight months of 1995. For those lucky enough to keep

[18] Many citizens are not familiar with the precise set of events that set off the depression of 1995. Substantial numbers of people, for example, would not recognize the terms *currency devaluation* or *capital flight*. Most place the beginning of the economic crisis sometime in 1995, rather than in December 1994, because most began to feel the effects of the devaluation only two or three months after the devaluation, when prices in central Mexico began to rise in earnest.

[19] Specifically, the problem of falling sales applied to businessmen in industries geared to domestic markets, or to people employed in services and nontradeables. Exporters stood to benefit from a devalued peso only if they did not use high proportions of imported primary materials. Few businesses actually were non-import-dependent. At the beginning of the devaluation crisis, for example, a business survey showed that some 83 percent of manufacturing firms in Mexico used imported goods in production processes (Gutiérrez 1995). Exports rose in the year after the peso devaluation, and a relatively small number of firms took in the profits from these sales. In July of 1994, the *Financiero* reported that in the first six months of the North American Free Trade Agreement (NAFTA), the national total of $2.57 billion in profits went to 252 firms producing about twenty-five products (Domville 1994).

their positions, incomes largely stayed the same while prices on basic consumer goods skyrocketed. By 1995, the crisis had uniformly constricted the net income of workers, small businessmen, and farmers. The Zacatecas Barzón, having already extended its membership from agriculturalists to debtors, now had an issue that spoke to vast numbers of people. For millions of people in the wake of the currency crash, interest on their debts would accumulate faster than they would be able to pay them off.

In hindsight, it is clear that the Barzón movement was in the right place at the right time: mobilizing debtors at the outset of an unforeseen national crisis of massive proportions. However, as I will argue in the next chapter, it would be a mistake to attribute the emergence of the Barzón as a national force simply to the existence of a severe economic crisis. Such post facto analysis could not answer a number of important questions, such as how the Barzón movement in particular moved to the forefront of opposition politics in 1995 and after, or how the movement managed to transform its image from a group of farmers who did not want to pay the banks to a front of citizens fighting to save Mexico from graft and corruption. It is tempting to attribute the Zacatecas Barzón's lightning-fast success in expanding to other parts of the country to structural factors alone. And yet, expanding from one locality to another, and one sector to another, the Barzón was actually a new and uncertain thing. It was not a clear successor to corporatist collectivities (peasants, workers, business, popular sectors) etched by the constitution and the ruling party in the early part of the century. The notion of a diffuse national community of people identifying themselves as "debtors" was not without its problems as a recruiting device, evoking images of mismanagement, personal irresponsibility, or, even worse, inability to take care of one's family. In addition, Mexico had produced few widespread movements of people using fiscal or financial categories (e.g., taxpayers, home-owners, or consumers) to identify themselves as a group and simultaneously link themselves to a cause.[20]

The following chapter will extend the discussion of the Barzón movement begun here, demonstrating how the Barzón expanded its membership in Zacatecas and beyond and, in the process, how it created new spaces for its opposition campaign.

---

[20] Since the 1988 campaign, a number of these types of identities have begun to emerge. The most prominent example is the Alianza Cívica, a group committed to clean elections. In that case, novel collective identifiers are those of "voters" and "citizens."

6

The Barzón Movement: From a Farmers' to a Debtors' Insurgency

The Barzón movements that staggered out of the fractious September 1994 meeting faced uncertain prospects. The Zacatecas Barzón, despite its claim to represent the organizing hub of ten state chapters of the Barzón movement, had ample problems just managing its own affairs in Zacatecas. A rented second-floor office in the capital city with one spare desk and filing cabinet constituted the "state headquarters" of the Barzón; no central list of members had been compiled in Zacatecas, let alone all of Mexico; no routine method of collecting revenue or information had been devised. Actions, commented a lawyer who did work for the group, were done *ad hoc*. "We just decide to do something and then we go do it . . . ," he said (Interview with Juan Hernández 1995). The Barzón movement, in fact, was still a loose confederation of farmers' groups mobilizing around debt. Leaders led successful day-to-day campaigns of protests, meetings, visits to journalists, and popular actions by knowing first-hand who was around to participate and what their stakes in the protests were.

The Barzonistas were hard pressed at times to find resources for large actions. The high-profile marches and long occupations that brought the movement new recruits and valuable press coverage depleted the members' scarce cash resources. Demonstrations were relatively expensive for participants, requiring farmers to pay their passages to town and to buy food for the days and weeks in which they had to remain in demonstrations or occupations. For farmers who drove their tractors into town for protests, the price of gasoline was also a considerable expense. In addition, protest also carried at least a perceived risk of high future cost: farmers demonstrating with the Barzón voiced fears that they might be legally harassed or excluded from government

TREGUA ■ Helguera

Deferral Agreement, **by Helguera** Guillermo Ortiz, Secretary of the Treasury, cowers behind a thuggish bank and explains the government's debt relief program to a bank customer, "You pay until the year 2035; we cut public spending until the year 2000, and the bank here promises not to repossess your property from now until January." From *La Jornada*, August 25, 1995. Reprinted by permission.

programs,[1] or that they might even face violence at the hand of thugs or police.

The Barzón movement was developing its insurgency in a narrow corridor of opportunity. Despite some factors – discussed in Chapter 5 – that made farmers and merchants more likely to join forces with the Barzón organization, there were other factors that stood as powerful disincentives to participate with the Barzón. These included perceived risk of repres-

---

[1] Recalling anecdotes of machine-politics in U.S. cities, informants report that the officials who wished to single out troublemakers for harassment might, as an example, direct bureaucratic authorities to "misplace" an individual's loan application or entitlement documents, thereby delaying disbursement of funds and so forth indefinitely.

sion, as well as a traditional reluctance of the middle class to participate in aggressive public protest.[2] Maintaining the movement and dodging reprisals from the government were constant challenges. As in the case of Local 271, the Barzón movement drew on solidary support from sympathetic individuals and groups. Barzón chapters made deals with political parties to supplement visibility and/or to gain friends in government. They also deployed visible actions in order to gain sympathy among onlookers, and they developed decentralized and fairly democratic practices inside the organization. Different from Local 271, however, there was heavier emphasis in the Barzón movement on gaining external audiences and influencing general public opinion, and less emphasis on pooling demands and resources with other farm organizations. The remainder of this chapter will chronicle the strategies employed by members of the Barzón movement in their attempt to win political fights with the government and the private banking sector, to evade repression, and to expand the movement.

As has been noted thus far, leaders of the Barzón movement began to address certain initial weaknesses in the movement by broadening its issues and making its protest activity less erratic. Recruiting urban merchants and consumer debtors was one measure that made year-round protest easier. When supported only by farmers, the movement had been constrained by the annual agricultural cycle. Despite debt loads, most farmers had continued to farm at least a portion of their lands in hopes that the government might raise prices at harvest time. Therefore, at planting or harvesting time, farmers were unable to come to town for protests. The types of aggressive protest that had produced limited collective negotiating power for the organization generally took place just before planting when farmers needed loans and subsidies, and just before and after harvest, when loans came due.

In addition to agitating over Procampo checks and commodity-purchase disputes in the northern part of the state, the Zacatecas Barzón led regional protests against California's Proposition 187. As Barzonistas burned a monkey-effigy of Pete Wilson in the streets of the state capital, Juan José Quirino submitted a petition with twelve thousand signatures to the local branch of the Ministry of Foreign Relations condemning the proposition (*Imagen de Zacatecas* 1994b, 1994e). The protest served a double purpose. First, it generated sympathy among the vast numbers of

---

[2] The exceptions to this tendency are middle-class university students. Since 1968, marking the massacre of several hundred college students at Tlatelolco in Mexico City, numerous student movements have arisen over various political issues.

seasonal migrants in Zacatecas, a state with one of the nation's highest per capita out-migration rates to the United States; second, it framed the Barzón's fight as anti-imperialist and patriotic – less a battle waged by individual debtors trying to save their own skins than a crusade of citizens concerned with the well-being of the country as a whole.

Developing a "Culture of Barzón-ing"

The challenge facing the Barzón movement was making perennial protest worthwhile for participants. Through trial and error, ad hoc actions gave way to routinized systems of communication, mobilization, and revenue collection. The Barzón developed a three-pronged approach to protecting members. First, it engaged in collective civil resistance to police and the banks; second, it provided movement participants with personal legal assistance; and, third, it offered Barzón members professional advice on how to structure their businesses or farms to avoid further indebtedness.

By late 1994, it became more apparent that the Barzón's agitation was creating a certain breathing space for indebted farmers, gaining them restructuring terms with banks and/or a reprieve from property repossession. The Barzón's protests, along with protests by a number of other farm movements in other states over the issue of farm debt, prompted authorities in Mexico City to take some actions to conciliate farmers. The government presented farmers with two restructuring programs within a year of one another, called the System for Debt Restructuring I and II (known also by their acronym, the SIRECA). However, the Barzón's principal demands – namely debt pardon and reinstitution of subsidies – went largely unfulfilled.

As it happened, the lack of cash in many debtors' households served the Barzón movement in a number of ways. If, for example, an individual facing imminent repossession went to a local Barzón coordinator for help, he or she was recruited to become a member of the organization and, subsequently, was assisted by the movement through some combination of popular action and legal measures. Once helped out by the organization, the recruit – still having no cash to pay the Barzón's lawyers or the two dozen or so farmers who blocked police and other authorities attempting to repossess the recruit's property – was compelled to participate in other actions protecting others' property. The recruit, if he or she had something the organization needed, was also encouraged to pay in kind for the protection offered by the Barzón. In this way, the Barzón got small items such as typewriters and office supplies, as well as expensive items, such as office space and even an old school bus that was used to carry farmers to Zacatecas for protests. Many of motley items that the Barzonistas utilized to bring off protests and manage the organization were items that the banks claimed were, in fact, theirs.

There was also the issue of recruits' needs for ongoing protection from the bank. Because the Barzón's campaign of civil resistance only kept the banks at bay, but did not *solve* members' problems of falling income and compounding debt, members needed to establish their loyalty to the organization by participating fairly regularly should the day come when the police might arrive for his or her things again. Recruits' houses, farms, tractors, and storefronts were often spray-painted with big green lettering, declaring, "This property is now the Barzón's."

Generally, local leaders asked new recruits for a nominal membership fee (about ten pesos, or the equivalent of between two and three dollars), plus monthly dues. The lawyers who worked with the Barzón usually asked those who could pay some fee for the services to do so, although lawyers who worked for the organization earned little and were undoubtedly doing the work for ideological reasons (Interviews with Juan Hernández 1995, David Lugo Camacho 1995). However, because cash was so scarce, the organization often overlooked dues. Much of the cash the organization could collect came from the wealthiest members, usually ranchers or businessmen who still had assets and income, but who owed the banks substantial sums of money.

Very small-scale actions often proved successful when dealing with the informal[3] debt of the Barzón's poorer or more isolated rural members. A lawyer, an organizer, and a debtor might pay a visit to the offices of the loan shark's "lawyer." In rural areas, those lawyers were often shady characters with hand-lettered diplomas, whose offices usually consisted of a bare metal desk set in a room with no books in sight. Their authority emanated not so much from their courtroom skills, but instead from their

---

[3] By some definitions, "informal" refers to those transactions, services, markets, or institutions that do not rely on the legal system for enforcement (Mansell 1995, unpublished manuscript: Chapter 2). In Zacatecas, however, where it is estimated that about half of all loans are made through what is known as *agio*, or private lending, the courts and the police play a role in enforcing claims on informal loans. Mansell writes of this phenomenon in Mexico: "Moneylenders may extend a loan documented by a fully legal and enforceable letter of credit; yet moneylending *per se* is illegal. . . . The protection of the law is not a black or white, yes or no matter . . . the enforceability of a given contract . . . may be a straightforward matter for one individual, and not, in practice, for others."

prominent ties to the feared Judicial Police. Such lawyers, who often were only nominally better educated than the peasants or poor urban dwellers they were charged with pursuing, were easily intimidated when challenged by a Mexico City-educated lawyer, who would demand to see the aggrieved client's papers and summonses. As contracts between loan sharks and clients were most often oral and of dubious legality, the papers documenting the loan were often non-existent, or contained many irregularities. The loan shark's lawyer was then likely to come up with a solution for the client, or to forgive the loan altogether.

An additional means of harnessing material resources and new recruits for the Barzón movement in Zacatecas was through a "technical team," a group of radicalized extension experts who offered their services to Barzón members. Several agronomists and an agricultural economist joined forces in a small company to assist members in devising new production plans, cutting unit costs, and finding ways where possible to convert from corn and beans to higher value crops (Interview with Efrén Bañuelos 1995). The extension officers usually worked on some sort of minimal commission, and most often drew up the proposals that would accompany legal proceedings of individual debtors fighting bank repossessions. The agronomists then often accompanied Barzón members to bank meetings in an attempt to convince the banks that their clients realistically might be able to repay their loans if production adjustments were made in their farm operations. The banks, which were eager to recover at least part of past-due loans, often agreed to restructure the clients' loans.

Allies

Leaders of the Barzón in Zacatecas had received assistance from various individuals and groups at intervals. Besides groups directly organized by the leftist PRD, a number of other groups lent their support to Barzón protests by donating food or blankets to occupations, attending rallies and demonstrations, and also by denouncing intermittent police harassment and arbitrary arrests of movement members. Among workers' groups, the Barzón got support from the local university union (known by its acronym, the STUAZ) and a leftist faction in the teachers' union (the Magisterio Democrático de México). The Barzón was also assisted by two civil movements, which served as watchdog groups on elections and human rights – the Civic Movement of Fresnillo and the Civic Alliance (Interview with

Jesus Vega 1995). In addition, the Barzón occasionally worked in conjunction with farm groups in other states that were also mobilizing around production and debt problems. The most prominent of these groups was the Confederation of Chihuahuan Campesinos, whose own fight over farm debt in fact pre-dated any of the Barzón demonstrations.

Important as these alliances were, however, they did not play as crucial a role in the Barzón movement as they had in the steel workers' insurgency in Lázaro Cárdenas. First, many fewer organized groups in Zacatecas were willing to publicly challenge the state and the ruling party than in the state of Michoacán, which was the cradle of the PRD, the home of its leader Cuauhtémoc Cárdenas, and the former home of Cárdenas's father, Lázaro. Second, the Barzón, by virtue of its nonofficial status, could simply make supporters into members, while a union such as Local 271 could not. Finally, leaders deliberately chose not to make binding pacts with other groups in many cases. In interviews, leaders said that, in fact, the organization explicitly resisted mergers with already organized groups because, they said, they feared that factionalism might then tear the movement apart (Interviews with Jesus Vega 1995 and Juan Figueroa 1995). Particularly after the unsuccessful PRD electoral campaigns of Manuel Ortega and Alfonso Ramírez Cuellar in the summer of 1994, the Zacatecas leaders conspicuously avoided close affiliation with already organized groups, wary that the Barzón movement would be labeled a puppet of some unknown outside force.[4]

Ultimately, the most important means for the Barzón to harness resources for protest was through mutualism inside its ranks rather than through alliances with other groups. Barzonistas exchanged participation in collective actions for protection and legal help provided by the organization, and this provided the movement an inexpensive and effective way to stay visible and sustain its confrontational stance.

---

[4] One notable exception to this practice of avoiding the absorption of whole organized groups was in the western municipality of Sombrerete, where a great many of the associates of the Sombrerete credit union had joined forces with the Barzón movement. They had done so, most say, at the urging of the president of the credit union, who himself was facing forcible closure of the credit union by federal banking authorities because of the level of past-due debt on the rolls. Of this case, however, one of the state-level organizers pointed out that the credit union members were unlikely to form a problematic faction, because, he said, the Barzón had "Barzónized their thinking." The idea, he explained, was that the credit union members – most of them with outstanding debts to the credit union itself – were logically more likely to be loyal to the Barzón over the credit union.

For all that worked well in the Barzón movement, however, the fact remained that large and small farmers, ejidatarios, wealthy ranchers, grain buyers, urban businessmen, and pushcart merchants were strange bedfellows. The Barzón movement in Zacatecas was fraught with dormant hostilities. First, the membership contained people who had once been blood enemies. One individual who had fought in the early 1970s with groups of landless peasants demanding subdivision of large ranches noted that the Barzón included both peasants who had won land in those fights as well as members of large landowners' vigilante groups who had attacked those peasants (Interview with Luis Medina 1995). Also, notably, the organization included small farmers as well as grain buyers, known as *acaparadores*, who in other circumstances were at bloody odds with one another over prices and the terms of grain sales.

There existed substantial room for disputes not only over demands, but also over the movement's course and strategies. Interviews conducted among Barzón members in the summer of 1995 indicate that there existed some difference of opinion among different socioeconomic groups in the movement regarding the types of functions the Barzón as an organization ought to assume in the long run. On most questions of short-term strategy, members agreed. Interview respondents indicated, for example, that the organization ought to continue in its actions protecting members from repossession, fighting in the courts against usury, providing technical advice to members, and forming coalitions to oppose the government's economic policies. Members indicated almost blanket opposition to permanent affiliation with any of the existing political parties. On the other hand, members held measurable differences of opinion about whether the Barzón movement ought to use significant portions of its time and resources lobbying political candidates and/or negotiating with the federal government. In casual conversation as well as local meetings, members often debated with one another over whether the movement ought to put up candidates for office or to form a new political party. People also disagreed over whether the Barzón movement ought to form collective production and marketing schemes in order to circumvent bad government management. The latter notion was most vocally championed by smaller farmers, the radicalized extension experts on the technical team, and the credit union members. They felt that if members of the movement pooled productive resources, they might be able to *bypass* government agencies and private banks in financing their farm enterprises.

Media

Although differences of opinion did in fact exist over what long-term strategies the Barzón ought to pursue, the movement did not weaken because of them in the period under study from 1993 to 1995. Under such severe financial and political constraints as existed at that time, neither binding negotiations with the federal government nor the establishment of production cooperatives was likely to occur. By and large, the movement's survival and expansion were fueled by mutualist protection schemes through which movement participants kept the state and the banks at bay.

As such, however, the movement was only a stopgap system – a collective measure taken to keep people going under in disastrous times. As much as its immediate effectiveness lay in its ability to fight *against* government agencies, banks, loan sharks, lawyers, and the police, the movement faced criticism that it was damaging the regional financial system without proposing a clear set of solutions to producers' long-term problems.[5] This was true in particular because one of the movement's key defenses against repression and mass arrests was the sympathy it had generated among observers, many of whom were not debtors, but were simply fed up with the government and/or the ruling party.

From the beginning, the Barzón movement spent considerable resources pursuing media attention. Particularly in the print media, where reporters were under less pressure to suppress coverage of opposition movements, the Barzón movement went after and received a good deal of sympathetic coverage. Leaders actively cultivated press coverage, notifying newspaper and radio reporters of demonstrations before they happened, holding press conferences, and inviting visiting journalists to speak with members or attend local meetings.[6] When reporters wrote articles

---

[5] This line of criticism has followed the Barzón throughout its existence. In Zacatecas, PRI official Cuauhtémoc Jaime Espinosa complained that the Barzón had caused serious damage to the farm finance system, noting that many of the private lenders were refusing to lend money to anyone for fear of the Barzón movement. This, he said, in a state where perhaps one-half of all loans came from private lenders, would effectively prevent people from getting credit because many of the private lenders' clients did not qualify for loans from banks (Interview with Espinosa Jaime in Zacatecas 1995). In another instance, *La Jornada* reported a comment from the head of the National Federation of Bank Unions, who said that banks ought not to negotiate with the Barzón because then "nothing definite would be arrived at" (Calderón Gómez 1995).

[6] My own experience, in fact, reflected this phenomenon as well. Upon arriving in Zacatecas and making a number of inquiries, I was immediately invited to the movement's headquarters in Zacatecas. Invariably, I was asked whether I was a journalist. When I said that

that were sympathetic to the movement, local organizers would clip the stories and post them. They would also photocopy stories and use them to recruit new members, as well as to brief visiting journalists on the movement and its goals.

Raising Consciousness, Raising Hell: Peaceful Spectacle and Direct Resistance

Different protest actions served different ends. Some provided direct relief for movement participants: occupations of boarded-up stores or houses afforded individuals immediate access to repossessed properties. The group visits to loan sharks freed debtors from immediate obligations to creditors. Other actions were meant to create sympathy among onlookers: mock funerals or bank occupations were meant to convince onlookers of the inhumanity and the irresponsibility of the government and the banks in allowing so many businesses and farms to fail. Some actions, such as popular repossessions, could easily serve both ends, if the media were properly involved, or if many onlookers were notified of the action in advance. One example of direct-relief action that also generated broad public sympathy for the Barzón was a very visible group defense of an impoverished widow in the city of Guadalupe whose only collateral on her past-due loans to a local loan shark were her refrigerator and her pots and pans.[7] Another such "dual-purpose" action was the forcible requisition of a car from a hospital parking lot. A middle-aged local family man had lost his leg in an accident and could not afford to pay for his medical care. Doctors had demanded his family's car in lieu of cash (Interview with Jesus Vega 1995). Protesters then repossessed the car publicly and dared authorities to arrest them for what they saw as an illegitimate confiscation by hospital doctors.

In many instances, actions that involved direct resistance to the banks were complementary to the movement's other objective of cultivating sympathetic public opinion both inside and outside Zacatecas. Many of the types of actions the Barzón used, including marches, blockades of roads, popular denunciations, invasions of local officials' offices, and even popular

I was not, I was then asked whether I ever wrote columns for papers and, if I did, whether I wouldn't write something about the Barzón.
[7] This account was related to me in June 1995 by Imelda Castro, student activist in the Zacatecas Barzón movement.

"liberation" of goods that movement participants maintained had been repossessed unjustly, were drawn from a repertoire of actions used in the countryside in the past by groups resisting state or landed authority. The direct requisition of property (such as tractors and houses) echoed the waves of populist land invasions in the 1930s and the 1970s. Also, the Barzón's invasions of the Rural Bank offices and the Federal Electricity Commission were not very different from farmers' protests over grain prices in the 1980s, in which protesters had staged invasions of CONA-SUPO stores and Ministry of Agriculture and Hydraulic Resources (Appendini 1992: Chapter 4). Whereas the use of new media stunts gained the Barzón considerable press coverage, the use of traditional actions helped establish the movement in onlookers' minds as the heir to previous distributive movements.

Still other types of action – more risky, but still not unheard of – were used both to get publicity and to achieve an immediate result. For example, in one instance, Barzón members occupying the central square of Zacatecas announced that they would proceed with their protest in the nude if one of the ranking agricultural officials persisted in his refusal to meet with them over a slate of demands. The action proceeded in front of reporters' cameras, beginning with the removal of participants' shoes and socks, and moving on to jackets and shirts and hats. When the Barzonistas threatened to remove their trousers, a flustered aide to the official announced that the official had managed to free up his schedule and would take a moment to talk with them in his office after all. This form of protest, though not typical, occasionally had been practiced before in distributive disputes elsewhere in Mexico.[8]

The Barzón undoubtedly gained its greatest media exposure and its widest popular recognition when it put new twists on traditional forms of protest. The occupation of urban space – not in and of itself out of the ordinary by 1993 – was taken a step further when it occupied city plazas with farm machinery. This in turn gave the Barzón its trademark green tractor logo, which the movement continued to use even after the point when the movement's constituency was more urban than rural. The Barzón also utilized a new band of international media space created in the 1990s as the North American Free Trade Agreement (NAFTA) was

---

[8] The most famous case of this extreme protest occurred in the early 1980s by silver miners in Hidalgo. For a description of the miners' 1985 strike against the Companía Minera Real del Monte in Pachuca (Trejo Delarbre, 1990: 175)

being negotiated.[9] In the February 1994 meeting of state chapters, leaders announced that they planned to visit the United States, including California, Washington, DC, and New Mexico to speak with human rights organizations, congressmen, and leaders of the United Farm Workers' movement (Hernández and Amador 1994). Despite the fact that the movement received little if any international media coverage before the December 1994 devaluation – eclipsed as it was by the Zapatista movement in Chiapas that had begun the month before – the leaders' very announcement that they would seek to influence public opinion abroad lent additional strength to the movement because the announcement itself was newsworthy *inside* Mexico.

Later, one of the most innovative and effective forms of action that the Barzón developed was mass legal action. By the spring of 1995, the Barzón movement had transformed its legal work from a supplement to collective action, or perhaps what a political scientist or an economist might call a "selective incentive,"[10] into a front-line weapon that could be used for media exposure and recruitment. Utilizing little-known procedures from civil banking codes, lawyers working for the Barzón prepared legal documents for Barzón clients that were then presented en masse to banks, courts, or financial authorities as a means to stall repossessions as well as to generate publicity. For example, with the help of Barzón members, lawyers might prepare legal summonses for "account of payments" statements. Banks, technically required to provide such statements upon request to individual clients with past-due debts before proceeding with repossession, would normally forestall individual forfeitures by a number of days. However, when such summonses were presented by the hundreds to bank branches, the production of account statements was likely to gum up administrative resources for weeks or

---

[9] The number of correspondents from newspapers, news wires, and news magazines jumped in the 1990s just prior to the ratification of NAFTA. According to Paul Sherman of the *New York Times* desk in Mexico City, the *New York Times* bureau rose from one temporary reporter to two permanent reporters in the 1990s, and the *Wall Street Journal* bureau rose from one correspondent to three. The Associated Press now has eight people, and Reuters has five. Among foreign posts around the world, he said, Mexico is now considered one of the top news priorities, with only Tokyo, Paris, and London having larger international news staffs from U.S.-based media organizations (Interview with Sherman 1994).

[10] This is a reference to Mancur Olson's famous rational choice argument about collective action, in which he contends that economic associations must offer rank-and-file members selective incentives, such as special services or bonuses, to gain their participation in collective action. See *The Logic of Collective Action*.

months at a time. Barzonistas usually made a spectacle out of the submittal of legal documents. Barzonistas might accompany lawyers to the bank with the stacks of legal summonses and would hold simultaneous press conferences, marches, and raucous public street theater. In the latter, Barzonistas constantly sought to outdo one another. In one instance, movement members dressed up as surgeons, with signs around their necks that said "banker," and ran around in the street with giant syringes. They would then pretend to draw blood from other Barzón members, dressed as hapless patients, yelling to the crowd that they would extract blood from the debtor in lieu of cash. In other instances, debtors wore plastic chains or handcuffs, depicting debtors as slaves or prisoners of the banks. Still other common stunts were mock funeral processions, complete with papier-maché coffins, depicting the victimization of individuals by the banks and the government.[11]

The Barzón's relationship to the media was so central, in fact, that it becomes impossible to separate the development of the Barzón's stated organizational purpose from its publicity apparatus, particularly because the Barzón depended on media coverage not only for public opinion, but also for new recruits. A substantial percentage of Barzón members interviewed by the author – particularly those from urban middle classes – reported that they learned of the Barzón through the newspaper. Especially after the December 1994 devaluation, when domestic manufacturing and service industries became engulfed in a crisis similar to what already existed in grain agriculture, there was a widespread sense that the nation's economic policy had gone terribly wrong. The symbols that the Barzón utilized – oscillating between the serious and the satirical – resonated powerfully among rural and urban audiences alike. The farm imagery – the green tractor, the notion of family patrimony, as well as the Barzón name – lent the issue of debt a weighty historicism, connecting individuals' financial problems to issues of land concentration that had fueled the Revolution of 1910. One urban industrialist who joined the Barzón movement in 1995 explained the power of the movement's symbols and name, commenting, "It's hard to explain, but the very title of the group

---

[11] There was a more serious side to the funerals. Much as in the U.S. Farm Crisis of the 1980s, many dozens of desperate depressed debtors committed suicide during 1994 and 1995. The Barzón movement accused banks and loan sharks of having played a part in these individuals' suicide by harassing them and their families relentlessly. At mass meetings of the Barzón organization, leaders began with moments of silence for the "martyrs" of the movement who had committed suicide as a result of their indebtedness.

– the Barzón – it's perfect, because it's funny. It makes you laugh [because the song is funny], but it's also got a lot of meaning."

As Mexico descended into economic depression in 1995, the Barzón was increasingly able to cultivate public sympathy in rowdy public spectacles. Adding fuel to the Barzón's protests were a series of accusations and indictments against President Salinas, his family, his former cabinet, and several billionaires with close ties to his administration. Raúl Salinas, the president's brother, was arrested for the murder of the ex-governor of Guerrero, Francisco Ruíz Messieu. Later in the year, rumors of Raúl Salinas's involvement in narcotics trafficking were confirmed in the public mind when his wife attempted to withdraw $83 million under a false name from a Swiss bank account. This occurred only two months after the ex-president's sister had been implicated in a credit-union scandal involving tens of millions of dollars. Just outside the Salinas's immediate family, evidence surfaced that ex-Secretary of Agriculture Hank González had been involved in campaign finance fraud, as well as drug trafficking. Meanwhile, rumors continued about collusive deals and money laundering in the privatization of the country's communication systems. Accompanying the flood of scandals about ex-executive officials, news reports cast a pall over the nation's bankers. In one high-level scandal in that sector, one large bank, the Banpais (acronym for "the country's bank") was named in a class-action suit by U.S. investors when it was revealed that the bank had placed some 13 percent of all its lending capital in the hands of the bank's own board of directors and their family members. The president of the same bank was subsequently investigated for having made a personal loan of some $30 million to the ex-chief executive officer of another large bank, who in turn was under indictment for having stolen $700 million from his own bank, the Banco Cremi/Union (Poole 1995).

The juxtaposition of elites' corrupt enrichment with the middle and working classes' pauperization fueled popular perceptions that the crisis was a grand conspiracy of a few evil men. The public now had not only some *thing* to blame, such as unemployment and high interest rates and inflation but moreover had some *one* to blame. Such concentrated, personified evil as the ex-president and his peers represented reinforced public discontent that in turn lent legitimacy to the aggressive opposition stance that the Barzón had assumed. When the Barzonistas lampooned Carlos Salinas, his ex-cabinet, and the bankers, their actions underscored leaders' declarations that the Barzón movement was not so much a protection scheme for debtors as it was a peaceful army of citizen-patriots, doing what was necessary to restore legitimate order to the political and economic system. The sheer wickedness ascribed to the ex-president, the man who also been the architect of Mexico's transition to a free market system, cast not only Salinas but also neoliberal policies like fiscal austerity, trade liberalization, and privatization as sinister machinations of elites who would stop at nothing in their campaigns of personal enrichment. Indeed, by the middle of 1995, the Barzón's national demands included both a call for the trial and jailing of ex-President Salinas, alongside demands to renegotiate the North American Free Trade Agreement.[12]

At the same time that the Barzón was succeeding in reinforcing public discontent with the corrupt neoliberalism represented by Carlos Salinas de Gortari, leaders began in an even more focused manner to cast the movement as the virtuous successor to the predominating system. Leaders began to speak of cultivating a "culture of *Barzonismo.*" By this, they meant a spirit of solidarity and support among members, who were under great psychic strain as they watched their businesses and farms fail, and as they waited for lawyers to show up on their doorsteps to repossess their houses or cars or appliances. The culture of Barzonismo also was meant to apply to a mode of confrontational but nonviolent protest in which people used, alternately, the letter of the law and civil disobedience to fight the banks and the government.

When leaders spoke of such a culture, they meant that they hoped that people's involvement in the Barzón would change the way they thought and talked about their own rights in the context of national economic policy. "It is our own experience that will form the future," explained one regional leader in an interview, "The Barzón is a nationalist movement, and the Barzón is a family. . . . [The movement] has made me care more about Mexico, because it dignifies human beings" (Interview with Luis Velásquez 1995). By 1995, the movement leaders sought to do far more than restructure individuals' loan portfolios; instead, they sought to change the public's mind about who in society had a right to finance capital. Members were encouraged to wear white T-shirts during public actions and at assemblies, and leaders increasingly referred to the "army in white," which would, as Juan José Quirino declared in one press event, "save the Republic and its institutions from destruction."

[12] Demands issued by leaders at the June 25, 1995, general assembly in Mexico City.

Perhaps the most visible campaign was the so-called dialogue with the Church, undertaken by Juan José Quirino after he was elected president of the national Barzón in June 1995. In various parts of the country, bishops agreed to give masses for the Barzón; in other parts, more cautious church officials who declined to associate with the Barzón directly consented to give sermons to Barzonistas on the Bible's teachings regarding usury. Of the relative importance of this symbolic linkage of Barzonista and Catholic values, one local leader of the Barzón commented that the Catholic masses were tremendously important because some of the Barzón's strongest campaigns were in socially conservative parts of the country such as Zacatecas; they also held sway among a constituency that was normally politically reserved – the property-holding middle classes. "My parents," he pointed out as an example, "are very conservative. We're very Catholic. My mother goes to Mass every day, and she was very upset when I began to get involved in the Barzón. . . . But now that the Bishop is giving a mass for them, she thinks positively of the movement. . . . There are a lot of people like that here in the city of Zacatecas, and those are the people among whom we're trying to raise consciousness . . ." (Interview with Efrén Bañuelos 1995).

The Electoral Game

The Zacatecas Barzón experimented with various electoral stances, evolving from a self-declared "independent" movement, to a faction of the state-level Party of the Democratic Revolution (PRD), back to a self-declared "nonpartisan group," before once again returning in 1997. In actuality, the movement did not abandon electoral politics when it eschewed party affiliation; instead, it leveraged power at the edges of four different parties, including the Institutional Revolutionary Party (PRI).[13]

As discussed in Chapter 2, the unstable relationship between the Barzón and electoral politics reflected a more general trend among social movements after the 1988 presidential elections that opened up the field for serious interparty contention at local and state levels. Social movement groups often made election-time deals with local candidates from various

[13] The Barzón movement's stance on electoral politics changed several times after this field research was conducted. In 1996, the Barzón movement was at the forefront of an initiative of several political groups to form an opposition front between the PRD and PAN against the PRI. That project failed. Later, in 1997, the Barzón would again forge more exclusive ties with the PRD.

parties, exchanging blocks of votes for the parties' short-term protection and/or support.[14]

The Barzón's first foray into electoral politics ended in a sharp defeat in 1994. Manuel Ortega and Alfonso Ramírez Cuellar ran as PRD candidates for the federal offices of Deputy (to the lower house of the legislature) and Senator. Despite the Barzón's high profile, they both lost by large margins to both PRI and National Action Party (PAN) candidates. The defeats were so resounding that the Barzón movement itself suffered a setback, as it appeared that its message carried little legitimacy among the electorate as a whole. The leaders of the movement quickly distanced themselves from electoral politics and began to emphasize once again the movement's independence from political parties. Also, Manuel Ortega and Alfonso Ramírez Cuellar receded from visibility in the press somewhat while Juan José Quirino – who had not run for public office in 1994 – moved to front and center of the state movement for several months.

Despite wide-ranging sympathy for the demands of the farmer-Barzonistas, the movement had no means to do battle directly with the ruling party in the electoral arena. The Barzón's disastrous early experience with direct participation in state-level electoral politics demonstrated that even though opposition to the Institutional Revolutionary Party (PRI) was growing among wealthier farmers and better-off ejidatarios, things remained much the same among the poor. The Barzón protests did not spark a wave of dissent among those who had long been controlled and repressed by the PRI, namely landless peasants, minimum-wage workers, day-laborers, and subsistence farmers. Particularly in the countryside or in urban slum dwellings, many still feared that voting for the opposition party would result in punitive measures from the ruling party. In the elections of 1994, for example, a number of residents in one of the poor sections of the city of Fresnillo testified to the author and other members of the election observer team that their coupons for corn meal and meat had been suspended two weeks before the election. They were informed that the coupon issues would resume after the election if the PRI won in their

---

[14] Even if not in power in a given locale, political parties could offer some measure of protection and support to isolated social movements that approached them for help. For instance, the national party might call attention to a movement's campaign by introducing some sort of legislation in the national or state congresses. Since the 1977 reforms in the electoral laws, opposition parties were afforded at least token representation. A national party might also send a high-level delegation to meet with members of a civil organization, thereby generating press coverage and greater notice among local citizens in the area where the movement operated.

neighborhood. Similarly, ejidatarios nearby reported that they received only half their Procampo payments and had been told that the rest would arrive after the elections.[15] People also feared that votes for the National Action Party (PAN) or the Party of the Democratic Revolution (PRD) would result in long-term consequences as well. Exclusion from government block grants for municipalities, which paid for such basic necessities as wells for drinking water, school buildings, and hospitals, represented a threat of the most basic order.

The Barzón movement, which began in October 1993 and had denied that it was affiliated with any political party, had oscillated between this nonpartisan position and a pro-PRD stance for months before emerging as a bloc within the PRD in the summer of 1994. In part, this ambiguity was due to the fact that the original organizers had differences of opinion over party politics. Manuel Ortega, Juan José Quirino, and Alfonso Ramírez Cuellar were all activists in the PRD, but others of the ranchers were not participants in party politics or even had ties with local PRI organizations. But even more, the Barzón's willy-nilly dance between autonomy and partisanship reflected a long bargaining game between the Barzón movement and the state government. The Barzón movement emerged at a time when every municipality in the state was controlled by the official party. Therefore, it stood to gain little by subordinating itself at the onset to a party that had no power over public purse strings.[16] The banner of "independence" allowed the fledgling movement to resist national or state-level PRD officials who might meddle in the affairs of their movement if it were more closely tied to the party. It also helped the Barzón battle accusations that the movement was merely a ploy by the national PRD to gain a greater foothold in the state of Zacatecas.

In the fall of 1994, the Barzón finally declared that it would henceforth be a "pluralist" organization, open to persons affiliated with any political party. The Barzón would seek support among reformist or soft-line PRIistas, and more centrist PRDistas and PANistas. In part, it chose this strategy to bury an embarrassing defeat and to capitalize on a general distaste for party politics altogether. As reflected in interviews with rank-and-file members as well as leaders, party politicking was associated with

[15] Author's report to the Civic Alliance, submitted August 24, 1994.
[16] Interestingly, in the mid-term municipal elections of 1995, the PRI's monopoly over local government was broken. The PAN and the PRD claimed to have taken eleven of approximately thirty-five municipal elections, although long negotiations afterwards may have resulted in interim candidates being placed in office.

opportunism, collusion, and corrupt leadership. Despite the fact that opposition parties in Mexico were gaining force, many still felt that electoral politics was coercive, and that opposition parties replicated patron-client practices of the PRI. Whether or not this was true in great numbers of cases, many people believed or had heard that caciquismo operated in the PRD, the Labor Party (PT), and the PAN; they believed that grassroots leaders cum party activists would deliver entire blocs of votes from ejidos or villages or neighborhoods when they were working with opposition parties. As in Lázaro Cárdenas, comments such as "They're all the same," "The PRDistas are really PRIistas in disguise," and "They work the same way" were common and reflected a deep distrust of parties as appropriate vehicles for social organization or demand aggregation.

As I discuss in the epilogue to this chapter, the dilemma of party politics was never fully solved for the organization, and tensions related to the issue would eventually erode portions of rank-and-file support for the organization. Many rank-and-file members staunchly opposed party ties of any sort, but leaders – all holding past ties to the PRD – were convinced that long-term gains could not be won without legislative pressure at state and national levels. The Barzón movement, despite periods of declared party independence, always held some continuing interest in opposition politics. The state agencies that the Barzón was denouncing, after all, were inextricably linked to the ruling party, so the Barzón's protest against the state carried with it at least an implicit indictment of the PRI. When the leaders of the state PRI – namely Governor Romo – did not settle the Barzón's demands, the Barzón's threat to make things difficult for the government and PRI carried little weight if they did not follow up on their own ultimatum.

Making Decisions Collectively

The movement also faced dilemmas of internal decision making. Perhaps the greatest danger of democracy in the movement was that schisms might emerge among the various classes and sectors participating together for the first time. Disunity, in turn, jeopardized the leaders' ability to portray the Barzón to external audiences as a unified group of citizens whose ideals were patriotic and high-minded. Where disputes simmered between rival groupings in the Barzón movement, leaders privately worried about the possible division of the movement into *corrientes*, or factions.

Ultimately, the movement's lack of centralized organization resulted in a fairly high degree of local control over demands and forms of protest. Having lowered the cost of mobilization by impelling local cells to organize largely on their own, the movement also locked in a fairly significant degree of bottom-up decision making. This local control in turn, generally (though not always)[17] prompted a high degree of rank-and-file participation in the movement's day-to-day decision making.

In part, one reason many local chapters held as many direct votes as they did was due to the fact that they were compelled to have open weekly or biweekly grassroots meetings for the entirely separate reason of coordinating the movement. Most members in the countryside, as well a good number in the city, had no working phones or reliable mail service. Some did not read well. And the Barzón, unlike most distributive social movements, did not encompass entire farm regions or ejidos or neighborhoods whose own leaders or bosses might have served as conduits of information. Accordingly, the only way to inform members on a regular basis of what the movement was planning as actions or what it would demand of the government was to establish regular meeting times in the municipalities. Once at meetings, members usually expected to discuss issues and make binding votes on whether or not their cell would take part in actions.

Movement participants, who exchanged their support for protection from the banks, were encouraged to devise strategies of their own to thwart repossessions and harassment from police and loan sharks. In this manner, isolated local spaces where the movement operated were in many senses the domain of local members rather than of national or state-level coordinators. Where there were differences of opinion between local and national leaders over specific issues or strategies, local leaders would most often prevail, simply because the organization had little power to censure rogue local chapters.[18]

---

[17] The level of rank-and-file participation in decision making varied from place to place. Rumors abounded in the movement regarding local leaders here and there who were said to be autocratic or corrupt, intent on using the Barzón as the vehicle for their own interests.

[18] One notable example is the case of the Barzón chapter in the impoverished state of Durango. The leaders of the movement in that state encouraged members to carry out grotesque protests. In one instance, the Durango Barzón chapter protested farm repossessions by slitting the throat of a donkey. In another instance, members of the group applied local anesthetic and had their eyes and mouths sewed shut to illustrate how the authorities had been "blind and mute" to collusion between financiers' lawyers and judges in the local court system. Leaders of the movement in other state chapters disapproved of these actions and tried to distance themselves from the Durango protests.

The lists of demands presented to the government, in particular, tended to bear the influence of bottom-up pressure, with the results of local meetings carrying substantial weight in the formation of the movement's state-level petitions. National demands tended to be so broad as to be generally inoffensive to any state organization, but they also exposed the organization to the criticism that the organization had presented no serious solutions to Mexico's consumer banking emergency. National leaders' principally had control over the movement's choice of public actions at inter-state meetings, with leaders determining the timing and form of marches or symbolic actions.[19]

Somewhat apart from these internal dynamics was the question of public opinion. The vilification of ex-President Salinas and the PRI turned upon a number of accusations that fed upon one another. That is, if Salinas plundered the people's treasury, then clearly the system lacked accountability. Therefore, if the Barzón was to present itself as the army of citizens in white, restoring the Republic, the institutionalization of some sort of internal democracy became essential in making a convincing case for its claims to represent the solution for Mexico's woes.

Fairly soon after the Zacatecas faction of the Barzón had begun to establish substantial cells of support in Mexico City and other areas, leaders drew up plans to create a formal constitution for the organization. The formal organization was to include provisions for the election of national, state, and local leaders; the internal supervision of the use of group funds, the ratification process for major platforms of action, the collection of revenue, and the separation of the members' organization from the growing bank of professionals (mostly lawyers) who were providing their services through the Barzón organization for a fee.

The movement's constitution ceded considerable formal power to local and state organizations. Eighty percent of collected revenue was to remain in the states where it was collected, and 60 percent was to remain in the municipalities it came from. Leaders were to be elected regularly to fill representative office at the national, state, and local levels, with the decisions of the general assembly constituting the maximum authority of the organization (El Barzón 1995).

As things were in the heady period of movement expansion following the December 1994 devaluation, the national leaders of the Barzón had

[19] Data drawn from observations of municipal, state, and national general assemblies, as well as meetings between national and state leaders.

little means to formalize the national organization in the manner that the group's constitution implied. Without a professional staff and a more complete state-by-state accounting of membership, revenue, and resources, there was little means to poll or sample member opinion or to devise a more complex set of national demands on the basis of such information. What did change, however, with the approval of the constitution, was the frequency of interaction between state-level leaders who made up an intermediate representative body below the small national executive committee. In numerous meetings, state-level leaders met in Mexico, Guadalajara, Monterrey, and Puebla, where numerous issues were reviewed and debated. Such meetings, part strategy sessions and part public-relations opportunities, were often also accompanied by protests and marches attended by rank-and-file Barzonistas from the host state and neighboring areas.

Epilogue

Readers familiar with Mexican politics will recall that in the chaotic two years following the December 1994 devaluation, the Barzón movement exploded in size and influence. Dwarfing its original membership in rural regions in the center and west of the country, the movement mobilized massive numbers of people to suspend service payments on their debts. The Barzón emerged in a narrow corridor of opportunity afforded by the convergence of woes among farmers and then, through the use of pooled resources, print media, and innovative public actions, it developed into a troublesome opposition fixture in the state political landscape. As spaces widened considerably in the wake of the December 1994 devaluation, the Barzón leaders' campaign to expand the movement – already well underway by that point – spurred a flurry of decentralized organizing that made the once-parochial social movement into a troublesome national insurgency. What began as a local movement of landed farmers dissatisfied with worsening production conditions ended as a conduit of mass backlash against the official corruption and concentration of wealth that had accompanied Mexico's neoliberal transformation.

For a time, the movement upended the rules of normal finance, forcing private and public banks to restructure loans and to desist from repossessing land, equipment, houses, and businesses. Through multifaceted local campaigns that included direct action, legislative pressure, press conferences, and legal activism, the movement was able to provide members with protection from the banks while also pressing a public agenda for a variety of policy reforms. As I argue in this chapter, however, the movement's success in pressing demands in chaotic national conditions does not explain the movement's prior existence, nor does it explain the particular strategies and organizational forms that materialized. Other debtors' organizations formed in 1994 and 1995, for example, such as the National Association of Debtors and the National Association of Debtors Anonymous, remained small, local, and largely ineffective when they were not acting in conjunction with the Barzón movement.

Notably, however, the movement that exploded in 1995 and 1996 declined in numbers and strength in the following three years. This was attributed to a number of factors. First, due to the pressure exercised by the organization, many people were able to restructure their debts. While many continued working with the organization, others returned full time to businesses and farms. Second, legal channels narrowed sharply. The basis of many thousands of legal injunctions issued from 1995 to 1998 had been a claim that interest charged over interest violated the 1917 Constitution. After a 1998 Supreme Court decision ruling compound interest legal, many lower courts refused to hear debtors' cases.

The success of direct action in relieving some members' debts and the failure of court action in eliminating the basis of the others' debts explains some, but not all, of the movement's trajectory. As demonstrated in this chapter and the last, the strategies that enabled the movement to maintain protest also embedded lasting contradictions in the organization. Four years after the initial research on the Zacatecas Barzón was conducted in 1994 and 1995, the strains inherent in its various means of mobilizing and maintaining protest were apparent. On the one hand, the leaders of the Barzón had emerged over time as national opposition figures. On the other hand, the cells of local activism had dissipated in Barzón strongholds in the center part of the state.

As outlined in a recent study by Charnas (1999), leaders Alfonso Ramírez Cuellar and Juan José Quirino Salas became federal legislators in 1997. Jettisoning the organization's nonpartisan stance in late spring of 1997, the members of the National Executive Committee of the Barzón decided to launch candidates for the Senate and the lower house as candidates with the PRD. After two and a half years of negative growth, government scandal, as well as hard-won electoral reforms, conditions were auspicious for opposition party victories. In the July 1997 proceedings, which swept hundreds of opposition party members into Congress and

Cuauhtémoc Cárdenas into the mayor's office in Mexico City, Ramírez Cuellar and Quirino Salas won, respectively, a seat in the Chamber of Deputies and a senatorship. Notably, neither won seats through majority vote in Zacatecas but instead gained their seats through proportional representation.

With the PRI now occupying a minority in the lower house for the first time in its history, leaders of the Barzón viewed legislative activism as the newest, best means of securing universal reforms that would protect debtors and infuse farming and domestic enterprise with fresh capital. "Instead of staging protests directed at the Executive [branch]," Charnas contends, "El Barzón would influence the legislative agenda and pass bills which benefitted the debtors" (1999: 32). Fastening hopes for advances on an oppositional party alliance among the PRD, the right-wing PAN, and the center-left Green Ecologist Party (PVEM), and the Labor Party (PT), Barzón leaders sought to force concessions on debtors' issues by vetoing budgets and various other presidential initiatives on monetary policy and banking bailouts. The latter issue was of particular importance because substantial portions of the private banking sector were in chaos after the crisis of 1995 and 1996. Of eighteen banks that the government had originally privatized in the early 1990s, only five were still solvent under their original buyers. Six had gone under, three had been taken over by the government again, and the remaining banks had been partly or wholly purchased by foreign banks. The government, in the meantime, had staved off systemic financial collapse by buying banks' bad debt portfolios through the Fobaproa, or the Banking Fund for the Protection of Savings (akin to the FDIC in the United States). With the interest on those debts mounting, and collateral on many of the largest loans unrecoverable,[20] the amount of debt in the Fund rose from approximately U.S. $40 billion to over $60 billion by the middle of 1998 (*The Economist* 1998).

[20] Opposition parties in the federal congress ordered an audit of the banking system at the end of 1998. According to the *New York Times*, the 1999 report by Canadian auditor Michael Mackey characterized the Mexican banking system as "an incestuous banking system in which a small business elite controls the banks as well as many of the companies that want to borrow from them" (Preston 1999). Mackey found that government officials had been aware of banks' mounting liabilities for some time but had continued to prop up insolvent institutions, thus increasing the total cost of the bailout. He also concluded that officials overseeing the sale of the banks in the Salinas administration had failed to investigate the background of the individuals who purchased the banks, and that many "lacked the lending experience and technical expertise necessary for prudent banking . . ." (Preston 1999).

When the Zedillo administration proposed a set of policy reforms that included converting the debts in the Fobaproa to public debt – thereby leaving the tab to taxpayers – the Barzón leaders had their issue. They claimed that the bailout protected the banks and the country's billionaires, while punishing consumers and small enterprise. Ramírez Cuellar, as head of the Finance Committee in the lower house of congress, carried out high-profile congressional investigations, alleging that reckless government management and collusive lending practices had scuttled the economy. Private banks, he claimed, had funneled leveraged capital to the ruling party via bogus loans. Business cronies close to Salinas, in addition, had purchased government-owned enterprises with borrowed money, run them into the ground, and saddled the Fobaproa with bad debt. Notably, millions of borrowers had gone bankrupt, but the committee pointed out that 50 percent of the bad debts covered by Fobaproa corresponded to just 600 accounts (Rosen 1998: 13).

In place of the President's bailout proposal, which was backed by the ruling party, the Central Bank, and the Secretary of Finance, the PRD campaigned for an alternative bailout plan that would "punish the guilty" among bankers and billionaires and provide zero-interest refinancing to small and medium-sized debtors. In eighteen months of furious legislative work, however, the Barzón leaders emerged with no substantive policy victories. Hoped-for coalitions blocking increasingly austere budgets for 1998 and 1999 failed to materialize. In each major vote over budgets and the banking bailouts, the PAN sided first with PRD in public debates, gained minor concessions, and then voted as a bloc with the PRI.

During this period, the Barzón as a social movement organization waned in combativeness and numbers at regional and local levels. This had much to do with conflicting visions of the organization, and the inherent tension between aggressive direct actions by the base membership and leaders' new official roles as members of the government, where legitimate activism meant playing by prescribed rules of order. In Zacatecas, informants pointed out that participation in the organization declined markedly after the 1997 decision to launch leaders as candidates for national office. Despite leaders' arguments that reviving farms and businesses was contingent on reaching universal policy reforms, many members saw the decision as an autocratic back-room deal that betrayed earlier commitments to organizational independence. Debtors – many of whom had refused to restructure debts under official programs at the urging of Barzón leaders – now faced imminent repossessions and lawsuits by lenders. Such debtors saw the exit of leaders to Mexico City as an abdication of local responsibilities.

In a manner similar to environmental and urban struggles in Lázaro Cárdenas, debtors' contention was balanced in a tenuous location – outside corporatist channels – and not moving toward a new set of institutional matrices, with norms of access, bargaining, settlement, and enforcement. Local settlements that were reached regarding debt restructuring and new lines of production credit were ad hoc, reversible, and subject among the more desperate to the time-tested carrot-and-stick incentives of patron-client management. Whereas government retrenchment in farm finance had originally heightened combativeness and scope of debtors' protest, new jurisdictional voids made the outcomes of distributive bargaining more arbitrary than before. Protesters often had to mobilize petition and protest not only to gain small concessions on capital, machinery, or land but had to mobilize again and again to enforce any agreements reached with officials. In some cases, where banks and lawyers fought back, protest became violent, and debtors' struggles devolved into defensive campaigns against criminal charges. In November of 1998, for example, lawyers in the town of Jerez made criminal charges against Barzonistas, charging members of the organization with threats and assault (*Imagen de Zacatecas* 1998).

The most significant turn of events involving the Barzón and its leaders in Zacatecas, however, came in the spring of 1998. Quite unexpectedly, a rupture in the state ruling party organization provoked a spectacular defection of one of the PRI's most powerful regional leaders, Ricardo Monreal. Monreal, a former senator with a wide base of support in ejidal and small farm associations, expected to be named the PRI's candidate for governor in the 1998 elections. Passed over by national party elites, however, Monreal considered his chances of victory outside the party umbrella and began negotiating behind closed doors with national leaders of the PRD. Notably, Barzón leaders Ramírez Cuellar, Quirino Salas, and Manuel Ortega were key players in the negotiations, as was PRD national executive committee member, Amalia García (of Zacatecan extraction herself). On May 5, 1998, Monreal announced his defection publicly, and said that he would run independently on an "Alliance" ticket. In separate press conferences, leaders of the Barzón and leaders of the small state Labor Party announced that they would back Monreal through a broad citizens' campaign.

Noticeably, in this electoral insurgency, the Barzón was suddenly a junior partner. Despite the Barzón leaders' prominent roles as brokers in Monreal's new alliance with the PRD, Ramírez Cuellar and Quirino Salas had very limited power over the popular vote. This points to the peculiar nature of protest and systemic power in Mexico: Ramírez Cuellar and Quirino Salas derived their power in congress from their prominent position inside the national PRD. Their prominence inside the PRD, in turn, derived from their ability to mobilize protest and direct action across a broad but thin strata of middle-class debtors in the cities and countryside. In the state race in Zacatecas, it was Monreal's newly ex-PRI base of supporters that determined the stakes of the race.

Ironically, as leaders of the Barzón turned to electoral politics and legislative politics, the Barzón movement fell into severe disarray by 1999. Demoralized by the Supreme Court defeat on the issue of compound interest and broken financially by the paucity of fresh lines of credit, the Barzón's capacity to mobilize direct action dwindled to near-zero in many localities. The new prominence of Barzón leaders at national levels, in turn, accelerated decline in participation, as disgruntled Barzonistas accused national leaders of having capitalized crassly on the mobilization as a means of gaining office.

What ultimately will become of the Barzón as a social force nationally is unclear. Despite the exhaustion of some lines of legal resistance, and wide disillusionment with congressional action as a means of solving problems, the movement still has at its disposal a resonant critique of the banks, and a wide field of bankrupt farmers and businesspeople. Wages and demand have not recovered from the shocks of the mid-1990s, many businesses have never reopened, and a great many farmers have viable markets for basic grains.

An account of the Barzón as a contentious force invoking participation of individuals from previously unassociated sectors demonstrates much about the interplay of economic policy, regional market disruptions, and social response. The two localities discussed in Chapters 4 and 5, although quite different in terms of social class and historically bound understandings of the appropriate roles of the state in distribution and production, also demonstrate powerful points of comparison. In both cases, market-oriented policies and resulting volatility in local economics prompted vigorous popular responses. The relocation of state-society bargaining, in addition, affected contention by pushing protest and collective action into new, more experimental political arenas. In both cases, contention became more frequent. Significantly, however, the routinization of protest also exacerbated inherent contradictions in the strategies protesters used to mobilize and extend protest.

Conclusion: The Interplay of Movements and Markets

Theorists of politics and market transition differ in the long-term outcomes they predict for various classes and sectors in developing nations undergoing rapid market transitions.[1] Certain conclusions, however, are foregone. Most grain farmers on small or medium-sized plots, or combative workers in state-owned enterprises, for example, are somewhere in oblivion's waiting room. As subsectors, these workers and farmers are residual elements of an economic order that prevailing ideologies deem obsolete. As individuals, they are factors of production that are expected to become imminently mobile.

---

[1] The voluminous literature on the distributive effects of the transition to market-oriented economies in Latin America or even in Mexico alone cannot be adequately summarized here. Some economists have addressed the issue of whether austerity and structural adjustment actually increase poverty, rather than merely correlating with hardship. See J. J. Thomas (1993), Cornia, Jolly, and Stewart (1987), Zuckerman (1989), and Morley (1995). Interestingly many of those who put their energies into measuring the well-being of sectors or classes during market transition do not engage in the same discussions or use the same methodologies as the economists who design transition policies. The largely inductive methodology of leftist economist José Luis Calva (1993), for example, speaks past the deductive econometrics of Finance Ministers Pedro Aspe or Jaime Serra Puche or Guillermo Ortíz. Of this phenomonon, it has been pointed out that monetarist theorists who have urged adoption of inflation-control measures and structural adjustment programs tend not to engage such arguments on theoretical grounds precisely because they must portray measures such as cuts in real wages, social services, and subsidies as being technical imperatives, and therefore not negotiable on political grounds. On this issue, see for example Foxley (1983). Beyond these disputes, there is also a broad and sophisticated array of political economic works that analyze the roles of regime type and institutions in market transitions. Some of these works address the prospects of various social groups under democratic or authoritarian market systems; others do not. All, however, are germane if the issue of democratic participation is expected to condition distributive policy choices of leaders. See, for example, Haggard and Kaufman (1995), Freiden (1991), and Stallings and Kaufman (1989).

IRA ■ Helguera

Anger, by Helguera The thugs in the foreground are burning a photograph of ex-president Carlos Salinas de Gortari. "Wow!" exclaims the observer on the left. "Are they from the opposition?" "No," replies the observer on the right. "They're from the PRI." From *La Jornada*, March 7, 1995. Reprinted by permission.

The greatest number of grain farmers and industrial workers in Mexico both have faced a set of stark survival alternatives. In cases where workers have actually kept their jobs through periods of downsizing or where farmers have retained control of their production after credit and price liberalization, they have still not been able to halt the fall in real income and buying power. This, in turn, has provoked many to send one or more family members to more prosperous areas of the country or abroad to the United States or Canada to work; meanwhile, other household members sell goods out of the home or in informal markets. Market losers have also cut consumption drastically. Meat and vegetables are scarcer now in many families' diets. Children are expected to leave school at an earlier age to contribute to household incomes. There are fewer special occasions and more austere Christmas dinners.

As demonstrated in the previous chapters, some of those people whose economic activities ended up on official loss ledgers have fought back. Contention and social mobilization in the two localities described in Chapters 3 through 6 have many differences: workers and residents of Lázaro Cárdenas City made demands about employment, wages, housing, health, and the environment; farmers and merchants in the Zacatecas Barzón movement called upon the banks and the government to address problems of rising debts and falling profits in the countryside. Their trajectories during the period of market transition spanning the Salinas and Zedillo administrations were also decidedly different. Local mobilization in Lázaro Cárdenas City broke apart in a centrifugal fashion, moving from a worker-based core into myriad opposition efforts after the SICARTSA steel mill was privatized. Contentious politics were then taken up by many small citizen groups, including Party of the Democratic Revolution (PRD) party cells, environmental lobbies, unemployed workers' groups, and even local chapters of national debtors' movements. Local mobilization in Zacatecas, on the other hand, came together in a centripetal fashion after the collapse of the farming economy. Protest over consumer and farm debt drew together the efforts of both unaffiliated citizens as well as veterans of various student, worker, and campesino movements.

Despite their differences, however, fields of contention in the two localities merit comparison. Movements in both localities frequently sought to create a public consciousness about the relationship between local problems and national economic policies, disputing the idea that the demise of their communities or of their livelihood sources was inevitable. In so doing, protests formed a public lens through which people around them viewed governmental actions. The state's exit from the direct regulation of production and distribution of resources was seen by many after a time[2]

---

[2] It is important to note that the greatest number of people in Mexico were not categorically opposed to privatization of banks or industries per se (with the possible exception of petroleum, which, because of the circumstances of its nationalization in 1938, has remained a symbol of national sovereignty). Informants in Lázaro Cárdenas City, for example, even report that there was a brief time of some considerable optimism about market-based commerce and production during 1990 and 1991. Several informants reported that, at that point, thousands of workers and company employees at SICARTSA were exhausted and socially divided after the long strike of 1989; as such, many were willing to consider some sort of free market, business-led future for the community. Among

not as a liberation of markets, but as a surrender of family or public patrimony to an unworthy portion of the private sector. Despite people's long-suffering relationship with party-controlled state agencies, many people believed that government regulation of local industries was preferable to laissez-faire management by industrial and banking groups with faraway owners.

In Lázaro Cárdenas City, this popular conception was reflected in the belief that the local economy was being controlled by a shady set of individuals who had colluded with government officials in the transferral of the steel mill from public to private hands. Many people stated in conversations and interviews that the new owners of the steel mill, who were from an industrial group from Monterrey, Nuevo León, were actually *prestanombres* (literally name-lenders, or covers) for ex-President Salinas. Within several years after the privatization, few local institutions were beyond suspicion. Two informants independently declared that it was no coincidence that the bus service to Lázaro Cárdenas City from Morelia and other more central sites had a monopoly on certain routes and times. "It's actually owned by the ex-president's brother, you know," one said in confidence. In yet other conversations, people pointed out that the highway robberies nearby were being carried out by the state Judicial Police, who housed a large detachment nearby.

In the case of the Barzón movement, the idea that bank repossessions were in violation of constitutional principles of unalienable family patrimony was a major axis of recruitment and mobilization among indebted individuals from all walks of life. Interestingly, in the Barzón movement, while participants were quite contemptuous of the banks, the greatest disdain was reserved for hostile judges, lawyers, and private moneylenders (*agiotistas*), who often acted as collection agents of sorts for banks.

The accounts of mobilization in Lázaro Cárdenas City and the state of Zacatecas in Chapters 3–6 operationalize two general arguments. First, I contend that trade opening, domestic market liberalization, and privatization shifted the location of contention, the axes of mobilization, and constituencies of distributive movements. Market-oriented policies altered the way the government allocated scarce resources, and in so doing, they

these were even permanent workers who had been laid off. They had received substantial severance packages and were promised help in investing and starting small businesses. Feelings turned against the privatization project once again, however, after it became clear that local demand would not support hundreds more small businesses and that investments were being mishandled and stolen by unscrupulous officials.

augmented the ability of some groups to *mobilize* protest and diminished the capacity of many local representatives of the state to *quell* dissent and public disorder. Second, however, I argue that patterns of protest in this shifting environment were determined by more than structural changes. Protest against markets required great skill and astute knowledge of the political environment. Gaining any sort of settlement with the government required the activists to devise practices that captured resources and public sympathies and that held off repressive counterattacks by their opponents.

Opportunity

The ability of groups to sustain mobilization for any length of time in Mexico is generally linked to their ability to capitalize on perceived contradictions in governance. Thinking about this problem with respect to a changing economic system yields an interesting methodological paradox for the researcher. Whereas one can model opportunity for firms fairly confidently from above in a liberalized market economy, one finds that it is quite difficult to model opportunity for popular mobilization from a top-down perspective. On the one hand, theorists of market development can identify with greater certainty where people with money will and will not make gains over time. Though crucial profit margins change day by day, one can predict that firms will make gains in Mexico in the next ten years in industries such as tourism and export-processing industries, in public utilities and hospitals, and in the management of financial services and privatized pensions. Theorists intent on modeling political opportunity for domestic actors in distributive movements, on the other hand, find that market-oriented policy corresponds with a pared-down sort of state administration that tends to conciliate the demands of sectors outside the investor class in a piecemeal, case-by-case fashion. Union centrals recede in importance as political actors; agricultural and urban planning ministries pale as meaningful ombudsmen in the shadow of newly powerful treasury departments and central banks. The latter, of course, are generally reluctant to adopt policies that result in higher wages across the board or that distort prices in national markets. As a result, movements are more likely to forge pragmatic, nontraditional alliances and coalitions at local levels to compensate for declining power of corporatist representatives. Also, gains that are made as a result of state-group negotiation under such circumstances are likely to apply on a local basis and to carry an exceptionalist status. The study of markets and movements, then, must travel between top and bottom, nation and locality.

Markets structured by transborder flows of capital require policymakers to take steps to prevent disorder and political uncertainty. Maintaining protest in a system where the state seeks to create the perception of certainty among investors then becomes a game where movement actors must leverage demands in the crevices between powerful political institutions and the media and public performances that legitimize them. As detailed in the preceding chapters, straightforward measurements of political or distributive variables rarely give researchers enough insight into the particular nature of opportunity for local mobilizations against market-oriented policies. For example, the strength of opposition parties, land distribution, percent drops in average household income levels, or unemployment levels may or may not figure into the "push" forces that cause political insurgency.[3] For every local case in which such forces look as if they have contributed to recruitment and mobilization of resources – say, the EZLN in eastern Chiapas – there are several localities in which nearly similar conditions existed and no such movement appeared – say, in southern municipalities in Chiapas, or localities in rural Michoacán, Durango, Oaxaca, Guerrero, Puebla, and Veracruz. In this work, therefore, I argue that opportunity for protest occurs when a particular narrative of good and evil becomes available to a group of people *at a moment when* the state cannot produce an effective counternarrative and is constrained in the use of force against dissenters.

Political opportunity is not defined by material conditions alone. Opportunity for collective action arises when people make links in their

---

[3] Specifying the precise nature of political openings remains a topic of much debate among scholars of both revolutions and of social movements. For a number of historical reasons, scholars of Latin American politics seldom have drawn from resource mobilization and political process models that emphasize political opportunity structures, mobilizing networks, and collective action frames. Studies of social movements or contentious politics in Latin America drew heavily in the 1980s on European scholarship, notably what is broadly known as the New Social Movements school, which emphasizes the roles of identity-formation and discourse in fomenting collective action (Escobar and Alvarez 1992; Slater 1985). Other studies have integrated the study of social movements into urban studies or rural sociology and tend not to isolate social movements from a more general discussion of, say, class or gender politics, or of more general political trends on the left. See, for example, Zapata (1987). Authors of revolution and political violence, on the other hand, use a much more macrohistorical lens and often seek to identify those conditions that act as thresholds of tolerance or detonators of violence (Paige 1975; Wikham-Crowley 1992; Muller and Seligson 1987).

minds between material conditions and a particular set of processes or people that they believe to be responsible for them. In many cases, that link is formulated through long-term organization, such as in the case of Local 271 in the 1970s and 1980s. In that case, activists encouraged slum dwellers to hold the state responsible for the provision of basic services that they badly needed. In other cases, people may draw links between hardship and state culpability very rapidly, especially where the state's sudden failure to provide relief or where certain production or employment guarantees clashes with popular expectations, such as with debt protests in Zacatecas.[4] In yet other cases, a political opportunity may bring to life movements that were seemingly spent, reinvigorating experienced leadership and channels of resources around a new narrative. Taibo explained how this phenomenon contributed to the unexpected eruption of support that Cuauhtémoc Cárdenas received in the 1988 elections. "Underground *cardenismo* proliferates among those who are obliged to show public support for the official party – gardeners in the public parks, street vendors, state bureaucrats – all of them suffering the scourge of the economic crisis . . ." (1990: 766).

Beyond Opportunity: Tools of Insurgency

Groups of workers, farmers, debtors, urban dwellers, and petty merchants today persist in hundreds of local and regional distributive movements in Mexico, protesting the specific fiscal or regulatory policies that affect their incomes and well-being. The effectiveness of their campaigns is conditioned in good part by the longevity and resonance of their protests. In efforts to gain substantive negotiations with the government, they use a variety of strategies. Sometimes they merely have augmented the forcefulness of older forms of protest, blocking larger highways, writing more desperate or frequent letters to the president, combining occupations with hunger strikes, or combining marches with low-level violence. Sometimes they have traded old forms of action for relatively new ones, forming

---

[4] Gabriel Torres (1996) argues that this type of dissonance was crucial in the farm debt protests in 1993–4 in the western Pacific states. In his analysis of the Jalisco Barzón movement, he points out that many farmers had grown accustomed to a farm credit system in which the government periodically would bail out debtors in exchange for political support. When in the early 1990s the government ceased to forgive debts as in the past, many farmers who had long been considered PRI loyalists suddenly were participating en masse in aggressive public protests.

human rights groups or international delegations to make appeals to foreign audiences. Most often, they have combined old and new forms of protest. In so doing, they have linked themselves to historical struggles while emphasizing that they represent innovative and uncorrupted forces for social change.

How groups mobilize and maintain protest matters greatly. I have argued that one cannot understand why any extended social movement campaign emerges in a given situation if one does not first consider why that movement might *not* have emerged or persisted. Three forces militate against most extended distributive protests in Mexico: resource deficiency, cooptation (perceived or real), and repression. To minimize these obstacles, participants in social movements must take steps to establish inflows of money, goods, and services while they organize protests and recruit new members. In the meantime, they must make themselves too visible and too widely legitimate for their opponents to attempt arbitrary arrests, assaults, or assassinations. They must also devise innovative protests and movement practices that convince onlookers that the movement is not an instrument of self-serving elites in the government or the private sector; moreover, they must make the case that the movement's goals constitute a public good and/or a Revolutionary Constitutional imperative.

Many of the tools that participants in distributive movements use to offset resource scarcity, exhaustion, and fears of retribution from their opponents are quite ad hoc, evolving more through trial and error and even luck rather than through premeditated strategy.[5] I have argued that participants in social movements often gather material resources and

---

[5] Charles Tilly (1996) addresses the issue of intentionality and premeditated cost/benefit strategizing. "Most order in social structures and processes," he argues, "results not from rational action but from constraints on the correction of errors. . . . For the Invisible Hand, let's substitute the Invisible Elbow." He wryly offers the following metaphor: "Coming home from the grocery store, arms overflowing with food-filled bags, you wedge yourself against the doorjamb, somehow free a hand to open the kitchen door, enter the house, then nudge the door closed with your elbow (sometimes only to spill groceries all over the floor). . . . You, your elbow, groceries, and the kitchen have systematic properties that strongly limit the likely consequences of your attempted nudge. Over many trips to the grocery store, which of the outcomes forms a frequency distribution with stable probabilities modified by learning. With practice you may get your door-closing average up to .900." He argues finally, that as observers of social processes, "we must distinguish *ex post facto* rationalization . . . from systematic explanation. Systematic explanation requires much greater attention to errors, their consequences, and their rectification than social scientists have given them so far."

needed services (legal or medical, for example) by drawing on political networks of similar organizations or grassroots groups, and also by soliciting help from neighbors, family, and even sympathetic strangers. In Mexico, where it is likely that protesters will have to take their demonstrations to state capitals and even to the seat of the federal government of Mexico City, such channels of resources literally may be lifelines for individuals of very limited means.

Participants in movements also are likely to work hard at establishing some way of telling their side of the story to external audiences who may otherwise remain unaware that the protest exists. Gaining access to independent print media with a national or international readership or to principled-issue networks concerned with native cultures, human rights, the environment, or labor practices may be a crucial barrier against official violence or arrests, especially in the short term while a group's opponents remain in a negative spotlight.[6] Publicity also helps stimulate flows of resources and services to the protesting group. As individual protests are many, and official will to provide more resources to the populace is low, gaining sympathy among external audiences involves making a local movement relevant to national or international concerns. In order that a distributive movement seem neither random nor purely self-serving, publicists inside and outside the movement must frame the group's grievances in terms that seem emblematic of generally acknowledged problems.

Another important element in many but not all distributive movements is their relationship with political parties. Particularly after the watershed presidential election of 1988 in which Cuauhtémoc Cárdenas's opposition front posed the first serious challenge to the ruling PRI since the late 1940s, distributive movements have frequently forged implicit or explicit pacts with candidates running for local, state, or federal posts. The degree to which distributive movements attach themselves to parties or to individual candidates (who themselves may switch party affiliations over time)

---

[6] Findings by Margaret Keck and Kathryn Sikkink on principled-issue networks would emphasize the capacity of certain highly visible international nongovernmental organizations to reduce the levels of official violence in cases where domestic actors are highly mobilized. They show, however, that such networks have a considerably more difficult time weighing in on issues that go beyond such universally accepted principles as bodily harm and legal inequality of opportunity. "New ideas are more likely to be influential if they fit well with existing ideas and ideologies in a particular historical setting," they write. "Since networks are carriers of new ideas, they must find ways to frame these ideas to resonate or fit with the larger belief systems and life worlds within which the debates occur" (1997: 204).

varies considerably according to local circumstances. As many citizens remain unconvinced that any new party, once elected, will rule any differently than the ruling party did in the past,[7] I have argued that grassroots groups that have formed around material grievances often remain fiercely opposed to incorporation into political parties of the right or the left. Instead, links to parties such as the PRD, the National Action Party (PAN), and smaller parties such as the Labor Party (PT), the Cardenista Front for National Reconstruction (PFCRN), and Authentic Party of the Mexican Revolution (PARM, allied more frequently with the Institutional Revolutionary Party or PRI) tend to be pragmatic and conjunctural.

Above all, elections are often important moments for movements to manifest their grievances publicly, to gain allies and resources, and to frame their demands as being part of a larger opposition to the status quo. In cases where elections are suspect, movements with some relationship to opposition candidates are supplied once again with an opportunity to call into question the legitimacy of the government.

Yet another element that may be considered a strategic choice of distributive movements is that of internal decision-making structures. Some, but certainly not all, distributive movements decentralize leadership and democratize decision making.[8] While many who devolve decision making to many small cells of movement participants, or who practice some form of internal democracy in their movements profess that they do so out of

[7] People who are skeptical of whether any opposition candidate can or will make significant changes in governance from the mayor's office or the governor's palace often differ in their explanations as to why this is so. My interviews in Michoacan, Sinaloa, and Zacatecas prior to federal and local elections in 1994 and 1995 revealed two general types of skepticism. Some explained to me that the problem lay with politicians themselves. Opposition candidates, they explained, did not rule differently simply because the types of people who sought office in general were corrupt profit-seekers. Others, however, explained that opposition candidates had little hope of making substantive changes because the PRI still held the purse-strings at the federal level and withheld crucial fiscal outlays from municipalities and states held by the opposition. For a set of excellent analyses of opposition administrations in Mexico, see Rodriguez and Ward (1995).

[8] One should take very seriously Judith Hellman's recent thoughts on the issue of social movements and internal democracy. She argues forcefully that studies of social movements in Mexico have not addressed the issue of internal democracy systematically, and that, as such, it remains unclear how widespread or important participatory democracy may be in the majority of grassroots struggles. She argues, for example, that many newer movements, which are purported to be more democratic than PRI-sponsored grassroots cells or Leninist groups organized in the 1970s, are not necessarily more inclusive. "The assumption that new movements are automatically more democratic," she writes, "seems as ill-founded as the assumption that they inevitably promote democratization simply because they make demands on the system" (1994b: 135).

a normative commitment to fairness and equity, one may view such processes as having pragmatic value as well. In the cases of the Barzón movement and Local 271 – with the former being perhaps more decentralized than radically democratic, and the latter being both radically democratic and somewhat decentralized – one can observe several important phenomena. First, decentralization allayed many fears of recruits and potential recruits that, in a single blow, the movement could be leveled by a death threat, an arrest, an unfortunate accident, or simply a payoff delivered to a single charismatic leader. Second, devolution of decision making to rank-and-file or local committees on critical tasks encouraged a diversity of initiatives to emerge from committees and local cells. While differences of opinion among different cells as often as not also produced personality clashes and arguments, they also produced a wider variety of alliances and protest strategies than otherwise would have emerged. A variety of protests and accompanying schemes for gathering resources arose in both cases, making disorder more difficult for authorities to quell, and rendering settlement more costly and complex in cases where officials sought to negotiate with the movements.[9]

The findings and hypotheses presented in this work should shed light on the factors that provoked the emergence of political insurgencies among workers and later neighborhood dwellers and fishermen in Lázaro Cárdenas City, and farmers and later merchants and consumers in Zacatecas. The accounts also explain how an independent organization lasted for years at a time in those cases, spanning numerous episodes of protest that produced at least some material gains for the actors involved.

The two movements' outcomes to date also suggest new areas for further research and discussion. In the case of social protest and organization in Lázaro Cárdenas, I have shown how privatization, labor subcontracting, and divisions inside Local 271 ultimately exhausted the mobilizational capacity of the miners' union. Most of the leaders and the militant rank-and-file participants in the movement were fired by the company just prior to privatization. Of those, many dozens left the community because of high unemployment rates and blacklists that circulated among the remaining employers in the city. Some of the remaining ex-steel workers stayed and became involved in new political initiatives in the years after privatization in 1990. By 1994 and 1995, when field study for this work was being conducted, ex-union militants were leaders in PRD

---

[9] This situation is not unlike the two-level game described by Putnam (1988).

party politics, in environmental protests centering on contamination of river and coastal fisheries, in lobbies of unemployed persons, in debtors' groups, in housing and land invasion movements, and in citizens' lobbies against terrestrial pollution.

To date, the Barzón farmers' movement that arose in the Zacatecas on the cusp of widespread agricultural protest in the entire western and northern region of the country in late 1993 has not dispersed, but instead has gathered tremendous force nationally. As recounted in an earlier publication (Williams 1996), an unpredicted convergence of rural and urban debt problems, plus shrewd strategy, combined to transform the Zacatecas movement from a largely rural movement of mostly grain farmers[10] into a cross-sectoral movement anchored by an urban middle-class constituency. The leaders of the Zacatecas Barzón, having expanded their organizing from the agricultural sector into urban sectors just prior to the devastating peso devaluation of December 1994, soon became national figures making daily appearances in Mexico City's most important newspapers. In the first six months of 1995, in which interest rates on dollar-backed consumer and business loans skyrocketed to over 100 percent annually, leaders of the Zacatecas Barzón surged ahead in their crusade to organize their debtors' movement as a national crusade against the finance system and the government's economic policies.

Clearly, various characteristics of the Barzón farmers' movement made it particularly viable in the deepening stages of market transition in Mexico, as Mexico plunged into a period of negative economic growth. Political-structural factors explain a good deal: the workers' movement in Lázaro Cárdenas was alternately empowered and constrained over time because their union was also an official institution; the Barzón movement operated independent of any such statutory apparatus. Reinforcing labor analyses by Maria Lorena Cook (1990, 1997) and Ann Craig (1990), the account of the workers in Lázaro Cárdenas City demonstrates that laws and agencies and jurisdictions constitute a political terrain that unquestionably shapes what movements demand, when and where they level those demands, and, of course, who will lead crucial parts of any movement campaign. Labor's decline had much to do with the dissolution of protest and organization in Local 271. In a political economic environment in which

---

[10] In Zacatecas, most of the farmers in the movement reported that their principal crops were corn or beans. In Jalisco, it should be noted, however, an organizationally separate movement that actually coined the name of El Barzón and pioneered some of its trademark protest forms was formed by tomato growers allied with basic grain growers.

the Ministry of Labor and corporatist union representatives in Mexico City concentrated more on policing labor than on bargaining for any meaningful rise in wages and benefits with competing private sector interests, even combative unions were often overwhelmed by the forces working against them. Notably, those labor movements that still persist in confrontational distributive campaigns are in most cases seeking new sorts of alliances and pressure techniques that will allow them to circumvent a near-stonewall in the government over wage hikes, health and safety codes, and jobs policies.

Craig and Cook remind us, however, that structure as such is not the sole determinant of what happens to movements. In her study of the teachers' movement that arose inside the National Educational Workers' Union (SNTE), the official union that encompasses all public school teachers in Mexico, Cook argues that "the laws, procedures, organizational structure, and leadership of the union set boundaries for the movement's actions, shaping, though not fully determining its demands, strategies, organization, and what it was able to achieve" (1990: 200). As she and others point out, institutional frameworks may just as easily become a terrain of contestation. When laws are not applied effectively or consistently, people may mobilize against the institutions that are supposed to enforce them. The Barzón movement, for example, often protests what it sees as the banks' supposed impunity by tying up the court system with vast numbers of legal proceedings. Similarly, labor organizers often carry copies of the Federal Labor Law with them in order to remind recruits and rank-and-file workers of the government's legal obligations to protect workers on the shopfloor and to recognize their unions.

In this work, I argue that we can extend this perspective further into the realm of political economy. Transitions to market-oriented development also shape the material and ideational landscapes in which social movements operate but do not ultimately determine who protests and to what end. The theorist must conceptualize technocratic exercises and multilateral treaties, therefore, as more than disembodied policies and programs that alter the modes by which scarce resources are allocated; market transition also brings to the fore latent conflicts in how groups perceive themselves in relation to one another, in relation to capital, and in relation to the state.

I argue that distributive movements and market transitions intersect at three observable levels. First, markets affect the structure and location of social demands, rendering some targets nearly immune to challenge while rendering others more vulnerable in certain circumstances. Second, market transition is likely to alter social movement networks. No state, no matter how authoritarian, exists without channels of bargaining and representation. These change and often contract for a time under new allocational regimes. As a result, social movements may turn to unprecedented sorts of alliances, they may innovate new forms of social capital and exchange, and they may frame their struggles under different banners in order to be heard. Finally, distributive movements and market transition collide at the level of consciousness. Markets also inhabit human minds. People have understandings of what they deserve; in times when market transition removes the possibility of receiving certain goods or services or opportunities, the most unlikely candidates for protest may become vociferous voices of opposition. Market policies, at once, are formulas, obstacle courses, and performances. They tell people what they deserve and when; they direct people to produce and participate politically in certain ways; and they also implicitly suggest the terms of their own destruction.

I have attempted in this work to present market transition and social mobilization from an inside-out perspective, departing from accounts of those who have lost out so far and who have called upon the state to redress those losses. The analysis is clearly preoccupied with what market-oriented policies do not achieve, with whom they will not liberate, with the forms of production and public association they will not nurture. So be it. I have labored as well, however, to portray movements' campaigns as subjective, sometimes very flawed and parochial exercises in which people stumble from protest to protest with very imperfect information. I shall argue, though, that what made these groups dangerous to their opponents, especially the state, was not their material demands per se. What made them subversive forces was their ability to introduce mass dissent into a delicate new system whose success depends on the widespread belief that there is no alternative to a market-oriented future.

References

Amnesty International. 1999. *Mexico: The Shadow of Impunity*. Washington, DC: Amnesty International.

Comandante Ana María. 1996. Address before the Intergalactic Encuentro Against Neoliberalism and for Humanity. Lacandón Jungle. Author's records.

Appendini, Kirsten. 1992. *De la milpa a los tortibonos: la restructuración de la política alimentaria en México*. Mexico City: El Colegio de México.

Arteaga Domínguez, Efraín. 1993. "Esbozo económico del fraccionamiento agrario en Zacatecas." *Tópicos Zacatecanos, Tomo 1: La difícil modernidad*. Zacatecas: Maestría en Ciencias Políticas, Universidad Autónoma de Zacatecas.

Bacon, David. 1997. "Fight on the Border," *The Los Angeles Times*, August 31.

Baitenmann, Helga. 1998. "The Article 27 Reforms and the Promise of Local Democratization in Central Veracruz," in Wayne A. Cornelius and David Myhre, eds., *The Transformation of Rural Mexico*. La Jolla: Center for U.S.-Mexican Studies, University of California, San Diego.

Banco de Crédito Rural del Centro Norte. 1994. *Evaluación de créditos*. Gerencia de Planeación Estratégica, State of Zacatecas.

Barkin, David, and Blanca Suárez. 1982. *El fin de la autosuficiencia*. Mexico City: Nuevo Imagen.

El Barzón. 1995. "Ley Orgánica." Mexico City: El Barzón.

Bennett, Vivienne. 1992. "The Evolution of Urban Popular Movements in Mexico Between 1968 and 1988," in Arturo Escobar and Sonia Alvarez, eds., *The Making of Social Movements in Latin America: Identity, Strategy, and Democracy*. Boulder, CO: Westview Press.

———. 1995. *The Politics of Water: Urban Protest, Gender, and Power in Monterrey, Mexico*. Pittsburgh: Pittsburgh University Press.

Bizberg, Ilán. 1982. *La acción obrera en Las Truchas*. Mexico City: El Colegio de México.

———. 1990. *Estado y sindicalismo*. Mexico City: El Colegio de México.

Brooks, David, and Jim Cason. 1998. "Mexican Unions: Will Turmoil Lead to Independence?" *Working USA* (March/April): 23–91.

References

Bruhn, Kathleen Marie. 1997. *Taking on Goliath: The Emergence of a New Left Party and the Struggle for Democracy in Mexico*. University Park, PA: Pennsylvania State Press.

Brysk, Alison. 1996. "Turning Weakness into Strength," *Latin American Perspectives* 23 (2): 38–57.

Business Frontier. 1996. "The Maquiladora Industry: Still Going Strong," Issue 3: 1.

Calva, José Luis. 1992. *La disputa por la tierra: La reforma del artículo 27 y la nueva Ley Agraria*. Mexico City: Ediciones Fontamara.

1993. *El modelo neoliberal mexicano: costos, vulnerabilidad, alternativas*. Mexico City: Fundación Friedrich Ebert Stiftung.

Camp, Roderic. 1993. *Politics in Mexico*. New York: Oxford University Press.

Carr, Barry. 1991. "Labor and the Political Left in Mexico," in Kevin Middlebrook, ed., *Unions, Workers, and the State in Mexico*. La Jolla: Center for U.S.-Mexican Studies, University of California-San Diego.

1992. *Marxism and Communism in Twentieth-Century Mexico*. Lincoln and London: University of Nebraska Press.

Carroll, Paul B. 1994. "Mexico Stocks Tumble on Fighting in Chiapas." *Wall Street Journal*, January 4: C1.

Castañeda, Jorge. 1995. *The Mexican Shock*. New York: The New Press.

1999. *La Herencia: Arquelogía de la sucesión presidencial en México*. Mexico City: Extra Alfaguara.

Castells, Manuel. 1977. *The Urban Question*. New York: Edward Arnold Press.

1983. *The City and the Grassroots*. Berkeley: University of California Press.

Centeno, Miguel Angel. 1994. *Democracy Within Reason: Technocratic Revolution in Mexico*. University Park, PA: Pennsylvania State Press.

Charnas, Rebecca. 1999. "Shifting Strategies, Shifting Times: El Barzón, the Mexican Debtors' Movement, 1995–1999." Unpublished senior essay, Yale University.

Chávez, Marcos. 1994. "Limitado compromiso social," *El Financiero*, June 17.

1995. "Congelada, la inversión productiva; 60% de las empresas en riesgo de depresión," *El Financiero*, January 16: 42.

Collier, George. 1994. *Basta! Land and the Zapatista Rebellion in Chiapas*. Oakland, CA: Food First, Institute for Food and Development Policy.

Cook, Maria Lorena. 1990. "Organizing Opposition in the Teachers' Movement in Oaxaca," in Joe Foweraker and Ann Craig, eds., *Popular Movements and Political Change in Mexico*. Boulder, CO: Lynne Rienner Press.

1996. *Organizing Discontent*. University Park, PA: Pennsylvania State Press.

Cornia, Giovanni Andrea, Richard Jolly, and Frances Stewart. 1987. *Adjustment with a Human Face*. Oxford: Oxford University Press.

Craig, Ann L. 1990, "Legal Constraints and Mobilization Strategies in the Countryside," in Joe Foweraker and Ann L. Craig, *Popular Movements and Political Change in Mexico*. Boulder, CO: Lynne Rienner Press.

Daville, Selva. 1986. "Sicartsa: Historia de la Sección 271," in Bensusan, Graciela and Samuel León, eds., *Negociación y conflicto laboral en México*. Mexico City: Fundación Freidrich Ebert Stiftung.

References

Democracia Proletaria. 1981 through 1993. *Boletines de discusión*. Internal union flyers. Lázaro Cárdenas, Michoacán.

Domínguez, Jorge I., and James A. McCann. 1996. *Democratizing Mexico: Public Opinion and Electoral Choices*. Baltimore: Johns Hopkins University Press.

Domville, Lucia. 1994. "Concentran 252 empresas los beneficios de los primeros 6 meses del TLC," *El Financiero*, July 1.

Economic Commission on Latin America. 1995. *Economic Panorama of Latin America*. Washington, DC: ECLA.

The Economist. 1998. "About Turn." December 18: 45.

Escobar, Arturo, and Sonia Alvarez, eds. 1992. *The Making of Social Movements in Latin America: Identity Strategy and Democracy*. Boulder, CO: Westview Press.

Ferree, Myra Marx. 1992. "The Political Context of Rationality: Rational Choice Theory and Resource Mobilization," in Aldon Morris and Carol McClurg Mueller, eds., *Frontiers in Social Movement Theory*. New Haven: Yale University Press.

Fideicomiso Lázaro Cárdenas. 1980. *Proyecto Integral de Desarrollo Urbano*. Mexico City: FIDELAC.

Foweraker, Joe. 1993. *Popular Mobilization in Mexico: The Teachers' Movement 1977–87*. Cambridge and New York: Cambridge University Press.

Fox, Jonathan. 1992a. "Democratic Rural Development: Leadership Accountability in Regional Peasant Organizations," *Development and Change* 23 (2): 1–36.

1992b. *The Politics of Food in Mexico: State Power and Social Mobilization*. Ithaca, NY: Cornell.

1994a. "The Difficult Transition from Clientelism to Citizenship: Lessons from Mexico." *World Politics* 46 (2): 151–85.

1994b. "Latin America's Emerging Local Politics," *Journal of Democracy* 5 (2), April: 105–16.

1994c. "Political Change in Mexico's New Peasant Economy," in Maria Lorena Cook, Kevin Middlebrook, and Juan Molinar Horcacitas, eds., *The Politics of Economic Restructuring in Mexico*. La Jolla: Center for U.S.-Mexican Studies, University of California-San Diego.

Foxley, Alejandro. 1983. *Latin American Experiments in Neoconservative Economics*. Berkeley: University of California Press.

Freiden, Jeffry A. 1991. "Invested Interests: The Politics of National Economic Policies in a World of Global Finance," *International Organization* 45 (4): 426–51.

Gitlin, Todd. 1980. *The Whole World Is Watching: Mass Media in the Making and Unmaking of the New Left*. Berkeley: University of California Press.

Gledhill, John. 1993. "Michoacan is different?" in Neil Harvey, ed., *Mexico: Dilemmas of Transition*. London, New York: the Institute of Latin American Studies, University of London, and the British Academic Press.

Gómez Flores, Laura. 1999. "El sectoral informal abarcara 40 por ciento del empleo urbano," *La Jornada*, June 3.

223

Gómez Salgado, Arturo. 1994. "Según INEGI, en 5 años se duplicó el número de ocupados en busca de ingresos adicionales," *El Financiero* June 29: 28.

Gómez Tagle, Silvia. 1994. "Electoral Violence and Negotiations," in Neil Harvey and Mónica Serrano, eds., *Party Politics in an Uncommon Democracy.* London: Institute of Latin American Studies.

González de la Rocha, Mercedes, and Agustin Escobar Latapí. 1991. *Social Responses to Mexico's Economic Crisis of the 1980s.* La Jolla: Center for U.S.-Mexican Studies, University of California-San Diego.

Goodwin, Jeff, and James M. Jasper. 1999. "Caught in a Winding, Snarling Vine: The Structural Bias of Political Process Thoery," *Sociological Forum* 14 (1): 27–54.

Gourevitch, Peter. 1986. *Politics in Hard Times: Comparative Responses to International Economic Crises.* Ithaca: Cornell University Press.

Greenpeace. 1993. Petition to the Ambassador of Norway.

Grindle, Merilee, S. 1977. *Bureaucrats, Politicians, and Peasants in Mexico.* Berkeley: University of California Press.

Guillén, Tonatiuh. 1991. "Elecciones de 1989 en Baja California," in Arturo Alvarado, ed., *Insurgencia Democrática: elecciones locales.* Guadalajara: Universidad de Guadalajara.

———. 1995. "Balance de la transición democrática en Baja California," Research Seminar at the Center for U.S.-Mexican Studies, University of California-San Diego.

Gurr, Ted Robert. 1970. *Why Men Rebel.* Princeton, NJ: Princeton University Press.

Gutiérrez, Elvia. 1995. "Aporte inflacionario por importaciones del 83.3% de las actividades manufactureras," *El Financiero,* January 11.

Haggard, Stephan, and Robert B. Kaufman. 1995. *The Political Economy of Democratic Transitions.* Princeton, NJ: Princeton University Press.

Hamilton, Nora. 1982. *The Limits of State Autonomy.* Princeton, NJ: Princeton University Press.

Harvey, Neil. 1994. *Rebellion in Chiapas.* La Jolla: University of California-San Diego.

———. 1998. *The Chiapas Rebellion: The Struggle for Land and Democracy.* Durham: Duke University Press.

——— and Monica Serrano, eds. 1994. *Party Politics in an Uncommon Democracy: Political Parties and Elections in Mexico.* London: The Institute for Latin American Studies/University of London.

Hellman, Judith Adler. 1983. *Mexico in Crisis,* 2nd ed. New York and London: Holmes & Meier.

———. 1994a. *Mexican Lives.* New York: The New Press.

———. 1994b. "Mexican Popular Movements, Clientelism, and the Process of Democratization," *Latin American Perspectives* 21 (2): 124–42.

Hernández, Evangelina, and Angel Amador. 1994. "Advierten con moratoria total de pagos," *La Jornada,* February 27.

Hernández Navarro, Luis. 1990. "Las convulsiones rurales." *El Cotidiano* 34 (March–April): 13–22.

References

1994. "Chiapas: reestructuración y cambio." *El Cotidiano* 61 (March–April): 5–10.

and Ramón Vera Herrera. 1998. *Acuerdos de San Andrés.* Mexico City: Era.

Hewitt de Alcántara, Cynthia. 1976. *Modernizing Mexican Agriculture: Socioeconomic Implications of Technological Change 1940–1970.* Geneva: United Nations Research Institute for Social Development.

Hiernaux, Daniel. 1982. "El Estado y las polítcas urbanas," in Ivan Restrepo, ed., *Las Truchas: Inversión para la desigualdad?* Mexico City: Centro de Ecodesarrollo.

Horizonte. 1995. "Resistencia civil contra embargos," No. 24, January 14.

Huntington, Samuel. 1968. *Political Order in Changing Societies.* New Haven: Yale University Press.

Imagen de Zacatecas. 1993a. "Campesinos protestan contra políticas agrarias," October 4.

1993b. "Banco Rural confirma reestructuración de adeudos," October 30.

1993c. "Barzón anuncia bloqueo de carreteras aquí," October 9.

1993d. "El Barzón coquetea con priístas," November 4.

1993e. "Barzón se reúne con dirigente priísta," October 29.

1993f. "Bloquean manifestaciones taxistas," October 11.

1993g. "CNC: Herberto Flores: 'Campesinos nunca estarán solos," October 26.

1993h. "PRI rompió relaciones con el Barzón," November 7.

1993i. "Romo: Pro-Campo brindará 615 millones," October 6.

1994a. "Accidentada visita de Hank a Zacatecas," July 14.

1994b. "Barzón convoca a solidarizarse con indocumentados," October 31.

1994c. "El Barzón presiona compra frijolera," January 8.

1994d. "Barzón rompe negociaciones con Banco Rural," February 17.

1994e. "Barzonistas rechazan iniciativa 187," November 8.

1994f. "Campesinos priístas demandan apoyo presidencial," October 4.

1994g. "FPLZ anuncia plantón," June 21.

1994h. "Marcha, protestas y plantones barzonistas hoy," February 24.

1994i. "Perredistas critican postura de Pérez Cuevas," May 11.

1994j. "Problemas en Vetagrande, Salvador, y Sombrerete," March 4.

1998. "Abogados contra Barzonistas," November 18.

La Jornada. 1988. "El gobierno desistó de la venta de AHMSA," June 6.

1989. "Se prevé el despido de 800 obreros: Este viernes concluirá la revisión del CCT en SICARTSA," August 16.

1992. "A la opinión pública," July 28: 2.

1994. "No se ha reducido la morosidad con la restructuración de carteras," August 26.

Katz, Friedrich. 1991. "The Liberal Republic and the Porfiriato, 1867–1910," in Leslie Bethell, ed., *Mexico Since Independence.* Cambridge and New York: Cambridge University Press.

Keck, Margaret. 1992. *The Workers' Party and Democratization in Brazil.* New Haven: Yale University Press.

and Kathryn Sikkink. 1997. *Activists Beyond Borders: Transnational Advocacy Politics in International Networks.* Ithaca, NY: Cornell University Press.

and Kathryn Sikkink. 1998. "Transnational Advocacy Networks in the Movement Society," in David S. Meyer and Sidney Tarrow, eds., *The Social Movement Society*. Lanham, MD, and Oxford: Rowman and Littlefield.

Klandermans, Bert. 1988. "The Formation and Mobilization of Consensus," in Bert Klandermans, Hanspeter Kriesi, and Sidney Tarrow, eds., *From Structure to Action: Comparing Social Movement Research Across Cultures*. International Social Movement Research, Vol. I. Greenwich, CT: JAI.

La Botz, Dan. 1988. *The Crisis of Mexican Labor*. New York: Greenwood Press.

1992. *Mask of Democracy: Labor Suppression in Mexico Today*. Boston: South End Press.

Latin American Newsletters. 1986. "Regional Report/ Mexico," March 7.

Laurell, Asa Cristina. 1989a. "Sicartsa: la esencia de la modernización salinista." in *El Cotidiano* 32 (November–December): 41–8.

1989b. "The Role of Union Democracy in the Struggle for Workers' Health in Mexico," *International Journal of Health Services* 19 (2): 279–93.

and Mariano Noriega. 1987. *Trabajo y salud en Sicartsa*. Mexico City: Sección 271 del SNTMMSRM, Sindicato Independiente de la UAM, Maestría en Medicina Social UAM-Xochimilco.

Lawson, Chappell. 1997. "The Elections of 1997," *Journal of Democracy* 8 (4): 13–27.

Lipsky, Michael. 1968. "Protest as a Political Resource." *American Political Science Review* 62 (4): 1144–58.

López Ortíz, Heriberto. 1995. "La agricultura mexicana en el marco de la apertura." *La Jornada del Campo*, June 27: 10–12.

López Sierra, Pilar and Julio Moguel. 1998. "Ejido Reform in the Isthmus of Tehuantepec: The Case of Juchitán," in Wayne A. Cornelius and David Myhre, eds., *The Transformation of Rural Mexico*. La Jolla: Center for U.S.-Mexican Studies, University of California San Diego.

McAdam, Doug. 1982. *Political Process and the Development of Black Insurgency, 1930–70*. Chicago: University of Chicago Press.

Magagna, Victor V. 1991. *Communities of Grain*. Ithaca, NY: Cornell University Press.

Mainwaring, Scott. 1987. "Urban Popular Movements, Idenitity, and Democratization in Brazil," *Comparative Political Studies* 20 (2): 131–59.

Martínez Aparicio, Jorge. 1992. "Sicartsa: De la reconversión a la modernización, 1986–1990." *El Cotidiano* 45 (January–February): 34–51.

1993. "La articulación regional del espacio rural en condiciones de enclave: Lázaro Cárdenas, Michoacan." Unpublished Master's thesis, University of Chapingo, Guerrero, Mexico.

Méndez, Cuautémoc. 1992. "Devastación pesquera," *Motivos*, August 3: 22–3.

Méndez, Luis. 1987. "El primero de mayo: celebración triste," *El Cotidiano* 18 (July–August): 262–6.

Méndez, Luis, and José Othón Quiroz. 1994. *Modernización estatal y respuesta obrera: Historia de una derrota*. Mexico City: Universidad Autónoma Metropolitana-Azcapotzalco.

Mexico Service. 1992. "Mexico Report," On-line version.

References

Meyer, David S. 1993. "Protest Cycles and Political Process: American Peace Movements in the Nuclear Age," *Political Research Quarterly* 46 (3): 451.

Middlebrook, Kevin J. 1989. "The Sounds of Silence: Organized Labour's Response to Economic Crisis in Mexico." *Journal of Latin American Studies* 21 (2): 195–220.

Mizrahi, Yemile. 1995. "Entrepreneurs in the Opposition: Modes of Political Participation in Chihuahua," in Victoria E. Rodríguez and Peter M. Ward, eds., *Opposition Governments in Mexico*. Albuquerque: University of New Mexico Press.

Moguel, Julio. 1987. *Los caminos de la izquierda*. Mexico City: Juan Pablos.

Moore, Barrington, Jr. 1967. *Social Origins of Dictatorship and Democracy*. Boston: Beacon Press.

Morley, Samuel. 1995. *Poverty and Inequality in Latin America: The Impact of Adjustment and Recovery in the 1980s*. Baltimore: Johns Hopkins University Press.

Moyssen, Gabriel. 1993. "El *Betula*, un buque-tanque *carcacha*; es más barato hundirlo que rescatarlo," *El Nacional*, July 4.

Muller, Edward N., and Mitchell Seligson. 1987. "Inequality and Insurgency," *American Political Science Review* 81 (2): 425–51.

Myerson, Allen R. 1994. "In El Paso, A Reluctance to Buy Shares," *New York Times*, April 2: 33.

Myhre, David. 1998. "The Achilles' Heel of the Reforms: The Rural Finance System," in Wayne A. Cornelius and David Myhre, eds., *The Transformation of Rural Mexico*. La Jolla: Center for U.S.-Mexican Studies, University of California-San Diego.

Nolasco, Margarita. 1984. "La ciudad de los pobres," in Ivan Restrepo, ed., *Las Truchas: Inversión para la desigualdad?* Mexico City: Centro de Ecodesarrollo.

Núñez, Oscar. 1990. *Innovaciones democrático-culturales del movimiento urbano-popular*. Mexico City: Universidad Autónoma Metropolitana.

Oberschall, Anthony. 1978. "Theories of Social Conflict," *Annual Review of Sociology* 4: 291–315.

Olson, Mancur. 1965. *The Logic of Collective Action*. Cambridge, MA: Harvard University Press.

1982. *The Rise and Decline of Nations*. New Haven, CT: Yale University Press.

La Opinión de Michoacán. 1995. "Solo el 50 por ciento de las colonias del municipio están habitadas al 100 por ciento," October 18.

1996. "Cinco obreros han muerto en accidentes laborales." May 2.

1997a. "Demandan acciones para hacer respetar precio de la tortilla." February 13.

1997b. "Impiden pescadores el relleno de un estero." July 23.

1997c. "Mineros piden a Zedillo castigo a desfacadores," April 4.

1997d. "Resultados finales," July 8.

1998. "Resultados oficiales del IFE," November 8.

1999. "Restringe el Fidelist programa de subsidios," January 13.

227

References

Paige, Jeffrey. 1975. *Agrarian Revolution: Social Movements and Export Agriculture in the Underdeveloped World.* New York: The Free Press.

Paz, Octavio. 1985. *The Labyrinth of Solitude and Other Writings.* New York: Grove Weidenfeld.

Pérez, Matilde. 1994. "Creció 2000 por ciento la cartera vencida." *La Jornada,* July 24.

——— 1995. "CNA: asciende a N$6.6 mil millones la cartera vencida del agro." *La Jornada,* July 18.

Piven, Frances Fox, and Richard A. Cloward. 1979. *Poor People's Movements: Why They Succeed, How They Fail.* New York: Vintage Books.

Poole, Claire. 1995. "On the Brink," *Mexico Finance,* June: 10–14.

Portes, Alejandro. 1990. "Latin American Urbanization during the Years of the Crisis," *Latin American Research Review* 25: 7–44.

Preston, Julia. 1999. "Runaway Banks Without Brakes: Mexico's $71 Billion Lesson," *The New York Times,* July 23.

Putnam, Robert. 1988. "Diplomacy and Domestic Politics: The Logic of Two-Level Games," *International Organization* 42 (3): 427–60.

Quiñones, Sam. 1995. "The New Federalism," *Mexico Finance* (June): 8–10.

Reforma. 1995. "Marchan miles sin CTM," May 2: 1.

Restrepo, Ivan. ed. 1984. *Las Truchas: Inversión para la desigualdad?* Mexico City: Centro de Ecodesarrollo.

Rodríguez, Leticia. 1994. "Caen 70 por ciento las ventas del comercio del DF," *El Financiero,* June 15: 28.

Rodríguez, Victoria E., and Peter M. Ward, eds. 1995. *Opposition Governments in Mexico.* Albuquerque: University of New Mexico Press.

Rodríguez Gómez, Guadalupe, and Gabriel Torres. 1994. "El Barzón y COMAGRO: dos estrategias frente a la modernización neoliberal del campo." *Cuadernos Agrarios* 10 (July–December): 70–94.

Rogowski, Ronald. 1989. *Commerce and Coalitions: How Trade Affects Domestic Political Alignments.* Princeton, NJ: Princeton University Press.

Rosen, Fred. 1998. "The $55 Billion Bank-Bailout Scandal," *NACLA Report on the Americas* 32 (3): 11–14.

Rubin, Jeffrey. 1997. *Decentering the Regime: Ethnicity, Radicalism, and Democracy in Juchitán, Mexico.* Durham, NC: Duke University Press.

Rudiño, Lourdes Edith. 1993. "Exigen Pescadores Indeminazación por los Daños Provocados por la *Betula,*" *El Financiero.* July 30.

——— 1994. "Bajó 60 por ciento la superficie agropecuaria dotada de asistencia técnica del gobierno," *El Financiero,* June 23.

——— 1995a. "Aumentan las carteras vencidas los juicios mercantiles en Zacatecas." *El Financiero,* February 13.

——— 1995b. "Insuficiente el financiamiento de Banrural para productores." *El Financiero,* February 2.

Rueda Peiro, Isabel. 1994. *Tras la huellas de la privatización: El caso de Altos Hornos de México.* Mexico City: Siglo Veintiuno.

——— María Luisa González Marin, and Lucía Alvarez Mosso. 1990. *El capitalismo ya no es de acero.* Mexico City: UNAM.

References

Sánchez, Sergio Javier. 1999. "Incertidumbre sesion consejo universitario," *El Universal*, April 8.

Sanderson, Steven E. 1981. *Agrarian Populism and the Mexican State: The Struggle for Land in Sonora*. Berkeley: University of California Press.

Schneider, Anne, and Helen Ingram. 1993. "Social Construction of Target Populations: Implications for Politics and Policy," *American Political Science Review* 87 (2): 334–47.

Scott, James C. 1990. *Domination and the Arts of Resistance: The Hidden Transcripts*. New Haven, CT: Yale University Press.

1985. *Weapons of the Weak: Everyday Forms of Peasant Resistance*. New Haven: Yale University Press.

Senzek, Alva. 1997. "The Entrepreneurs Who Become Radicals," *NACLA Report on the Americas* 30 (4): 10–13.

Servicio Universal de Noticias. 1996a. "Dia Ecologia, Estados." June 6.

1996b. "Pescadores contra Pemex." May 18.

1998. "Bloqueo Termoeléctrica Guerrero." March 17.

Shaiken, Harley. 1994. "Advanced Manufacturing and Mexico: A New International Division of Labor?" *Latin American Research Review* 29 (2): 39–72.

Sheridan, Mary Beth. 1996. "Zedillo Government Thinks the People Protest Too Much," *The Los Angeles Times*, August 31.

Skocpol, Theda. 1979. *States and Social Revolutions: A Comparative Analysis of France, Russia, and China*. Cambridge and New York: Cambridge University Press.

Slater, David. 1985. *New Social Movements in Latin America*. Amsterdam: Center for Latin American Studies.

Smith, Peter. 1991. "Mexico since 1946: Dynamics of an Authoritarian Regime," in Leslie Bethell, ed., *Mexico Since Independence*. Cambridge and New York: Cambridge University Press.

Snow, David A, and Robert D. Benford. 1992. "Master Frames and Cycles of Protest," in Aldon D. Morris and Carol McClurg Mueller, eds., *Frontiers in Social Movement Theory*. New Haven: Yale University Press.

Snyder, David, and Charles Tilly. 1972. "Hardship and Collective Violence in France, 1830–1960." *American Sociological Review* 37 (October): 520–32.

Stallings, Barbara, and Robert Kaufman, eds. 1989. *Debt and Democracy in Latin America*. Boulder, CO: Westview Press.

Taibo, Paco Ignacio. 1990. "Cardenismo in Mexico: A New Politics with Deep Roots," *The Nation*, December 17: 764–7.

Tarrow, Sidney. 1993. "Social Protest and Policy Reform: May 1968 and the Loi d'Orientation in France," *Comparative Political Studies* 25 (4): 579–607.

1994. *Power in Movement: Social Movements, Collective Action, and Politics*. New York: Cambridge University Press.

1999. "Paradigm Warriors: Regress and Progress in the Study of Contentious Politics," *Sociological Forum* 14 (1): 71–8.

Thomas, J. J. 1993. "The Links Between Structural Adjustment and Poverty: Causal or Remedial?" *International Labor Organization Working Papers*, No. 373, Santiago, Chile.

References

Tilly, Charles. 1992. *The Contentious French*. Cambridge, MA: Harvard University Press.
1996. "Invisible Elbow," *Sociological Forum* 11 (4): 589–601.
1999. "Wise Quacks," *Sociological Forum* 14 (1): 55–62.
Torres, Craig. 1994. "Mexico's Bolsa Rebounds on Signs of Possible Dialogue with Rebels." *Wall Street Journal*, January 12: C1.
Torres, Gabriel. 1996. "El derecho de barzonear." Unpublished paper, CIESAS-Occidente.
Torres Oseguera, Carlos. 1992. "La industrialización de Lázaro Cárdenas está provocando un giro en el ecosistema." *El Quijote*, March 31–April 6.
Trejo Delarbre, Raúl. 1990. *Crónica del sindicalismo en México, 1976–1982*. Mexico City: Siglo Veintiuno.
Uno Mas Uno. 1991. "Acuerdan 268 organizaciones del agro apoyar las reformas al 27," December 3.
Vilas, Carlos M. 1997. "Participation, Inequality and the Whereabouts of Democracy," in Douglas A. Chalmers et al., eds., *The New Politics of Inequality in Latin America*. New York: Oxford University Press: 3–42.
Villareal, René P. 1988. "La reconversión en la siderurgia paraestatal en México." *Comercio Exterior* 38 (3): 191–201.
La Voz de la Costa. 1976. "Sicartsa aseguró su abastecimiento de acero," July 7: 1.
La Voz de Michoacán. 1988a. "Auditoría a SICARTSA, exigen los mineros de la Sección 271," June 10.
1988b. "El cambio del ISR ocasionó a SICARTSA pérdidas por 600 mil millones de pesos," June 15.
Walton, John, and David Seddon, eds. 1994. *Free Markets and Food Riots: The Politics of Global Adjustment*. Oxford: Blackwell Publishers.
Warman, Arturo. 1980. *We Come to Object: The Peasants of Morelos and the National State*. Baltimore: Johns Hopkins University Press.
Wickham-Crowley, Timothy P. 1992. *Guerrillas and Revolution in Latin America*. Princeton, NJ: Princeton University Press.
Williams, Heather. 1996. *Planting Trouble: The Barzón Debtors' Movement in Mexico*. La Jolla: Center for U.S.-Mexican Studies, University of California-San Diego.
1999a. "The Barzón Movement in Mexico and Its Vision of a Democratic System of Finance," forthcoming, *Latin American Perspectives*.
1999b. "Mobile Capital and Transborder Labor Rights Mobilization," *Politics & Society* 27 (1): 139–66.
Willis, Eliza, Christopher Da C. B. Garman, and Stephan Haggard. 1999. "The Politics of Decentralization in Latin America," *Latin American Research Review* 34 (1): 7–56.
World Bank. 2000. "2000 World Development Indicators." Washington, DC: The World Bank.
Zacatecas Governor's Office. 1992. "1986–92, Seis años de progreso y confianza." Zacatecas: State Government of Zacatecas.
Zanella Figueróa. 1994. "Carece de prestaciones sociales el 46% de trabajadores urbanos," *El Financiero*, July 4: 38.

230

References

Zapata, Francisco, ed. 1978. *Las Truchas: Acero y sociedad en México*. Mexico City: El Colegio de México.

———. 1985. *Enclaves y polos de desarrollo en México*. Mexico City: El Colegio de México.

———. 1987. "El nuevo carácter de los movimientos sociales en América Latina," *Estado y Sociedad* 3: 85–101.

Zuckerman, E. 1989. "Adjustment Programs and Social Welfare." World Bank Discussion Paper No. 44.

Interviews Cited

"A" series (Workers and ex-workers at the Sicartsa Steel Mill), in Lázaro Cárdenas City, June and July 1994 and January and February 1995, and in June 1999.

"B" series (Management personnel, contract personnel and bosses), in Lázaro Cárdenas City, June and July 1994 and January and February 1995.

"C" series (Political activists outside Local 271), in Lázaro Cárdenas City, June and July 1994 and January and February 1995.

"D" series (Journalists, businessmen, city residents), in Lázaro Cárdenas City, June and July 1994 and January and February 1995.

Efrén Bañuelos (Activist in El Barzón, head of Technical Team), in Zacatecas, May and June 1995.

José Luis Castellanos (Labor activist, attorney) in Lázaro Cárdenas, Michoacán, July 1994, January 1995.

C. Espinosa Jaime (Diputado Estatal, ex-head of state CNC, PRI activist), in Zacatecas, May 1995.

Juan Figueroa (Secretary of Organization of El Barzón, and head of the Agro-Barzón), in Zacatecas in May 1995, in Mexico City in June 1995, and in Guasave, Sinaloa, in July 1995.

Casto García (Fisherman and environmental activist), in Lázaro Cárdenas City, July 17, 1994.

Juan Hernández (Attorney for El Barzón), in Zacatecas, June 1995.

Faustino López (President of the Unión de Crédito de Sombrerete, S.A.), in Sombrerete, Zacatecas, May 1995.

David Lugo Camacho (Head of El Barzón-Culiacan), in Culiacan, Sinalóa, July 1995.

Luis Medina (Professor of Law, Universidad Autónoma de Zacatecas), in Zacatecas, June 1995.

Mercedes Murillo (President and founder, Frente Cívico de Culiacán), in Culiacán, Sinaloa, July 1995.

Manuel Ortega (President of state chapter of El Barzón), in Zacatecas, June 1995.

María Estela Ríos (Labor attorney), in San Diego, California, October 1996.

Renato Rodríguez (activist in the PRD), in Zacatecas, June 1995.

Isabel Rueda Peiro, Professor of Economics, Universidad Nacional Autónoma de México, in Mexico City, July 1, 1994.

Hilda Salazar (Support Group for the national Network of River Fishermen-José Valdovinos), in Mexico City, July 6, 1994.

Paul Sherman (Assistant to Correspondent Tim Golden, *New York Times* Mexico Bureau), in Mexico City, June 27, 1994.

Jesus Vega (Executive Leadership, state chapter of El Barzón), in Zacatecas, June 1995.

Luis Velásquez (President, local chapter of El Barzón), in Los Mochis, Sinaloa, July 1995.

Index

Index

Urban Popular Movement, 65
Urban Transport Workers' Union
   (SUTAUR), 69

Valdovinos, José Luis, 143
Velásquez, Fidel, 162

wages and buying power, 3
Walton, John and David Seddon,
   10
Wilson, Pete, 181

Zacatecan Front of Popular Struggle
   (FPLZ), 77
Zacatecas city, 167
Zacatecas municipality, 155
Zacatecas state: conditions in, 151,
   157, 158; elections in, 49, 50; land
   tenure law, 169–70
Zapatista Army of National
   Liberation (EZLN), *see* protest,
   Chiapas and Zapatistas
Zedillo Ponce de León, Ernesto, 50

www.ingramcontent.com/pod-product-compliance
Ingram Content Group UK Ltd.
Pitfield, Milton Keynes, MK11 3LW, UK
UKHW010040140625
459647UK00012BA/1500